MASTERS
OF BADASSERY

Praise for Masters of Badassery

"Reading it was like sitting with a mirror that spoke back. Like kintsugi, Marta's words illuminate the fractures, each page a golden seam reminding us that healing is honoring, not erasing, what's been broken."
— Farah Ismail

"A holy invitation to wake up and live the life that's been waiting. For anyone who has felt invisible, unworthy, or stuck, this book is your permission slip to begin again."
— Luke Harris

"Every word carries Marta's raw, unfiltered heart. What she shares here is pure possibility."
— Bradley Davidge

"SOUL NUTRITION: raw, real, and powerful. This book will change how you see your fears—and your life."
— Raghav Parkash

"Sacred. This is not just a book, it's the way home."
— Sam Smith

MASTERS OF BADASSERY
RECLAIM YOUR WILD AND WORTHY SELF

Marta Czajkowska

RED AUSSIE
— PUBLISHING —

Copyright © 2025
Marta Czajkowska
Masters of Badassery
Reclaim Your Wild and Worthy Self
All Rights Reserved

No part of this publication may be reproduced, distributed, or transmitted in any form or by any means, including photocopying, recording, or other electronic or mechanical methods, without the prior written permission of the publisher, except in the case of brief quotations embodied in critical reviews and certain other non-commercial uses permitted by copyright law.

Published in the United States of America by
Red Aussie Publishing, a division of Red Aussie Multimedia
22424 S. Ellsworth Loop Rd., Unit 898
Queen Creek, AZ 85142

Contact the Publisher:
Joy Fluckiger, CEO Red Aussie Publishing
redaussiepublishing@gmail.com

Cover Design and Illustrations by Marta Czajkowska
Front Cover photograph by Karl Kelley
Marta's childhood photograph - Family Archives
Back Cover photograph by Sierra Farquhar
Interior design by Hanna Szeliga-Czajkowska

Printed in the United States of America
First Edition, 2025

ISBN: 978-1-990090-20-2 (paperback)
ISBN: 978-1-990090-21-9 (ebook)

Summary

Foreword	VIII
Prologue	1
Introduction	3

Part 1: Roots & Echoes — 9
Where the Roots Begin — 10

Root 1: The Goodbye I Didn't Understand	13
Echo 1: The Wall	17
Root 2: Tiny Acts of Disappearing	20
Echo 2: The Vanishing	22
Root 3: The Shrinking Years	27
Echo 3: Beer Run	30
Root 4: Nature of Belonging.	33
Echo 4: One Last Ski Trip	35
Root 5: Initiation by Stone	37
Echo 5: The Invisible Fixer	44
Root 6: Replanted and Thriving	47
Echo 6: The Leads I Gave Away	55
Root 7: The Summer of Mythic Yes	59
Echo 7: From Comfort Coffin to the Exile of the Open Road	65
Root 8: Windswept to the Soul	69
Echo 8: The Forest That Fed Me	76

Part 2: The Path to Badassery — 80
Trunks & Branches: A system for becoming wild, worthy, and whole — 81

Trunk 1: Know Thyself — 88

Branch 1: Drop Their Plan and Make Your Own	90
Branch 2: Understand Your Feelings and Needs	96
Branch 3: Recognize Your Protective Patterns	99

Branch 4: Practice Embodied Presence	106
Branch 5: Follow Your Desire	111
Trunk 2: Tend Your Ground	**118**
Branch 6: Recognize Your CRASH State	122
Branch 7: Access Your COACH State	128
Branch 8: CRASH and COACH Integration	132
Trunk 3: Respect Yourself	**139**
Branch 9: Anchor in Your Higher Self	142
Branch 10: Practice Self-Forgiveness	145
Branch 11: Build Self-Trust	148
Branch 12: Live in Integrity	152
Trunk 4: Transmute the Challenge	**158**
Branch 13: Own Your Story	161
Branch 14: Reclaim Your Mythic Identity	164
Branch 15: Transform in Real Time	168
Branch 16: Train With Stress	171
Trunk 5: Action	**178**
Branch 17: Act Before You're Ready	181
Branch 18: Redefine Goals	185
Branch 19: Commit Boldly	189
Branch 20: The Process Is the Way	193
Trunk 6: Expression	**200**
Branch 21: Rest, Detox, Movement, and Nature	204
Branch 22: Mark the Thresholds, Celebrate the Milestones	209
Branch 23: Update Your Identity	215
Branch 24: Create from Truth	220
Bonus Branch 25: Make it Mutual – The Art of Conscious Agreements	224

Part 3: Fruits & Flowers — 229

    Fruit 1: The Universal Thumb — 232
    Fruit 2: Aegialis Awakening — 235
    Fruit 3: Knocking on 700 doors — 239
    Fruit 4: Her Breakthrough Was My Shortcut — 243
    Fruit 5: High on the ledge of love — 245
    Fruit 6: The Truth at 17,500 — 250
    Fruit 7: The Fall That Set Me Free — 255
    Interlude: Basket of Roots — 258
    Fruit 8: Not Just Free: 5.13 Committed — 261
    Fruit 9: Sparkling into Sovereignty — 265
    Fruit 10: When the Work Works You — 269
    Fruit 11: The Film That Didn't Make Me a Filmmaker — 274
    Fruit 12: After the Diagnosis, the Mission — 278
    Fruit 13: The Marriage is His Wildest Adventure — 283

Epilogue: The Soul, the Sky, and the Silence — 288

Next Steps / Getting Help — 290

Acknowledgements — 292

Glossary — 293

About the Author — 298

Foreword
by Stephen McGhee

The first time I read this manuscript, I didn't just read it.

I experienced it.

This is not a tidy story of triumph.

It's a raw, unflinching account of what it takes to move from survival to sovereignty. Marta doesn't hide behind abstractions or inspirational slogans. She takes you into the cold rooms, the hard choices, and the quiet awakenings where everything is on the line.

I've spent over thirty years coaching leaders at the highest levels. Transformation, in my experience, is never clean. It's messy. It's inconvenient. And it's always human. What makes this book remarkable is not just Marta's journey, it's her courage to tell it without looking away.

In Part One, you walk with her through storms that strip you bare, betrayals that rattle your core, and winters so long you forget the reality of spring. Every trial, every mountain pass, every reckoning, becomes a threshold, stripping away illusion and forging the sovereignty she now lives. And when she reaches the edge of her own transformation, she turns and hands you the map.

Part Two is that map. Not theory. Not wishful thinking. A proven blueprint, drawn from her lived experience and years of guiding others through their own rugged terrain. She knows the switchbacks that test your patience, the false summits that tempt you to stop, and the thin-air moments when you wonder if you can keep going. She won't carry you, but she will walk beside you until you find your own stride.

And then comes the truest ascent, walking into the life you were always meant to live, fully and on your own terms. Not the summit the world sells you, but the one your soul has been calling you toward all along.

Masters of Badassery isn't about power plays or performance.

It's about remembrance, returning to the truth of who you are before the conditioning, the compromises, and the performance for the world.

As you read, don't just listen to her voice. Listen for the inner mastery it awakens in you.

Let it confront you. Let it steady you. Let it remind you:

You are not here to prove your worth.

You are here to live it.

The next page is not just her story, it's your invitation.

If you're willing to take this step and keep going, you will not leave this book the same person who opened it.

The summit is waiting, but it will only appear once you take the first step.

Stephen McGhee
Author *Climb for Freedom*
Leadership Guide

Part 3
Fruits & Flowers

Part 2
Trunks & Branches

Part 1
Roots & Echoes

Prologue

SOME dreams begin with vision boards. Mine was conjured from hunger, luck, and one wildly questionable ride. Before I had a plan, I had a pull; something unnameable tugging me toward a life I couldn't yet imagine.

I could barely afford to feed myself that summer. I was twenty, broke, and hitchhiking to work.

Every day, I walked down National Street in Kings Beach, stuck out my thumb, and prayed. It was a strange cocktail of hope and humiliation. Hand outstretched, heart open, feeling like a sore thumb to the world: broke, foreign, invisible.

And still, I stood there. Vulnerable. Exposed. Asking the universe to catch me. Car after car passed. Not one slowed. Not one stopped.

But for the first time in my life, I didn't care how I felt. The urge to shrink and stop was still there, but something stronger pulled me forward; like a rope tied around my ribcage, tugging me toward a life not yet formed.

I had one focus: Yosemite. I had come to California for the summer on a student visa, working whatever job I could find to save just enough to make it to the Valley in the fall. Granite cathedrals were waiting for me. Calling me to climb them.

The air carried a faint mix of sun-warmed vanilla and butterscotch from the Ponderosa pines mingled with the sun-baked asphalt. The unmistakable scent of a Sierra summer.

Then, a sleek black sports car pulled over.

The driver looked like trouble. Disheveled. Bleary-eyed. A man who'd been up all night chasing demons or dice. I hesitated. Then I got in. Twenty and clueless: that's how you learn.

He barely spoke. Just asked, "What's your story?"

"I'm from Poland," I said. "Here in Tahoe for the summer, working. But the real goal is to climb in Yosemite. Half Dome, and then El Capitan; I want to climb the biggest, cleanest granite wall in North America. It will take me days. I want it more than anything."

I looked up at him. "Nothing can stop me."

He listened. Quietly. Then, without another word, turned his car toward Squaw Valley. Out of his way, but straight toward mine.

When we got there, he reached into his pocket and handed me a wad of cash. "I won big last night," he said. "Your dream is cool. I want to help. No strings."

This wasn't just generosity. It was a portal. A stranger's belief cracked open the door to the life I quietly told myself I'd never have. I didn't get his name. I ducked into the nearest bathroom and locked the door; to count. To cry. To hide. I was sure that if I blinked, the universe would hit "undo".

But it didn't.

Every great story has a threshold. That ride was mine.

I didn't know it yet, but the road ahead wouldn't just lead to Yosemite. It would take me deep into the wildest part of me; the part still starving to hear her own voice, and believe it mattered.

Introduction

I **DIDN'T** grow up thinking I could have a big life. I was poor, from a country no one talked about, in a body that learned early to disappear. By seven, I'd mastered invisibility. I felt cut off from the world I longed to enter, and I resented my parents for being born.

I internalized a story: that survival was best I could hope for. That my role was to support others, to stay small, to never take up space. And I wore that story like the truth. For a long time I believed it… until I did not.

Life had other plans for me. By sixteen, I heard the unmistakable call of my soul. I didn't know where it was leading, only that I could no longer live someone else's version of my life. So I left.

By twenty, I stood at the edge of the world: no map, no clear direction. Just a dream I couldn't yet name, and a backpack that held everything I owned, except the weight of the old story I was finally learning to put down.

If you've ever felt your worth tied to what you give, and not who you are, this book is for you. If you've settled for the sidelines, aching quietly inside, or you're secretly waiting to be called forward, or have stopped hoping altogether, this is your call. You don't need to feel ready. All that it takes is to make yourself available to listen to that spark in your belly whispering: maybe there's more.

If you wander these pages like another checklist, you may pocket a few bright stones. But if you hold them to your soul like a mirror, letting each line align with your own heartbeat, a portal opens. Sit in silence and sing with what sparks or stings, where the pulse falters or erupts, where old ash flares back into flame.

This friction is your doorway. Step through, and this book ceases to be my tale; it unfurls as your mythic map, guiding you back to the wild. To the worthy, to the whole being you have always been.

The world cheers for the high achievers, the relentless, the invincible, the ones who grind through pain with a smile. But what if you are not one of them? What if you've spent more time shrinking than striving, more time surviving than shining?

What about those who haven't yet stepped into the arena, the ones still seated in the stands, quietly convinced they were never meant to play? Today's arena might be launching the company, finishing the manuscript, or finally asking the brave question that keeps tugging at your soul. Have you almost made peace with being a spectator, even as something inside still burns for more?

There's a place within many where the yearning to matter glows fiercely, yet that fire is too often smothered by the heavy blankets of fear and inadequacy. I know this place well. I've lived in the numb ache of believing my dreams were never meant for this world. I convinced myself that other people's stories were more important, their goals more worthy, their light more luminous.

I thought my value lived only in the shadows of others' brilliance. I watched their lives and quietly concluded that whatever magic they had was never going to be available for someone like me. I was only meant to hold the torch for others, never to carry it for myself.

But there's a whisper that never dies. A soft yet persistent murmur that refuses to be silenced. It says: you, too, were meant to enter the arena: not for applause or victory, but to finally meet the part of you that's still waiting to come alive.

This book is about following my myth. Not myth as fantasy, or fiction, or something we outgrow, but myth as origin, as the deep story our soul has been carrying all along. The way I use "myth" comes from the mythopoetic and soul-centric traditions: from rites of passage, from ancestral memory, from the wild edge of unfolding into our purpose. Myth not a story we make up, but a story that makes us. A living current that pulses beneath the surface of our lives, calling us to become who we were born to be.

For me, that myth sounded like granite walls and wind-stung plateaus, like languages I hadn't yet learned and places I couldn't yet find on a map. There were no instructions, just an unmistakable ache, a pull, and the wild hunch that if I followed it, I'd meet a version of myself not yet visible, a wild twin.

This book is a map of what I found on that trail. As Joseph Campbell said, "We must be willing to get rid of the life we've planned, so as to have the life that is waiting for us."

I'm writing this book for three reasons:

First, to share my story. From once believing I would never amount to anything, to building a life full of meaning, creation, and contribution.

A life I silently craved yet never imagined possible. For a long time, even in success, I played small, avoiding my brilliance, shrinking to stay safe.

The truth is, I have had to keep choosing to rise. I still do. Life began to reveal itself through me when I stopped striving to become and started allowing myself to be. My hope is that through my story, you'll see reflections of your own. That you'll wake up to where you've been hiding or holding back. And that you'll remember, it's never too late to choose something different.

Second, because I know, without a doubt, that the life you're yearning for, the one that feels aligned, joyful, and deeply yours, is waiting on the other side of your biggest fear. That fear is a door, on the other side is freedom. No one else can walk through it for you. The moment you cross that threshold, everything begins to shift. You start to feel your aliveness again. I want to help you find the courage to walk through that door. I promise you this: it's not as hard as the story you hold in your mind.

Third, I'm writing this book because I believe humanity stands at a crossroads. Our world is on the brink, our ecosystems are collapsing, our social fabric is fraying, and our spirits running on empty. These aren't isolated issues. They're part of one interconnected crisis we can no longer ignore.

I believe the answer lies in a collective awakening. We must rise above ego-driven thinking and begin building from a place of wholeness, love, and connection. We need leaders who are healed. While powerful work is being done in politics, activism, and business, it won't be enough, unless we also start to heal from within.

My work is to help people wake up and remember who they really are. To stop building their lives from avoidance and fear. When we operate from wholeness, love, and truth, we heal everything around us. Your joy is not selfish, it is a planetary upgrade. This work can't just live in our heads; It must be lived in the real world. It must be chosen, again and again.

The Title? It Came From a Client.

We had just mapped out a bold, yearlong journey: transformational coaching with a mountain backdrop. Every fear mirrored in a cliffside ledge or a thinning trail above the clouds. Her outer climb catalyzing the inner one.

"I feel like I'm getting my Master's of Badassery" – she said one night, her eyes submerged in firelight. And I knew, this wasn't just coaching. We were remembering who we really were. This wasn't about the summit, metrics or milestones. It was about integration of courage, truth, of wild, untamed original aliveness.

Out there, beyond the treeline, she remembered her myth that has been buried in her bones, waiting for movement and fire. That's the real Master's program. And now, if your breath catches at the thought, it's yours too.

So who is a Master of Badassery?

It's not the one who charges in loudly, untouched by fear. It's the one who feels the quake, and rises anyway. A Master of Badassery is someone who stops apologizing for their presence, stops shrinking to fit a story that was never theirs. Someone who dares to tell the truth, with their whole being. They know that purpose is the ultimate power. And from that knowledge, they boldly create peace, love, and impact, not just for themselves, but as a living invitation to everyone around them, stewarding the frequency of love.

You don't need to be perfect. You don't need to hold a position of power. There is no arrival point. You only need to stop waiting, decide, and act.

This book won't give you a blueprint. It will hand you a mirror, a match, and a machete. It will help you come home to your fire, your power, your voice. You don't need to be someone else. You don't need permission. There was never anything to fix. You only need to remember who you already are.

How This Book Works

This book unfolds in three parts: a journey from remembering, to embodying, to rising. Instead of traditional chapters, I use the organic structure of a tree: Roots and Echoes, Trunks and Branches, Flowers and Fruits. This is more than architecture, it's a living metaphor.

A tree doesn't grow in a straight line, it spirals, expands, and deepens with each season. So does your healing. So does your truth.

Part 1: Roots and Echoes

Every rise begins below the surface, in the quiet, unapologetic remembering of who we were before the wounding, before we learned to forget ourselves to survive.

The roots are my formation: the experiences, environments, beliefs, and ancestral legacies that shaped me, especially those I absorbed before I had language to name them. They anchored me in my protections: people-pleasing, hyper-achieving, surviving on performance. They held me long enough to gather the strength and resources I'd need to one day truly thrive.

The echoes are how those roots reverberated later, showing up as patterns in my relationships, reactions, and choices. Echoes don't ask for blame; they ask for awareness. They whisper, then shout until I finally listen. Until I choose to dispose of what no longer serves and root more deeply in what does.

This section doesn't move in straight lines, because growth and healing don't follow calendars. They spiral, they loop, they repeat, until the fears get dissolved into love.

This part of the book is about remembering. Not nostalgia, but re-remembering: gathering the pieces of myself I forgot, abandoned, or silenced. The goal isn't to stay buried. It's to reclaim a foundation strong enough to hold our rise.

Part 2: Trunks and Branches

This is the embodiment. The midpoint of the tree, solid, visible, lived.

The trunk represents your inner alignment: integrity, self-trust, and embodied presence. It's the spine of who you are becoming. From that sturdy center, your branches reach outward, expressing, stretching, and interacting with the world around you.

Every boundary you honor, every truth you speak, every time you return to your center in the midst of chaos, you add another ring to the tree of your becoming. Layer by layer, you become more yourself.

This section is practical. Experiential. You'll move beyond reflection into action. You'll get simple, potent practices designed to bring you back to your truth in real time. To help you live from your center, even when the winds blow.

Part 3: Flowers and Fruits.

This is the bloom. The beauty. The integration.

Once you've rooted deeply and embodied your truth, expression becomes inevitable. This section explores the fruit of your becoming, not as a reward, but as a natural result. Joy, clarity, creative contribution. Flowers are those glimpses of grace, when life suddenly feels aligned and whole.

This part shares stories, not just mine, but also those of others who dared to follow their own myths, cross their thresholds, and rise. Their blooms are not prescriptions, but invitations, sparks to ignite something uniquely yours.

This is not a book of steps. It's a spiral of return. If you read it as a self-help book, you'll gain insight. But if you read it as a mirror, if you let it be about you, you may emerge fundamentally changed. This is a reclamation. A rewilding. A reminder that you were never broken, only living like you were.

The Vertical Lexicon

Throughout the book, you'll come across climbing terms, jargon born at campgrounds and shouted on belay ledges. These words aren't just technical; they carry the rhythm of the vertical world. They're how climbers mark effort, describe fear, and celebrate triumph. If any of them feel unfamiliar, I've included a glossary at the end for those curious to dive deeper. Think of it as your passport into a parallel language: of trust, risk, and the poetry of stone.

Turn the page only if you're ready to be undone and remade in your own truth.

Let's begin.

Part 1:
Roots & Echoes

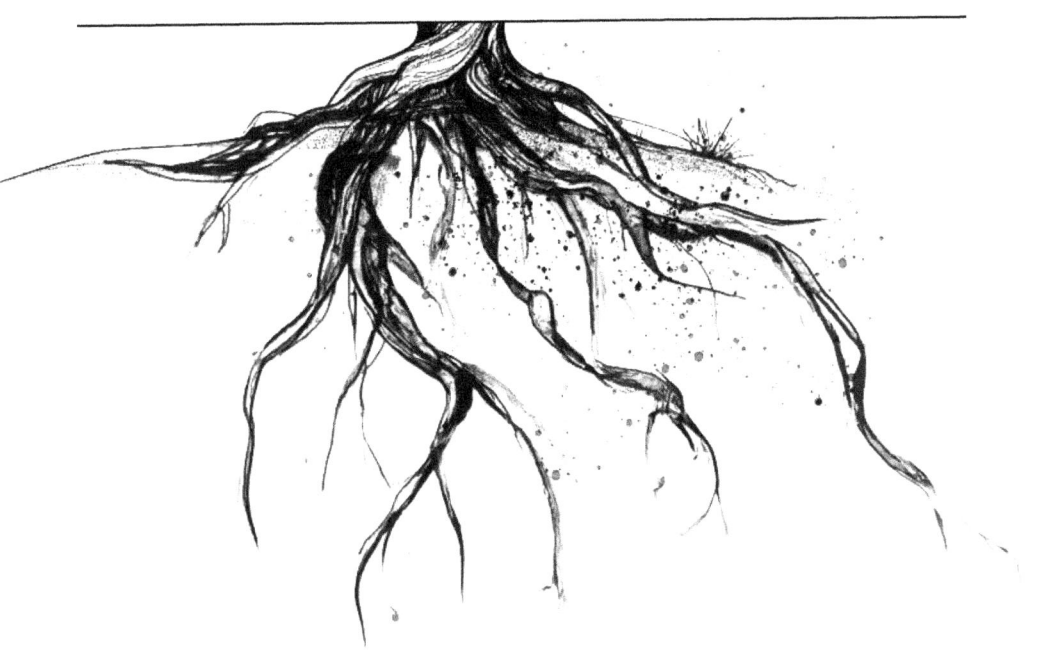

Part 1

Where the Roots Begin

Before I could rise, I had to go to the basement and find the girl I left behind. The one who went silent so I could survive. The one who learned to hide her grief, her pain, and her dreams behind a wall built from small yeses and going with the flow.

My childhood was filled with tiny wildflowers pushing through cracks in concrete, abandoned cats hiding in stairwells, and the quiet shame of always being the poorly dressed cousin. The one people felt obligated to include.

There was love. There was laughter, warmth, and joy in my home. This isn't about making that time wrong. There's so much I'm truly grateful for. And I also need to tell the truth. Naming the hard parts doesn't erase the goodness. It lets me be whole. Because wholeness isn't choosing one part of the story over another, it's having the courage to hold them both.

Beneath that beauty were stories I learned to breathe like air. Messages I didn't know I was absorbing. That shaped how I saw myself. Quietly. Completely.

I grew up in Communist Poland, on the eastern side of the Iron Curtain. In Warsaw, 1985, promise tasted like tangerines, because at Christmas, if you were lucky, that's what you got. A mountain-shaped bar of Swiss chocolate was a portal, a scent of magic from a better world.

All the kids looked the same in their state-issued coats and identical backpacks. We carried the same stiff, gray notebooks, and colored inside the lines with the same set of four dull crayons. To have anything different, a pencil case from the West, bubble gum with English writing, a shiny plastic toy, was to be instantly special, exotic, envied. There was only ever one version of everything, and it came in shades of gray.

We had no colorful playgrounds full of fun slides and swings. No ethnic restaurants or shiny shopping malls to wander through. Just long lines curling around grocery stores with bare shelves, and the clatter of ration cards in cold hands.

Parents clutched those food stamps like lifelines, only to exchange them for wilted cabbage and half-bricks of sour lard. The craving for more, more flavor, more color, more life, wasn't just material. It was spiritual.

Behind closed doors, grown-ups whispered what couldn't be said out loud. Bureaucracy was its own game: bribes folded into passports, favors traded for meat or car parts. Corruption wasn't the exception; it was the way things worked. Borders were closed. Voices censored. Grainy television full of lies spun with confident smiles in grayscale.

My parents bore the weight of pretending. Pretending they believed in the slogans. Pretending they weren't scared. Pretending they could protect their kids from a truth that always leaked through. No matter how hard you worked, how long you stood in line, how good you were, there was nothing you could ever do that would make your life better.

Uniform on the outside, freedom starved on the inside. A place where longing lived in the body like static, and even a piece of foreign chocolate could break your heart. The West meant freedom and possibility. It meant you could want things, and you might even get them.

And somewhere in all of that, I came to believe I was born in the wrong place. Other people's lives mattered more than mine. Their dreams were allowed to be big. I didn't get to have any.

That belief followed me across oceans, into new languages, into relationships where I became the quiet supporter of someone else's dream. It echoed through the ways I learned to measure myself, as a woman, an immigrant, someone always trying to earn love through silent sacrifice.

I'm not writing this to cast blame. I'm writing to understand, to bring clarity to how I made sense of the world around me, and who I had to become in order to survive it.

I became easygoing, helpful. I buried my needs, and swallowed my voice. I took pride in not needing anything, in never being the problem. I told myself that was a strength.

Yet all along as I curled inward to survive, something eternal in me simply observed. It didn't judge. It didn't fear – It waited.

At first, I didn't know I was doing it. When I discovered it, I admired it. Eventually, my soul stirred beneath the silence, whispering that even this cage was a chrysalis in disguise. Now I understand; these weren't flaws. They were intelligent adaptations. The universe wasn't testing me, it was entrusting me.

My stories sprawl like a root-system, not a staircase. They hop across decades in a single breath, because roots don't care about calendars, and echoes arrive on their own schedule.

Roots are the moments that took hold early: some planted for me, others I drove into the soil myself. The earliest reached deep and taught me to shrink. Those that came later split rock and taught me to speak. Somewhere in the dark, a wild root kept pulsing, Come find me.

Echoes are the shoots that surfaced another time in my life with the same DNA. Parental abandonment echoes in compulsive traveling. A group exercise during zoom training triggers an old wound. A childhood whisper makes me quit a climbing project.

Track the echo. Trace it downward. Compost what no longer serves. Every new choice enriches the soil for what comes next.

So this is where we begin. In the roots. In the distortion. In the stories that made me disappear. Before we can rise, we have to dig down into the soil so that we can understand what we are rising from. We rise not in spite of the roots, but because of them.

The roots run deep. The echoes ring long.
And the bloom – inevitable.

Root 1: The Goodbye I Didn't Understand
Warsaw, Poland, 1984

My earliest memory is a goodbye I didn't understand. My dad disappeared before I could even form the words to ask him to stay.

It's strange, the things I remember. Sometimes they come more like vague glimpses: blurry visions emerging from faded, sepia-tinted photographs of the eighties. My memories from those early days are fragmented but deeply felt. Small moments of intimacy and closeness. Did I make them up from the photos? Why these particular stories? What are they trying to tell me?

The first thing I remember is a bedroom in my grandparents' apartment, on the fourth floor of a gray, concrete building with no elevator. My parents and I shared that tiny space. My dad, Maciek, stayed home with me while my mom, Hanna, went to work at the publishing house. I remember sitting beside my dad on the bed, feeling safe and close, unaware that all of it was about to vanish.

On a sunny day we picked up my mom from her driving lessons. He bought me lemonade in a little plastic bag while we waited. He was happy, joking. Those early days felt perfect. A brief, bright window of closeness between my dad and me. The kind neither of us would ever know again.

I don't know how much time passed, but suddenly everything changed. One day, my dad was there, the next gone without a trace. North America.

Somewhere impossibly far away for my two-and-a-half-year-old brain to comprehend.

I imagined him fighting off polar bears, my childish fantasy echoing the fear and confusion I couldn't name. They said he left to chase a dream. A chance to make more money. Build a better life. But I only understood one thing: He wasn't anymore.

That day could've been the first time I pressed the Locator Button, even before I knew it existed. You will learn about the Locator Button in part two. What did I feel? Abandoned. What did I need? Safety. But I was decades away from having the language or the tools to cope with this emotion.

In the days of Communist Poland, getting a visa to the United States meant freedom. And my dad, adventurous and unconventional, wasn't about to let that chance pass him by. Freedom and breaking the rules were his top values.

Before I was born, he graduated with a degree in physical education and taught PE in school. He was a highly skilled hunter and a distinguished member of the Polish Hunting Association, often traveling around the Eastern Bloc to compete in trap shooting competitions.

Those years, traveling with his team, visiting foreign places, made up much of his identity. Yet behind that adventurous spirit was a boy who grew up in terror. His father, Stanisław, was an abusive alcoholic. My dad sometimes had to physically protect his mother from being beaten. When other kids in his kindergarten drew their homes, he drew a black hole.

Years later, we sat together in my dad's living room, flipping through an old photo album. We laughed easily as he told stories from his younger days and shared glimpses into moments of warmth with his mother and sister. It felt precious, like holding something fragile and fleeting.

As we turned to the final page, a loose photograph slipped out, unattached to any page, an outsider. My dad picked it up, and suddenly his face drained of color. His hand shook slightly as he stared down at the image. "My old man," he whispered, his voice cracking, thick with a terror that had never fully left him.

I now understand how deeply my father craved freedom. Freedom from a past filled with abuse, poverty, and oppression. But in pursuing freedom, he unknowingly sacrificed intimacy, the kind he would never again fully experience. I didn't know that then. And neither did he.

What I remember next, vividly and painfully, is the phone call. Back then, international calls had to be arranged in advance. Imagine the operator patching through my dad's voice from America, and suddenly, he was on the other end of a cold plastic telephone. A ghost I couldn't touch. I held that receiver, heavy in my tiny hands. His voice thin, faking cheer, crackling through static. All I could hear was a whisper: People leave because of you.

The tears came uncontrollably. I couldn't speak. I couldn't comprehend how someone I loved so dearly could now exist only as a disembodied voice, but not be close enough to see or touch.

While my dad was working construction in Chicago for the next two plus years, my mom and I moved to a different apartment and quietly adjusted to life without him. My aunt and her family lived next door and I was happy to have my two older cousins nearby.

Then, one day he came back. I remember clearly the Barbie dolls he brought me. And, strangely enough, duct tape. He was convinced that duct tape was the most remarkable invention in America.

His return couldn't mend what had been broken. The closeness, the easy bond we once had was irreversibly gone. He'd missed too much. I'd changed too much. The damage of feeling discarded was already done. And I still had no words for it. Must have been hard for him, too. Returning to find his daughter grown, different, and distant.

At the same time, my mom was facing her own challenges. She had finally passed her driving test and I vividly remember her anxiety the first time she drove alone across Warsaw. She asked me to be quiet during the ride. To stay still. Not to add to her stress. As we drove, her hands nervously gripped the wheel, I remember the voice in my head: you must be quiet. You must not make any trouble. She needs your help.

Without realizing it, I planted a seed inside myself that day. I was a burden. I had to earn love by being quiet, helpful, invisible, and perfect. Because if I wasn't, people I loved might leave. Just like him. At the same time, something else had taken root – a tiny seed of defiance. One day, I would stop saying yes. And when I did, I would build something wildly different.

The world kept asking me to stay quiet, and I kept answering yes. I lived the story of being unwanted and abandoned. From then on, that story ran quietly in the background of my life. A silent current beneath every relationship, every choice, every dream. A belief I didn't question for years: People leave. It's your fault. Don't be a burden. Sacrifice yourself. Be helpful. Be perfect. Don't let them know you're scared.

Years later, gently and courageously, I began to see it for what it was. I could not change the goodbye. But if I could go back, I'd place my small palm on my heart and promise the child in me, I'll never hang up on you.

That goodbye carved a canyon in me. But now I see it wasn't abandonment. It was an initiation into resilience. Into empathy. Into the very medicine I now carry for others.

Soul Note:

You were never the reason he left. You were the reason you remained. Beneath the sadness you were learning the sacred skill of staying with yourself. That goodbye was not the end but a door into your own heart. Into the part of you that learned to hold space for something nobody taught you. The canyon it carved in you? It became a riverbed for empathy. A place where others now find water. You were the soul who stayed when it mattered most.

Echo 1: The Wall
Warsaw, Poland, 1993

A wall is built not out of bricks, but of silence, survival, and a decision to never need too much. That wall will take decades to notice, and even longer to tear down.

I was eleven, sitting in math class, staring out the window, with a thought circling over and over: *How terrible of a person I must be. How could I not feel anything? Not even sadness?*

The evening before, my parents had told me that my cousin Karolina fell to her death on a school trip in the Tatra mountains. Her group was off-trail and trying to navigate steep terrain without the right equipment or skills. We never discovered what actually happened.

I didn't feel anything. It wasn't because I didn't know her or love her. We were close. Our families lived back-to-back in a duplex for several years. We spent afternoons playing in the yard and whole summers together at my grandparent's cabin.

She was six years older, my good big sister. She braided my hair, taught me how to make flower crowns, and coached me on how to perform in theatre plays we put on for our parents.

Her death rippled through our family, each of us swept into our own private currents of grief and coping. Her parents, hollowed by loss, became withdrawn and fragile, their sorrow an invisible burden. My parents and grandparents quietly struggled, mourning privately while trying to shield me from their sadness.

My cousin Ola, at fourteen, bravely took on the impossible task of raising her younger siblings. Zofia, the youngest, was robbed of a childhood, her parents transformed into grieving ghosts unable to see past their loss. The twins, born just a year later, inherited a silent, heavy expectation to heal wounds inflicted before they took their first breath.

Slowly and quietly, the family fractured, not in dramatic arguments or explosive confrontations, but through pockets of silence, whispered conversations behind closed doors, and emotional distances that stretched across years.

Some armored themselves with detachment, numbing out the pain. Others spiraled into anxiety, haunted by helplessness and dread of another loss. Each crafted their own protection, silently paying a high price just to survive.

I was strangely untouched, as if I stood outside the swirling currents of trauma, immune to their pull. Her loss didn't break through; it didn't even crack the surface. It was as though I had already hardened myself with an invisible shield. You couldn't hurt what had long ago gone numb.

Her passing wasn't my first experience with death. The year before, my father's mom Krystyna whom I called "Babcia Krysia", had passed. Rapid onset Leukemia took her away in less than a month. One day after school I stopped by her place for dinner and my favorite lingonberry whipping cream biscuits. The next, she was gone. Like gone-gone. Me pretend-crying at her grave.

And still, I felt nothing. I knew enough to act sad, thinking, If I show no feelings, they might think it's weird. That might cause concern. Make it easy for them. That story was already running the show. I knew my only worth was in not needing anything.

Later, I began to notice something else. Every time someone said, I miss my mom or I wish my friend were still here, I felt this wall go up inside me. A kind of glass shield between their grief and my understanding.

My gut reaction? Really? That's your problem? Get over it. People die. They leave. This isn't about you.

Have you ever judged others for feeling what you were too afraid to feel?

I didn't know what the emptiness meant. I only knew I couldn't feel what others felt. I couldn't mourn like they did. Later, when more of my friends died; MC and Roberta (who you will meet later), Sean, Dean, JD; some I truly loved, all I felt was the wall.

It took years to realize that the wall wasn't protecting but imprisoning me. And even longer to dismantle it, brick by brick, belief by belief.

As a kid, I was told I was too sensitive. So, I made a quiet decision: Not feeling made me strong. Strong was good. Strong was safe. Years later, when I became a coach, that sensitivity, now unburied and reclaimed, became my greatest asset. What was once too much is now a precious gift that I get to share with the world.

Years later my climbing partner and great friend Aimee passed. The numbness came. Why don't I feel this? "I don't think I know how to mourn," I said out loud to a friend. (first crack in my masonry).

That's when it finally hit me. The goodbye I didn't understand, my dad vanishing across an ocean, was a moment I stopped trusting anyone would stay. I decided if people were going to leave, I'd leave first, on my terms.

Something in me had shut down permanently. I learned not to count on anyone. I made a pact with myself: Don't feel too much. Don't need too much, don't get too attached. Just deal with it. Nobody cares. There's no time for your tears. Handle it. Move on.

So, I built a wall around everything, trying to hide the brutal truth: What I called strength was survival. And my way of dealing with it? I was forcing myself to deny who I really was.

Have you ever built walls of silence or perfection to avoid being left behind?

I wasn't broken. I was building a wall to protect the sacred flame within. Even numbness was an act of devotion to the part of me still surviving.

Now I see her, the one behind the wall, not as weak, but as wise. She knew what the world could not yet hold. Her silence was a shield. Her detachment, a doorway. And because of her, I have something to return to. Something untouched by performance or pain. That sacred flame? It never went out: it waited. And the wall I once cursed? It was the sanctuary that guarded my sacredness.

Soul Note:

You weren't numb because you didn't care, but because you cared so deeply and had nowhere safe to put it. That wall you built was wisdom. Every brick – a quiet act of protection for the sacred flame you carried.
You don't have to pretend to be strong. You already are. The truth beneath the pain is that you've always been whole. Sensitivity is your sacred power.

Root 2: Tiny Acts of Disappearing
Warsaw, Poland, 1987

Abandonment taught me that love leaves. But that was not the only lesson I learned. The world taught me to lose, and then it taught me to hide.

The seed that whispered you're too much and you don't matter, didn't just grow on its own. It was watered every time I swallowed my truth, stayed quiet, and played nice. It grew in silence in the quiet moments no one noticed. Moments that taught me how to disappear, one choice at a time.

It's wild how vividly certain childhood memories etch themselves into your soul, holding onto you long after you've grown. As I write this, I wonder: How do we pick the memories? Why do some feel as clear as yesterday, while others blur away?

One clear memory was in kindergarten in Warsaw's Northern Żoliborz neighborhood. Unlike today, where children are carefully dropped off and signed in, my mom simply left me at the building entrance, trusting I'd find my way to the classroom on my own. I always did… except on Tuesdays.

Tuesdays meant dance class, first thing in the morning. And I dreaded it. Not because I hated dancing, but because of a boy who decided he liked me. He said things I didn't understand. Yet even at five years old, I knew they were wrong; I felt the unsettling weight of his words in my small body.

Nobody seemed to notice, or maybe they just didn't know how to respond. Perhaps they didn't care. Either way, I learned quickly: keep quiet, no one is coming, no one will help.

Have you ever learned without realizing it – that silence felt safer than speaking out?

One Tuesday morning, after my mom dropped me off, I didn't go upstairs. Instead, I sat silently in that cold doorway, the chill from the concrete creeping into my legs, faint music drifting down from the classroom above – each cheerful note a painful reminder that something was wrong with me.

At five years old, I had already decided it was better to hide. Better to disappear than to face the shame of that boy's attention. I chose to stay out and stay silent, never once thinking I could ask for help.

What would it have meant to say "I need help", and know that someone would listen?

I had other problems, too. Our clothes, all secondhand, arrived in care packages from beyond the Iron Curtain: West Germany, France, England. My mom, always resourceful, patched up my jeans with care, lovingly sewing heart-shaped patches onto the knees. She thought they were adorable.

I was mortified. The patches screamed weakness to me – too girly, too vulnerable. But I didn't dare hurt my mom's feelings by telling her I hated them. So instead, I walked through kindergarten with my hands awkwardly covering my knees, desperately trying to hide what I believed was broadcasting my weakness to the world. Don't let them see. If they do, they'll know you're weak. It was pre-rejection at its finest: disappearing before anyone could reject me.

All those little moments stitched together an invisible truth I began to carry everywhere. I built an entire rulebook in my young mind, and it screamed loud and clear:

You're alone. Don't speak up. Never be weak. Don't cause trouble.

Then came the kindergarten dance performance. They dressed me up in a fuzzy white dress with little bunny tails, exactly the image I dreaded. During the performance, that same boy ignored the choreography, skipped past the other girls, and insisted on dancing with me. Humiliated and ashamed, I did and said nothing. Again, I chose silence over confrontation, swallowing the shame I felt. I didn't just feel shame; I became it.

I wonder how many of us learned to survive by shrinking.

Thirty years later, every time I want to shrink, I whisper to that younger version of me: Speak up, you are safe here, little one.

When my dad finally returned from Chicago, life got complicated in new ways. He started taking me on runs through the woods. I hated it. My small legs burned, my chest ached, the cold air sharp in my lungs – but I never dared stop. My heartbeat pounded in my ears, louder than my shouting thoughts. Don't disappoint him. I remember wishing I'd trip and fall, just to get out of it without being a disappointment. Even then, I was never brave enough to go through with it.

Over and over, my childhood delivered the crystal clear message: Your needs come second. Your feelings are too much. And no matter what, you'll never get it right.

I don't believe this was anyone's fault. It was just the story I patched together to create safety for myself.

Looking back now, I see how brave that five-year-old girl was; brave enough to protect herself the only way she knew how: by hiding.

Slowly, I crafted a version of myself that could survive those invisible rules. My protections were born: a Marta who stayed quiet, helpful, and unseen. A Marta who believed, deep down, that who she really was would never, ever be enough. I thought I was broken, but I was actually adapting. Doing the best I could with what I knew.

Many of us craft these versions of ourselves to survive. We shrink, swallow our voices, cover up our truth, believing it's the only way to be safe. These beliefs don't just shape our childhood. They follow us into adulthood, into our passions, our partnerships, our friendships.

It isn't until later, if ever, and only if we dare, that we realize how much of ourselves we've lost along the way.

Years later, I began to ask the question that would change everything: What if I didn't have to shrink anymore?

Soul Note:

You were never too much. You were simply too vast for the container you were given. Hiding was not a weakness, it was a sacred strategy. Now, the soul who once hid is ready to step forward and be seen. No more shrinking. No more wondering how much is the right amount of you.

Echo 2: The Vanishing
Squamish, British Colombia, 2006

She offered her hands, her food, her rope, her heart – believing being needed was love. But when the story was told and her name wasn't in it, she finally saw the truth: she got edited out of the very tale she helped craft. And worse: she had done it to herself.

Fast-forward twenty years, from kindergarten dance class to Squamish, British Colombia; an idyllic town of lumberjacks and adventurers tucked between the sea and the mountains, just an hour north of Vancouver. Granite walls rise like cathedrals from the rainforest, and climbers from around the world come to test their will against the stone.

I was twenty-four, beyond excited to finally climb there. My partner D-Griff and I had a truck, a stash of gear, and a plan. We were meeting some of my Polish climbing friends who were already here. It all felt like a dream: Climbing in Canada with the people I'd started my climbing journey with, my hot boyfriend by my side. I pictured shared meals, big laughs, long days on granite, and the kind of connection that only deepens in the wild.

What unfolded bore little resemblance to the dream I'd carried in. The guys were broke, without transport, and mostly focused on themselves; on what they wanted and needed. D-Griff and I became the drivers, the planners, and the pack animals. We carried the literal and emotional weight of the trip.

After a few weeks, we rerouted to the Bugaboos, an alpine cirque in British Columbia's Purcell Mountains, where jagged granite spires shoot into the sky high above ancient glaciers. I'd never climbed anywhere like it. Six of us crammed into our truck; four in the front cab and two in the camper bed, pounding beers to survive the ride. I still clung to my vision: if I just kept showing up, kept giving, it would all click.

But the energy had shifted. The guys were not offering gas money or food. D-Griff was irritated. I kept smoothing things over, telling myself I was being generous. Trying to keep the peace, to hold it all together.

It would be years before I'd learn this pattern had a name. That what I called generosity was something else entirely, a legacy of protection and self-erasure passed down through my family. Codependence.

Have you ever mistaken self-sacrifice for kindness? Stayed silent to keep the peace, even when something in you was quietly breaking?

In the Bugaboos, we camped close but barely spoke. We hoped that giving each other space would somehow fix what words hadn't. It helped, temporarily.

After the Bugs, we made the 20-hour drive back to California. The tension in the truck was thick enough to cut with a knife. D-Griff had clearly reached his limit. But I wasn't ready to face what was becoming obvious. "Let's invite the guys to Reno," I said. "Let's regroup before Yosemite."

He agreed… reluctantly. I told myself I was doing it for everyone. Truth? I was still trying to hold it all together for my self worth. At my own expense.

And then, in the morning, I saw it.

An article appeared in a Polish climbing magazine, written by one of the guys. He called the trip a great success. "Amazing ascents," he wrote. In his version, they had done it all on their own. I wasn't mentioned; not once.

Not the routes I'd led. Not the meals I'd cooked. Not the way I'd quietly held it all together when it was falling apart. I was invisible again.

Betrayal hit like a punch to the gut, this time, it cut deeper than ever. I collapsed onto the bathroom floor and cried for hours, body shaking, heart split open; not just because I'd been erased from the story, but because I saw how I created it all. At dinner, I said nothing. Later in my journal, I wrote the first boundary of my life: I am done earning my belonging.

I emailed the magazine my own version of the story. Even though I had no interest in appearing in magazines, I was hoping it would help set things straight and expose the truth about what had actually happened. I thought it would make me feel seen. I thought my friends would finally acknowledge my part in the story, freeing me from my anguish. No one said anything.

As William Blake wrote: "You never know what is enough unless you know what is more than enough." That was my threshold. I had to cross the line; to overgive, overextend, overfunction, before I could see the cost. And once I saw it, I couldn't unsee it.

This is how codependence looked in me: a double standard. I made sure everyone was fed, driven, cheered on… and never asked for anything in return.

I thought it was normal and how everyone should be, that's how women were in my family. I judged those who weren't doing it. Now I see I was acting out of survival. I needed them to need me, because I didn't know who I was without it.

This realization was painfully clear… and it was the first time I experienced witness consciousness. Just beyond the pain I saw a pattern. I saw a lifetime of trying to earn love by disappearing, a pattern passed down through generations. For a moment, something beyond me simply watched. Not in judgment, but in grace. It whispered: *You did what you knew. And now, you know better. And a vow: this ends with me.*

My nervous system had wired itself to equate usefulness with safety. If I wasn't needed, I feared I'd be left behind. So I overgave, hoping someone would give back. But they didn't. They saw me as trying too hard. And like so many codependent women, I was taken for granted.

What I really wanted wasn't credit in the magazine. I wanted to matter to my friends. I wanted them to notice the ways I'd shown up. I wanted to feel like I belonged. In the end, I made up an excuse and they had to find their own way to Yosemite.

Did they know I was hurt? I honestly don't know, I never asked. I wanted to be cool and didn't want them to know I cared. I thought if I voiced disappointment, they would abandon me. But here's the irony: I had already abandoned myself.

There was never another trip, never a second chance. I realized I was never a part of their story. I had imagined something that wasn't real.

In time, I would learn to break the codependence, with tools, boundaries, and a truth deeper than belonging. It took years to learn how to stay with myself, name my needs, and make decisions rooted in self-respect.

I see now: I wasn't being left out of their story. I was being invited to craft my own. One not written for applause, but as a hymn to the truth. For this invaluable lesson, I'm eternally grateful.

Back then, I thought I was being kind. I thought I was being strong. But really, I was just disappearing again. No wonder no one noticed.

Soul Note:

I watched you give and give, hoping it would earn you a place. I watched you disappear with a smile, thinking that it was love. But you were never meant to vanish: you came here to take up space, to speak your brilliant mind and to lead. To be known, not for how useful you are, but for who you are. You don't have to prove your worth by carrying what isn't yours. You are not here to earn love – you ARE love. And it's safe now to stop performing, stop pleasing, and come home to yourself.

Root 3: The Shrinking Years
Warsaw, Poland, 1988

That quiet girl covering heart shaped patches on her knees?

She was about to walk into a classroom that would confirm her worst fear: not only was she too much, she might also not be enough.

Before I decided I wasn't enough, there was a time when I believed I was capable, fast, fierce, and full of possibility. The world would eventually convince me otherwise.

I was one of those kids who developed quickly, especially when it came to language. By the time I was one, I was speaking in full sentences. Before I could even walk, I could express myself clearly and with conviction.

My mom loves to tell the story of taking me grocery shopping when I was a baby. She'd sit me on the checkout counter, barely old enough to hold myself steady. Then, to the amazement of everyone around, who expected baby talk I'd suddenly start speaking in full, complex sentences.

I was sharp, curious, and eager to understand the world around me. So when I turned six, my mom decided to send me to school a year early. My mom, having been bright and bored during her own school years, didn't want the same for me. She saw my potential and believed in it. More than wanting to keep me occupied, she wanted to give me something to grow into.

My mom was a stay-at-home mother. She was present, careful, and intentional. She gave me her full attention and made decisions from love. I felt it. And to this day, I honor it.

To her, I was full of promise. To others, I was a problem to correct.

My first-grade teacher believed my mom made a mistake, and she took it personally. She seemed more committed to proving my mother wrong than to educating me. She treated me differently, ignored my raised hand, humiliated me when I spoke up, she left me out of games, handed back tests with failing marks and no explanation. I was convinced I was stupid and unwelcome in the room.

Already too much, or not enough, or both.

I got bad grades; not because I didn't know the material, but because my teacher didn't think I belonged there. And to the six-year-old me, the truth was simple and devastating: I must be stupid.

I don't remember much detail of that school year, but I vividly remember the feeling: The tightness in my throat as I walked into the classroom. The hot flush of shame when she called on someone else. The quiet vow I made to myself not to try so hard next time.

I learned to shrink before someone else could shrink me. I remember the voice clearly: You will never be like the smart people, what's the point in even trying.

The following year, we moved across town. New school, new teacher, new classroom; but by that time, the damage was done. I was still a "good" kid, so I did the work. But I didn't believe in myself – school was just something I was bad at, and there was nothing I could do to change that.

I stayed in the middle. Not failing. Not shining. There was no spark, no wonder. My priority was not getting hurt and remembering that showing interest wasn't safe.

The only thing I learned in school was that it wasn't a place to learn or grow. It was a place to survive. A place where it was best to lay low, because being noticed only led to pain.

Have you ever stayed quiet and invisible because who you really were was dangerous?

My first teacher didn't accept me, and after that, I stopped expecting anyone to.

I was shy. Insecure. I didn't disregard school, I just didn't believe I belonged there. Belief was planted: I will never have what it takes.

That quiet belief followed me for two more years. By the time I entered fourth grade, something had shifted. Poland had undergone a peaceful revolution sparked by the Solidarity movement which was transforming the country into a market economy.

My parents, far from wealthy but deeply aware of my struggles, enrolled me in one of the country's first private schools. It was a financial stretch, but way worth it to them. They wanted me in an environment where I could finally thrive.

That school gave me room to breathe. I had a kind teacher, and I made friends. I didn't suddenly transform into an academic superstar, but I stopped dragging myself through the day. I discovered little sparks of curiosity. I began to feel safe enough to speak up. The fog of survival started to lift. For the first time, I was showing up.

A small door cracked open, and I chose to step through.

Soul Note:

You were never stupid – you were symphonic. A soul of uncommon cadence, born into a world deafened by its own limitations. They mistook your originality for error. But the brilliance they overlooked became the bedrock of your becoming. The silence was not surrender, it was a seed. And now, it flowers into wisdom. You never lost your light. You stashed it for safekeeping. Now it is time: Retrieve it. Speak it. Let the world relearn what brilliance looks like.

Echo 3: Beer Run
Rifle Mountain Park, Colorado, 2022

A climb awaits: silent, unmoved, indifferent. It won't meet you halfway. It is not your enemy, nor your ally. When you reach for it, it reveals exactly where you stand: with your body, your worth, your story.

This was supposed to be hard, but not this kind of hard. The question: Will I stay with myself, even when everything inside me screams to disappear?

Rifle Mountain Park is a narrow limestone canyon nestled in western Colorado's high country. The winding gorge is framed by dense green forests, vibrant wildflowers, and the soothing sound of East Rifle Creek flowing toward the Colorado River. It's also one of the world's most renowned climbing destinations, a proving ground for elite climbers and devoted seekers alike.

In my thirties, I uprooted my life and moved across the country, to live as close as possible to Rifle. I wanted to submerge myself in the canyon's cryptic, demanding style, to let its limestone walls become both teacher and mirror along my evolutionary curve.

Beer Run is Rifle's classic 5.13a*– a serious climb for very advanced climbers, like me.

I picked Beer Run as a project*, because that's what climbers do. Attempt what we perceive as impossible to test our limits. We choose

---

* For explanations of climbing terms, see the glossary at the end of the book.

routes that push us just beyond our current ability and return to them, again and again. Projects are full-body puzzles. We study the moves (called beta*), rehearse the sequences, build muscle memory over days, weeks, and sometimes even years.

One day, if everything aligns, we send*; climb from the ground all the way to the top anchors* without falling or hanging on the rope.

I showed up with commitment, energy, and determination to give it everything I had. The first 80 feet was extremely demanding and technical. Still I was able to imagine piecing most of it together.

Then came the upper crux*: the Tombstone.

On almost every single move of Beer Run, I was coming up short. In climbing, a few inches can make or break you. I had to jump, lock off*, and strain for holds others reached with ease. It felt punishing, the kind of hard that makes you question why you're even trying.

I threw myself at the tombstone sequence again and again, hoping to unlock some crucial beta that would let me through. Below me, a group of shirtless guys lounged at the base, relaxed, at home in their long-limbed bodies.

They were projecting Beer Run too, and while I was thrashing and falling in dismay, they were laughing, sipping beers, and casually spraying* out beta that worked for them, but not for me. They weren't trying to be condescending. They simply had no idea that their sequences wouldn't work for someone short like me.

Hanging at the end of the rope I was collapsing inside. Why was I on this route? Why did I move across the U.S. to live close to this canyon? Why was I even born?

Have you ever been overwhelmed by inadequacy because someone else made it look easy?

My body; short, and female, wasn't built for Beer Run. I didn't belong here. But this wasn't about the rock climb. It was me against every silent story I'd swallowed without question: You're not built for this. You'll never be strong enough. You'll never be enough to love. A distant echo of running in the forest with dad.

After falling more times than I could count, I finally lowered back to the ground. I felt broken. I hadn't just failed at a rock climb, I'd failed at remembering who I was. I let the outside noise convince me my effort didn't count. I let their ease make me question whether I even had a right to be there.

I went home and did all the things I knew would help me: nervous system grounding, lengthy talks with my coach, convincing myself I had cleared it.

I returned with hope laced through my ribs, daring to believe I could outclimb my own skin. This time, I'd escape the sentence of being me. I tried a hundred times. But each reach ended the same, fingers grasping absence, chest echoing with ache, anchored in the same quiet no. The wall: silent. Indifferent. Unmoved.

And then, one moment, I imagined the canyon not as an obstacle, but as a mirror. The stone didn't reject me, it reflected me. My own doubts, my own distortions. And as I saw it, I softened. The wall had never been against me. It was simply holding the line until I could meet myself.

There was a time I believed strength meant trying harder. Once I would have come back stronger, more determined. Fixating on sending the route to find redemption.

But this story isn't about triumph – it's about worth. About staying with yourself through discomfort. About refusing to outsource your value to a crowd that doesn't see you.

The real win was walking away, saying "enough," lowering off, untying, and choosing to love myself without the send.

What if self-respect was saying to yourself, not today, and meaning it? What if strength was knowing when to say, this is enough, and truly believing it?

Because the climb? It's never just about the reach. It's about meeting yourself at the edge of your limitations, welcoming your body, your history, your hurt, and giving it everything you've got anyway.

Soul Note:

The wall wasn't the test. You didn't come to prove your worth, but to remember it. You didn't fail, you witnessed. You touched the raw edge of your story and chose tenderness over conquest. That is not defeat – it's devotion. The canyon didn't need your send, it needed your presence. And so did you.

Root 4: Nature of Belonging
Małe Ciche, Poland, 1990

And then there were the mountains.

We lived in an apartment in the heart of Warsaw, surrounded by flat grey stretches of city, sprawling concrete blocks that gave way to the endless flatness of Mazovian farmland. But once a year, we were called somewhere else. A different, magical land – my favorite.

For as long as I can remember, we had a Christmas Day tradition. Still stuffed from our Christmas Eve feast – gelatin fish, pierogies, and poppy seed rolls – and dressed in new winter clothes hand sewed by my mother, bright neon patchwork – an 80s dream, we would pile into our tiny Fiat and head south. Six hours of winding roads and nausea, all for that first breathtaking glimpse of the snowy mountains.

Some of my most treasured memories are from those ski trips to the Tatra Mountains. We traveled with a lively crew; my father's friends from the Physical Education department – a rowdy bunch of aunties and uncles who doubled as extra parents to us kids. Meals were communal, laughter was constant, and we all squeezed into a tiny guesthouse in Małe Ciche – a village tucked against the slopes. Our days were spent on a single ski hill.

It probably wasn't much, but to me it was the edge of my known world. It was there that my dad taught me to ski. It was magical; by far the best times we ever had together since he came back from the U.S. He was cheerful, funny, sober (at least during the day), and fully in his element.

He loved skiing and he loved teaching me to ski. In those moments, he was completely himself, alive in a way I rarely saw.

Something took root on those trips. I learned to cherish nature, movement, laughter, and the joy of shared adventures. A seed was planted: reverence for the wild and a delight in moving my body through untamed places. That seed would one day crack open a future I couldn't yet imagine.

It grew into the kind of wealth you can't measure in numbers. It lives in your lungs when you're lost in the wilderness and dances through your muscles as you cross a river. It whispers: you belong here. You are good. That was my father's greatest gift. He passed on something he loved deeply, and now it lives in me. For that, I'm forever grateful.

Soul note:

You were claimed by the wild long before I tried to earn it. The gift was always first. It took you years to remember that the belonging was always yours.

Echo 4: One Last Ski Trip
Warsaw, Poland, 2020

When it was time for their final journey, it was not the peaks that mattered, but the feeling they once forged together. For this was their cosmic pact: to taste life side by side, to steal joy from the dark seams of lineage, to meet again at the edge of life and death. In that silent accord, love needed no fixing, only remembering.

Maciek was a mixed bag of a father. He gave me two things: one a gift, the other a curse. The gift was his love for the mountains, the joy of being in nature, of feeling alive out there. The curse, likely passed onto him by his ancestors, was an unspoken rule: To be loved, I had to perform.

Skiing was joy, but there was always a shadow. I needed to be tough, to prove I was worthy of his pride, and that I could keep up. That seed grew into a twisted core inside me for years. Nature became both sanctuary and stage. I found refuge in forests, in lakes, and in the foraging. While at the same time I was always chasing summits, miles, and harder grades, hoping that conquering them would finally make me enough.

Was it a drug, or was it medicine?

It took me decades to understand and feel the difference: adventure as addiction versus adventure as aliveness. Eventually, I learned to draw an invisible boundary within myself: The need to perform is an ego trap. The wild was never meant to be where I proved my worth. It was always meant to be where I simply got to be myself.

My dad's health had been declining for years, and when it suddenly collapsed, I flew home from the U.S. with a heavy heart, suspecting this might be the last time I would ever see him. He was in constant pain and mostly bedbound. I carried so much grief that I never really had a dad, anger at his illness, anger at the world.

I needed a goodbye. So, I came with a clear intention, to go on one last ski trip. I found him frail and sunken into the couch. I joined in, scared, unsure, and conflicted, yet determined to spark up that old feeling.

His shame, his brokenness, and his wish that things were different, hovered in the room.

He reached for the remote, flipped through some channels, landed on Eurosport. Downhill skiing. I closed my eyes and breathed deep. I recalled the snow, the crinkling of the neon clothes, the sun's rays shooting down the hill.

Slowly, I was there again. He was there with me. The same wonderful, wild, charismatic, magnetic man who used to come alive in the mountains. His only refuge. His medicine.

Dad and I sat on the couch bantering about skiers, the outfits, the forest, and old trips to Małe Ciche. "Remember the time we almost died?" he said, a grin spreading. "The car slid down that icy road, spun a couple times on the curve, then just stopped. Right at the edge of that huge cliff. One more foot and we would have been dust!"

"You were maybe 8, but looked at me with wide eyes, aware of what could have happened."

"I remember! Did we ever tell Mom?" I laughed. "No way," he shook his head laughing with his full body. "She'd never let us go again."

At that moment, I understood. He didn't need to be healthier, happier, or finally quit his addictions. He was perfect. I was perfect too. It didn't matter if we never skied together again.

We were perfect, right there on that couch, sitting inside everywhen, on our timeless ski trip.

Soul note:

The mountains are more than a landscape. They are myth, written into our bones, calling us to chase something neither of us could name. And in the end, it was not summits or grades that mattered, but this quiet moment, where wounds turned to medicine and we found each other perfect at last.

Root 5: Initiation by Stone
Warsaw, Poland, 1997

If school made me question my intelligence, life at fifteen made me question my existence. I had stopped believing I could shine in a classroom. Now I was wondering if life had any shine at all. The days were always gray, and I felt like I was dying of nothingness.

Teenage years are rough for most, but for me, it felt like everything I loved was being stripped away. My parents decided to build a house outside the city, chasing a dream of country life that they believed would fix everything. To me, it was a brutal exile. I was being evicted from my own life. Everything dear to me was ripped away. I was being buried alive.

Just as I was finally feeling confident at school, they pulled me out and sent me somewhere new. My best friend, Ola Sawicka, who I'd built an entire world with, was one of the casualties.

We lived just blocks apart. We rollerbladed around the neighborhood, journaled side by side, woke before dawn for horseback rides, taught each other how to snowboard, dressed up in what we thought made us look cool, and talked about boys for hours. We watched MTV, invented our own language, and pieced the world together like a shared puzzle. It was the first relationship where I let myself be fully me. And moving away stole it from me.

Winter in Poland is dark, damp, and bone-chillingly cold. That first winter in the new house, we had no heating. Just a big metal barrel acting as a makeshift fireplace in the middle of the house. One day, while we were outside, the barrel caught fire, filling the living room with flames. My dad managed to put it out, but as I watched the smoke rise, I remember thinking, I hope this stupid place burns.

We had moved only fifteen miles outside of Warsaw, but with no phone line, no bus connection, and no internet or cell phones yet, it might as well have been another planet. Our house stood alone in a vast, flat cabbage field, the first of many to be carved into a suburban sprawl.

My parents bought a big lot with a group of their ski friends. It was supposed to be the dream of communal living, away from the chaos of the city, surrounded by nature and a close-knit community. But no one else had begun building yet.

It was just me, and the long, aching silence of isolation. The absence of connection felt like a life sentence.

I enrolled in a new school, which wasn't that bad, but I resented it anyway. I joined the swim team, and it was the one thing that brought a flicker of excitement. My parents dropped me off at school in the morning and my grandfather, Leszek, picked me up in his tiny red Daihatsu Charade in the afternoons.

If I was even one minute late, he'd drive off without me, no warning, no second chances. I'd be left to untangle a maze of buses, then walk or hitchhike the final miles home. His life had been built on hardship and discomfort, and he was passing down his lessons the only way he knew: through the school of hard knocks. And it worked. "Old men don't wait around for young girls," he'd grumble, foot on the gas, as I ran behind the car waving, too late again.

Life in the cabbage field was a dull nightmare, devoid of inspiration or excitement. School. Home. Homework. Repeat. I felt like a prisoner inside in a colorless suffocating routine.

The atmosphere at home wasn't warm anymore, it was quiet in all the wrong ways. My parents were unraveling under the weight of financial strain and a slow, silent collapse of their marriage. The contractor they'd trusted had vanished halfway through building the house, taking their money with him. Now they were scrambling to find someone else to finish what was left. They couldn't afford much, certainly not my private school. And the silence between them grew thick and heavy, a void all three of us avoided like a cracked foundation no builder dared to touch.

My dad coped by disappearing. His remedy of choice: beer. Just enough to blur the edges. To be there but not really there. He'd drink and vanish into the TV. My mom checked out in her own way: disappearing into her work. She came home late then buried herself in books. Even when my parents were home, I felt completely alone.

The place felt like a Siberian exile: unfinished drywall and dusty plywood. We couldn't afford flooring or furniture for the first few years. Every afternoon, I sat by myself for hours, waiting for my parents to return from work.

I tried numbing out in front of the TV like everyone else, but the brainless shows and flashy commercials only amplified the emptiness. I felt like a ghost haunting the shell of a life. A girl wasting away. Idling through each day. Hating myself for not knowing how to fix it.

I remember coming back from a weeklong swim meet, riding a bus full of kids, all happy to be going home. I sat there, dreading the return to loneliness, to silence, to my sadness.

The weeklong swim meet gave me a temporary escape from the dull ache of my life. But the return was inevitable.

At some point during those years of emptiness, I made a silent vow: If I ever find something that can carry me out of this, I will hold on to it for dear life.

That was the first time my soul began to whisper.

If there's a season I'm most grateful for, it's that one: the moment I stopped trying to fit into a life that drained me. Instead, I began to follow the current of something alive inside me.

It was around this time when my parents' marriage finally snapped. Their divorce didn't just split a household, it shattered the last illusion that kept me tethered to being the good, quiet daughter. If they could break their vows, I could break the rules.

It echoed a deeper fracture I'd witnessed when I was seven and Poland broke its own rules, shedding communism overnight for a new, uncertain system. In both my family and my country, the message rang clear: everything is made up. And in that collapse, a wild permission emerged. If the world could reinvent itself, so could I. I could write my own story.

And then the wild whispered. A friend of mine, Filip, told me about a weekend trip his Boy Scout troop had taken to go rock climbing. I'd never heard of rock climbing and, as he was describing it, a deep, electric yes lit up in me. I didn't understand it, but I felt it. This isn't stupid. It isn't average. And it sure as hell isn't empty. It was absurd, courageous, anarchistic and wild. Everything I craved. My whole body responded. And underneath it all was something even deeper, what I now call soul truth.

What I didn't know then was that climbing would give me what I wanted more than anything: a wild curriculum designed to evolve me into my truest self. A space where the fight was mine to choose. Where the struggle had rules I could understand. On the rock, I wasn't at the mercy of adults, moods, political systems falling apart, or a crumbling household. I had control over one thing: me.

I begged the Boy Scouts to take me. I wanted in…bad. And when I finally scraped together enough Polish Zlotys, I bought my first pair of real climbing shoes: Boreal Stingers. Yellow leather, black laces. Like a bee in a corset. They looked dangerous. Fierce. Like they belonged to someone who meant it.

My mom supported my new fascination and imagined me in proper mountain footwear. Sturdy boots with thick soles. Something sensible. Something that looked safe. So when she saw those tiny little slippers, she cried. Those weren't practical. They were a foolish indulgence, expensive, and unthinkable. An extravagance no kid like me should dare to want.

In her world, dreams were dangerous. You didn't chase after them – you chased them away to survive the day. When she saw me spend every last coin on something so bold, so bright, full of hunger, it terrified her. She did not value her own dreams, so how could she support mine?

Even my teenage climbing friends thought I was nuts. They climbed in old worn-down soccer cleats with the studs shaved off. But I didn't care. Those Stingers weren't just climbing gear. They were a declaration. A badge of hope.

Proof that I still believed my life could change.

I bought them so tight, I gave myself permanent nerve damage. Years later, someone gifted me the same shoes, two sizes up, and I couldn't even squeeze my feet in. That's how tightly I'd been clinging to the hope that something better was possible for me.

I bought those shoes before I'd ever even tied into a rope. But despite that I was already telling everyone, "Watch me. I'm going to be a rock climber." I didn't know what that meant. I just knew I needed it.

Have you ever said yes before you knew why, simply because something deep in your bones whispered: this is the way?

The Boy Scouts finally cracked. We took a two-hour train ride south from Warsaw to Zawiercie, one of Poland's climbing meccas* nestled in the Kraków-Częstochowa Jurassic Uplands. We called it Jura. I spent most of the ride bouldering* around on the interior walls of the train in my too-tight shoes, like a kid playing cosmonaut or pirate. I wasn't a climber yet, but I was rehearsing what it might feel like to become one.

There were four of us: Filip, Tomek, Vava, and me. We didn't really know what we were doing, just a dream, a flicker of something wild, and hearts pounding with anticipation. All we knew was that we had to follow it.

When we arrived, the landscape looked like a coral reef rising from green fields: gently rolling terrain dotted with ancient white karst towers, their jagged faces full of pockets and edges perfect for climbing. I eagerly asked someone to show me how to tie into a rope. I had been dreaming of this moment for weeks, imagining how glorious, how life-changing it would be.

But the moment I stepped onto the rock, the fantasy collapsed. It was brutally hard. I had watched others and thought, I can do that. I was wrong: my feet skated, my hands slipped, and I flailed. I wasn't good. Not even close. The reality of climbing hit me like an anvil: I wanted it to feel natural, and heroic. But it didn't. It was the hardest thing I'd ever tried. And the wall didn't care.

They say if you like sucking, you'll love climbing. I guess I was in the right place. Yet I didn't quit – quitting meant going back to the cold house, to the silence, to being invisible again. Despite the pain and humiliation, something deeper whispered: this is it. This is the way out. It didn't matter how hard it was. I had to find a way. I had to make it work.

I struggled. I cried dry tears no one could see. I swallowed my pride, especially after announcing to the whole train that I was basically an expert. But after thrashing my way up the hardest part of the route, the climb began to ease. And for the first time, I felt it: the rhythm, the reach, the flow. I stole it back, my right to be here, one fingertip, one shallow breath at a time, until I reached the anchor*.

At the top, I was both utterly defeated and wildly triumphant. I've felt that same paradox nearly every time since: agony, exhaustion, frustration, and joy. The joy of being the one who didn't quit. Who whispered I will into the roar of you can't.

In climbing there were no teachers to impress, no grades to earn. No one I had to shrink from or perform for. It was just me and the rock. I liked that.

I don't remember much else about that trip, probably more climbing, campfires, sleeping in hay, and the kind of nonsense talk teenagers live for. But one memory burned itself into me like the first sunburn of summer: huddling with the others on the cold floor of the room around a dusty old TV, watching Masters of Stone IV on scratchy VHS.

Though the tape was worn out and skipping, the film was unmistakably a portal. It featured the rock gods of the day: bold, shirtless, flying up impossible routes, taking insane risks, screaming with effort and joy. Living a life worth risking it all, their climbing a dance with gravity. Every move said: This is what freedom looks like. I watched wide-eyed, heart pounding, something calling me in, lighting me up. This film was a declaration. A protest flag against the gray 9-to-5 prison.

It's when I first heard of Yosemite. I didn't know how I'd get there. But I knew I would, no matter what.

Later that summer, I signed up for a weeklong intermediate rock-climbing course. There I learned how to place gear* in cracks, build anchors, and lead* climbs. That winter, I completed speleology training, learning how to move through, map, and understand underground cave systems.

By the next summer, I was alpine* certified: specialized training for moving confidently in the mountains across snow, ice, and exposed rock.

I was now seventeen, and climbing had become the center of my life. I could read topography, understand weather patterns, plan routes, and execute complex rescue techniques. I had become a climber.

Many of my early climbs were done in those same Boreal Stingers – two sizes too small. A perfect metaphor: trying to grow and willing to endure pain to prove I belonged to my dream. For years, I shoved myself into versions of success that crushed my toes and cut off my circulation, because they looked like they'd get me where I wanted to go.

Have you ever thought that suffering meant you are doing it right?

But just like those shoes, what looks powerful on the outside doesn't always support you on the inside. You can only contort yourself for so long before something goes numb.

The fifteen-year-old girl watching TV alone in a cold, unfinished house, convinced she was nothing, was gone. In her place stood someone who had found her purpose. Climbing didn't just teach me how to move. It taught me how to take responsibility. How to bet on myself. How to put everything on the line for something that mattered.

For years, I believed climbing gave me purpose. That the mountains saved me. But now I know the truth: I gave that purpose to myself. I saw the lifeboat, and crawled into it. What began as an escape became the nurse and the tutor, the cure, and a lifelong initiation into what it means to be fully, fiercely human.

So many people wait to find their purpose, like shoppers scanning a shelf, hoping to spot the one thing that finally fits. But the purpose can't be found. It's forged in risk and devotion. In the moment you say yes to a life no one else can dream up for you.

Whether it's climbing, quilting, starting a business, or raising a child, meaning isn't something we find. It's something we build. One hold, one hope, one heartbeat at a time.

This was only the beginning. But I didn't want just a bite – I wanted to eat up the whole damn mountain. That first hit of aliveness and challenge ripped the lid off something dormant inside of me. And when the next invitation came; unexpected, urgent, the only answer was yes. I had no idea how far it would take me.

Even after finding my footing, the old ghosts still lingered. For years the patterns crept back in again and again. Healing isn't a straight line.

Choosing to climb was choosing not to vanish. My turning point.

In the years that followed, I kept moving, always chasing the next trail, the next climb, the next thin thread of aliveness. I lived with a restlessness I didn't yet know how to name. I wasn't lost, exactly. But I hadn't yet landed anywhere that felt like mine. Climbing grounded me. The mountains made me feel real. But there was still something missing.

Soul Note:

The moment you chose your hunger for life over your fear of pain, a new world was born. That girl didn't give up. She climbed through the silence and summoned a future where her joy was non-negotiable. You owe her nothing less than your full aliveness.

Echo 5: The Invisible Fixer
Yosemite Valley, 2016

And when once again no one noticed, when the credit passed her by, the drop overflowed. Not with rage. With clarity. She finally saw "If I don't stop this pattern myself, no one ever will." To walk away, not in defeat, but in power, reclaimed.

We were camped at Yellow Pines Campground in Yosemite Valley, working on a film shoot about climbing legends. I'd been hired to help in the kitchen and keep basecamp running smoothly. In the mornings, after the crew had left for the day, I'd ventured off to free solo* routes on the Manure Pile Buttress, a classic granite formation known for its approachable multi-pitch climbs. It was my private ritual, a way to claim the day before dissolving back into support mode.

One morning, the film crew happened to be filming at the same crag. I showed up as usual, and soon, found myself back in my old role. A woman who gives all of herself to keep things from falling apart. The one who handles it.

I told myself to stay out of it, to just climb, as I watched the whole production completely unravel. There were lives at stake. The rigger*, responsible for building life-critical anchoring systems, didn't know how to build an anchor. His equally unqualified assistant, pulled me aside to ask how to use a belay device*.

These were the men being paid to keep people alive, and there I was; unpaid, uninvited, quietly stepping in to do their job. No hesitation. No question. Pure muscle memory: step in, save the day, swallow the ache.

Later that day, their audio setup failed. I offered a solution, soloed up the wall, and repositioned the receiver exactly where it needed to be. By sundown, I'd saved the production more times than I could count.

There's a backstory to this.

Before that fiasco on set, I had applied to work for that company; multiple times. My resume was stacked: technical rigging experience, years behind a camera, a film degree from Brazil, and a documentary I had shot, edited, and produced on my own. On top of that, I had a proven climbing record and fluency in the vertical world that most people could only dream of.

I never got a response. I didn't expect a parade, but I didn't expect silence either.

That evening, as I walked away from the buttress, I saw the lead producer loading equipment into his car. I stopped by to say goodbye. He looked up, smiled politely, and asked, "Aren't you part of the kitchen crew?"

Have you ever given everything, hoping they'd notice, while knowing they never will?

He had no idea what had transpired that day. No one told him. No one noticed. All the weight I had carried, completely unacknowledged. That stung. I didn't need praise, but I had earned recognition for saving the production that day.

I wanted him to say "Wait, you applied to work with us? After what I saw today, you're a no-brainer. That was masterful. Thank you for saving our ass! You're in."

Instead of telling him about what happened, I just nodded, smiled an awkward grin and walked away. Invisible. Again.

I resented that day for a long time but I don't any longer. Now I bless it. Their blindness was the gift that showed me where to stop handing over my brilliance. It taught me to claim my light fully.

As much as I once wanted to be a part of the climbing production world, I had had enough. It was the last time I auditioned for their approval. It didn't end in failure. It ended in clarity. I finally saw the truth.

I had more important things to do in life than proving I'm extraordinary.

That night, I felt the old urge stir, the one that says, try harder, prove it, earn your place. But instead I zipped my sleeping bag closed, exhaled centuries of silence, and whispered: "We're done auditioning. My brilliance was never meant to echo in the background of those too afraid to face its light."

Soul Note:

Somewhere deep in your grandmother's bones, a silence was broken. Rage turned into release. They, too, carried the weight of the work without witness. You are the one who gets to lay it down. You remember that your worth is more valuable than applause. That your brilliance was never meant to beg. That your "yes" is a gift, and your "no" is a line that is not to be crossed. This is not rebellion. You are walking back to yourself.

Root 6: Replanted and Thriving
Minnesota, 1999

After I found my savior in climbing, I knew I could never go back, not just to the cold house or the lonely routine, but to the smallness I had been surviving inside. I had touched something real and I needed more of it.

The call came out of nowhere. No time to plan, no chance to prepare. I had no idea that this one wild yes would completely change my trajectory.

I was seventeen, camping with friends in Hel, a narrow peninsula on the Polish coast, learning to windsurf on the Baltic Sea. The summer sun was golden and wide, the air thick with salt and possibility. Each time the wind caught my sail, I felt the song of my soul humming.

Freedom maybe, or the first flickers of power. It was nearly idyllic, if not for the quiet throb of teenage ache. But even in my angst, with questions whirling, I had already begun my slow, deliberate ascent toward something vast and more truthful.

Two years earlier at fifteen, I had completed my first climbing course and hiked across the Polish and Slovakian Tatras with two friends. I was shaping my life around wilderness and movement, but I still unconsciously carried old beliefs about worth, invisibility, and needing to earn my place. The thoughts underlying these beliefs were nothing new, but something else had begun to stir. Not loud, or certain, but unmistakable.

A different flavor to the ache: less desperation, more desire. I was beginning to get a glimpse of what it might feel like to have a life, instead of just surviving one.

Maciek called me out of the blue. "There's an opportunity," he said. "Someone canceled, and your name came up. Do you want to go to the U.S. for a year?" He meant now. As in...tomorrow.

His wife was involved with the Rotary Club's student exchange program. I had been drifting between train stations and trailheads, barely staying in touch with my parents when another student dropped out from the program at the last minute. She instantly saw this vacancy as an opportunity for me, sensing that this program could offer me something invaluable. Maybe even lifesaving.

Before dad finished his sentence I already knew the answer. Like him, I was quick to leap, willing to risk. I had one condition: I'd go, but only after I finished my alpine climbing certification. Non-negotiable.

As soon as I got home from Hel, I applied for my visa, repacked my bag, and left for the Tatras with Filip and Tomek for three weeks of alpine training, climbing, and learning to survive in the mountains. I would not have missed this trip for the world.

The Tatras are a compact, rugged mountain range straddling the border between Poland and Slovakia, the highest stretch of the Carpathians. With sharp granite peaks, emerald valleys, turquoise alpine lakes, and serrated ridgelines, they formed the perfect crucible for a young climber on the cusp of becoming.

The climbing there? Technically mediocre, the approaches long, the weather often moody and unpredictable. But to us, it was sacred ground. We weren't chasing grades, we were chasing godlight: those fleeting moments when the mountain opens up and says: you belong here.

Our instructor, Wojciech Jedliński, was a legend. An old-school alpinist from Łódź, he had climbed in the Himalayas and Hindu Kush, opened virgin routes in Norway, and claimed first ascents of nearly twenty unnamed peaks in the Peruvian Andes. He wasn't some plastic gym hero; he was the real deal. We worshipped him.

He taught us the basics of knots and techniques. But more than that, he taught us how to BE in the mountains. How to carry ourselves with reverence and reliability. How to suffer with grace. How to honor the terrain and your partners like your life depends on it; because it does. I still carry his values to this day. They live in the way I move, the way I lead, and the way I return to the wild again and again.

Three weeks of grit, glory, and pain led us to the final trial: a brutal exam with a 5% pass rate. We made it through. We earned our alpine climbing cards, and with them, a new identity. We were climbers now.

Then it was time for me to go.

One day I was rappelling* into icy couloirs*, gripping granite with bloodied knuckles and full lungs. The next day, I was stepping off a plane in Minnesota. Gone was the crisp alpine air scented with pine and wild laughter echoing off the ridgelines. In its place: endless cornfields, and a land so flat and still it felt like the world had been muted.

I had gone from dancing with death on sharp peaks to walking the halls of a Midwestern high school, where no one knew what to make of the girl with a strange accent and euro pants. More than culture shock, it was a soul clash. A collision between worlds. From boldness to blandness. From sacred landscapes enveloped in thin air to the stuffy perfume haze of the Mall of America. From belonging to bewilderment. The wild in me felt caged.

The curriculum was a joke. I came from one of Warsaw's top academic high schools, where excellence was expected, not applauded. Now I was in classes I could ace in my sleep, surrounded by people who didn't know me, didn't share my history, and couldn't possibly understand what it took for me to say yes to this. No one here had seen fog roll over a Tatra ridge at sunrise. Most couldn't even find Poland on a map.

They were kind, in that quiet Puritan way, pleasant on the surface, distant underneath. Cheerful, yet restrained. Their world was safe, neat, and color-inside-the-lines predictable. Nothing like mine. I didn't fit, not because I didn't try, but because I had already lived a wilder truth. And once you have tasted that kind of aliveness, you can't un-know it.

Everything felt fake. I almost went home.

But after three months, I moved in with a new family: the Abbotts. Claire and James had three kids, two still at home, and they welcomed me like one of their own. Their house buzzed with funeral home humor, the kind you earn from generations of witnessing both grief and grace, and the kind of light chaos that feels unmistakably like love.

Back in Poland, my mom was having a baby; in January, my little sister, Maria was born. I missed her arrival, and the ache of that absence sat briefly in my chest like frost. But life with the Abbotts was full and generous, softening the sorrow reminding me that I wasn't running away from my life, but growing into a bigger one.

Mrs. Abbott, and I clicked fast. Claire got me outside every morning before school, even in the heart of winter when the temps sat in the single digits. First we hiked, then we started jogging. Somewhere between frozen eyelashes and thawing muscles, a switch was flipped.

The movement wasn't just physical; it was medicinal. A lifeline. Running turned into a ritual. A devotion. Six miles every morning before school for the rest of the year. Not for performance, not for approval, but to stay in touch with the fire inside me that refused to die, even in Midwestern America. And slowly, this strange land of corn and casseroles began to feel less like exile… and more like possibility.

The magic was emerging.

After a few months I was so far ahead in school, they told me I didn't need to come anymore. As an exchange student, attendance wasn't mandatory. So, Claire and I packed up the car and road-tripped across the U.S. making a quick stop in Mexico.

We drove cross-country through the flatlands of the midwest making random pit stops anytime we saw something weird or interesting. We saw the Phantom of the Opera in Phoenix, crafted the night away with Claire's nieces in Tucson, and wandered an art fair in Tubac. In Southern Arizona we stood staring up in awe at the giant saguaro cactuses, poised like sentinels over the ancient desert and I felt, somehow, a kinship. I wanted to be like them – rooted, resilient and reaching.

Somewhere along the way we ended up with a statue of Saint Francis of Assisi and a mannequin we named Lena, who leaned dramatically with every turn. The car became the "Freaking Black Car" for reasons no one remembers, and was our ship of fools and freedom. I remember taking tequila shots in the back seat as the sun dipped low, laughing until my sides hurt, and falling hard for the American West, its landscapes, its wildness, its raw, wide-open promise.

On the way back we stopped at the Grand Canyon and found it shrouded in fog, we marveled at the cliff dwellings in Mesa Verde, and I gleefully peed in all four states at Four Corners. We chatted with brawny ice climbers in Ouray, Colorado, gazed up at the Devil's Tower in Wyoming, and stood before the massive presidential faces at Mount Rushmore, utterly alone, in the heart of off season.

In South Dakota we detoured to see the Corn Palace and a giant roadside chicken (or maybe it was an eagle?), some of the random surreal Midwestern attractions that make you question whether you're dreaming or just very far from home.

That trip was a gateway. It wasn't just freedom, it was the scale of it all. The absurdity, the beauty, the invitation. The land itself felt like a dare to dream bigger.

Have you ever stayed with discomfort long enough for exile to turn into expansion?

Later that winter, one of the Rotarians invited me to join him and his seven grandkids on a snowboarding trip to Montana. Of course I said yes. It was my first time riding powder through trees. Pure, unfiltered joy. I carved fresh lines through snow so light it felt like riding on a cloud. This wasn't the bunny hill in the Tatras anymore – I was flying in the Rocky Mountains.

Back in Minnesota, not far from the Abbotts, I discovered a small bluff just outside Red Wing, overlooking the Mississippi River. It wasn't huge or famous, just a modest local crag. Now all I needed was partners.

One afternoon, I crossed paths with a crew – doctors and researchers from the Mayo Clinic. They welcomed me into their gang, and soon we were climbing together every week. I didn't have a car, so one of them, Mark, went out of his way to pick me up, week by week, without hesitation. They were generous with their time, gear, and encouragement. Those guys really helped me out, and in their own quiet way, mentored me. Before long, they invited me on a spring trip to Red Rocks in Las Vegas. They even wrote a letter to my exchange officer, promising to bring me back in one piece.

I had heard of climbing in Vegas, but nothing could have prepared me for what I saw. The sandstone rose from the desert like a fever dream, massive walls of burgundy, rust, and flame. When the first sunrays ignited it, the rock shimmered like it remembered the fire that first formed it. And in that blaze, I felt something ancient in me stir: the recognition of a soul speaking in stone. My heart was at home.

The guys handed me a T-shirt printed with the classic Red Rocks routes, starting with Cat in the Hat. It was meant to be a souvenir but it quickly turned it into a ticklist, a mission. By the end of the trip, I'd climbed every single one.

The Mayo crew taught me, believed in me, and nudged me forward, encouraging me to lead routes I never would have dared to lead on my own. It was definitely not as "safe" as they had claimed in the letter to the Rotary club. That was part of the magic: being trusted to rise. And I did.

The highlight of that trip was Crimson Chrysalis, a classic 5.8+ with over 1,000 feet of clean, vertical stone. Long, exposed and elegant, an ascending spine of light. I was hoping I might get to lead a pitch or two. But as we roped up at the base, Mark turned to me, handed me the sharp end*, and grinned.

"Take us to the top, rope gun*." Just like that, it was mine. All nine pitches!

The air was crisp, the rock still cold from the desert night. My heart thudded in my chest, not from fear, but from a deep, electric yes. Every move demanded presence. Every clip was a vow. Every belay, a celebration.

By the time we topped out; wind in our hair, grins lighting up our faces, the Mojave sprawling below, I wasn't the same girl who had laced up her tight Stingers at the base. I had always waited for some teacher to declare me worthy. Instead, Mark's rope hand-off forced me to decide for myself.

That climb wasn't just a vertical journey. It was a rite of passage. Climbing and claiming my capability, resilience, and my place in the world. That trip initiated me. After Red Rocks, I wasn't just a kid who liked climbing.

I was a lifer.

Not long after that, the Rotary Club funded a trip for the exchange students to Boundary Waters in northeastern Minnesota. A week of canoeing and wilderness travel.

Unlike most of the city kids who were nervous in the woods, I was in my element. Three years of outdoor experience have given me something most teens didn't have. I was at ease in the wild, I moved with confidence, I knew I belonged there. After the trip, our guide Charlie pulled my Rotary Club officer aside. "Marta could've led the whole thing herself," he said. For once, someone saw what I was capable of and said it out loud.

It makes me smile that Charlie went on to become a rock climber himself. A really good one. I sometimes wonder if that trip shifted something in him. If witnessing a teenage girl move through the wilderness with so much certainty, raving endlessly about rock climbing, set a silent seed stirring in him. If maybe, in some small way, I helped light his fire.

That wilderness trip was just the beginning. Next came a three-week bus journey down the East Coast, from the buzz of New York City to the warmth of Florida, with an educational pause in Washington D.C.

We started as a ragtag crew of exchange students from across the globe. Strangers from Argentina, Korea, Norway, Morocco, and so on.

But we were quickly stitched together through shared awe and cramped bus rides. We marveled at the grandeur of the Smithsonian, craned our necks at Manhattan's skyline, and screamed on rollercoasters at Disney World.

We traded snacks, stories, and dreams in every accent imaginable. Somewhere between the monuments and the motel breakfasts, I caught a new glimpse of myself. The world no longer felt so impossibly vast. It felt reachable. Navigable. Being on the road with those kids made the world feel smaller, but me, infinitely bigger. Like I had stepped out of the margins of my own life and into a future waiting for me to claim it.

I kept up my six-mile runs, my daily practice, a place to move freely and to be alone. It gave me a sliver of wildness inside the container of a tightly planned journey. And it planted a seed: I could totally do this alone.

By the end of that year, I wasn't just fluent in English, I was fluent in myself. I had crossed an invisible threshold. While others were growing heavy with homesickness or drifting into disconnection, I felt vividly alive. I ran at dawn, paid attention, and stayed awake to the wonder. What could have been a detour became a launch.

That year transformed me, maybe even more than discovering climbing. For the first time, I felt an unshakable belonging. Not just in language, but in life. Emotionally, spiritually, logistically, I was no longer orbiting someone else's gravity. I began to emancipate from my parents, not out of rebellion, but out of readiness. That year wasn't just a chapter. It was the beginning of a new book.

And just when I thought the magic had peaked, life surprised me once again.

On the flight home, I got upgraded to business class. I sat next to a German banker who was opening a branch in Poland. We talked the entire flight. By the time we landed he was so impressed, he offered me a job on the spot. He said I had "something." That I'd pick up the rest easily.

I went to the interview with HR, but I didn't take the job. They looked at me like I'd lost my mind.

I was eighteen, just out of high school. And while the offer was appealing, I had no intention of working full-time with serious bankers. I wanted to live more, explore more, and climb more. But the offer felt like a sign. A wink from the universe.

It was the year 2000, the world was opening up to me, and I kept saying "yes".

Something deeper was driving me now. I was no longer chasing scraps of belonging. I wasn't waiting to be chosen. I had found the pilot light. I wasn't reacting to life anymore – I was shaping it. That year was a launchpad: I felt powerful and worthy. I belonged, not just somewhere, but everywhere.

And no, that feeling didn't stay. I've lost my power a hundred times since, I've fallen into doubt, into hiding, into forgetting. But I knew something I hadn't known before: The magic was never out there. It was mine. It is mine. I had it all along. It rises when I leap. It returns when I choose. And every time I forget, life offers me another chance to remember.

That year was the beginning.

Learning to live from that power, consciously, consistently, courageously; that's where we're headed next.

Soul note:

You are not from nowhere. You are from the stars. Your life is not a string of accidents It is a constellation, shaped by movement and choice. You are the soul who said yes to life. The sprout who grew through cracked concrete. You bloomed and you will bloom again.

Echo 6: The Leads I Gave Away
Yosemite Valley, 2003

How many times will she give away her thread? Each time, forgetting the cost. Until one day, her hands are empty, and only silence remains, whispering: "It was always yours." The lead was never taken. If you gave it away, you can take it back.

We met in the meadow, under the shadow of El Capitan, as golden light spilled across the enormous granite wall. He had just topped out on a one-day ascent; sun-kissed, strong, a California hard man. He looked like he'd stepped out of a climbing movie. As it turns out, he had. I didn't know it yet, but that day marked the beginning of a love story that shaped nearly two decades of my life.

D-Griff was my best friend; cut from the same cloth, like echoes of the same ancient mountain song.

We climbed together, ascending El Capitan again and again, chasing granite and wind through vast mountain ranges and the western deserts. Wandering the U.S. in our camper truck like pilgrims, always searching for the next pitch*, the next lesson. That fall, he followed me to Spain while I worked on my degree.

At some point, we made our way to Hawaii. We kiteboarded between islands, made a documentary, and when my passport was too full for a Brazilian visa, we got married on a whim; half necessity, half cosmic contract. A few years later, we bought a house, and shortly after that we divorced. Yet somehow through it all, our bond outlasted the form.

From the first moment I met him, I could tell that this man lived by his own rules. And he would teach me, unintentionally, how easy it is to hand over the lead to someone who seems to already have it all figured out.

Fiercely adventurous, profoundly himself, yet quietly numbing a hidden ache with weed. D-Griff refused to give up magic, though I sometimes wondered if that magic came at the cost of being truly adult. I can already hear him laughing at that.

His untethered spirit oddly anchored me. It made me practical. It kept me clear. He was 15 years older, and felt like the father I'd longed for and the child I found myself caring for. Reckless, radiant, utterly unburdened. With him, I caught glimpses of what a life without apology could feel like, even as I carried the weight he chose never to hold.

Everybody loved him, including my family. My grandpa Leszek had a shirtless photo of D-Griff pinned to his wall. I used to stare at it and wonder: was it his charm? His wildness? Or his fearless refusal to fit in that no one could resist?

D-Griff taught me to cowboy up on big walls*, to laugh when things went sideways, to sound and walk like a Yosemite local, to meet panic with precision. He gave me so much.

And I gave him something too. Something I didn't even realize I was surrendering; my leads.

In climbing, leading means stepping into the unknown. You climb with the rope tied to your harness, clipping it into protection as you go. Every decision is yours; the path you take, the gear you place, your timing for when to relax and when to give it your all. You're exposed mentally, emotionally, and physically. A fall can have real consequences. It's a full-body act of trust: in your skill, your judgment, and your ability to respond under pressure. For the follower the experience is very different. They climb the same route, but the rope comes from above. The gear is already in place. The hardest choices have been made. There's still effort, still challenge, but far less risk. The second* can focus on movement, breath, and presence. It's the same terrain, but the emotional reality is entirely different.

When D-Griff and I started climbing together, I was already a solid lead climber. I had made my way to Yosemite on my own. Hauling my own gear, protecting my own falls. But once we were a team, I started defaulting.

At first, it felt like no big deal. "You'll be faster," I said. "I'm not up for it today." I told myself I was being practical. Efficient. Bit by bit, I handed it over. And each time, I gave voice to something much older.

Something quieter, and more dangerous.

The whisper that his strength mattered more. That my place was in support. That it was safer to follow than to ask for the front. That my dreams didn't deserve full pursuit. Because leading isn't just about strength.

It's about vision. Voice. Desire. And every time I passed him the rope, I passed on myself.

He didn't demand it. I handed it over willingly; shrinking without realizing it. And because I never said a word, he assumed I didn't want to lead. And maybe, at the time, I didn't. Because claiming the sharp end would've meant claiming my worth. And the old voices in me weren't ready for that. They said: Don't be too much. Don't take up too much space. Don't make it about you.

For how long have women been dimming their fire to avoid being burned?

Only after our marriage ended I saw it clearly. When I began climbing with others. Swapping leads. With each pitch, I reclaimed something I hadn't realized I'd lost. I didn't just want the sharp end. I needed it.

I needed to remember that I hadn't been pulled into this world; I had taken wild risks to be here. I had left everything behind to follow this dream. And it was mine to live fully.

D-Griff and I chose El Cap Meadow as our meeting ground, not just in this life, but in the timeless story of us. He once told me, "When you're waiting to meet someone, pick a place you already love. Then waiting is never a burden, no matter how long it takes."

For ten years, he returned to that sacred ground, an altar to the granite monolith above. Waiting, singing our future into the wind. I like to believe I was on my way there the whole time.

Years after our divorce, I walked into a room and saw a VHS flickering: Masters of Stone IV. And there he was: Young Strong Dave - wild, fearless, immortal. Not just a man, but the destiny I had once whispered into being.

I smiled a tear-salted smile, not out of longing, but reverence. I had manifested the man from the movie. In that moment I saw the arc completed: a girl spinning fantasies in the cabbage field on the edge of Europe, and a woman, sovereign and real, who walked into her own myth, not to be saved, but to remember her own fire.

The love and the shrinking came hand in hand, until they didn't. The leads were always there. I just had to stop giving them away.

And now?

Sometimes, I still hand over the sharp end. But never to disappear. Never to shrink. Never to trade my worth for love.

Every time I tie in now, I remember: the rope isn't just protection. It's a sacred thread. And I'm the one holding it.

I ask myself honestly: Is this silence or strategy? If it's silence, I take the lead.

Because my dream doesn't live in someone else's hands anymore. The dream, the lead, the life, it lives in me now. And I'm not handing it over.

Soul Note:

There is an ancestral inheritance inside of us: a long line of women who gave up the sharp end. Not from weakness, but from love, love that mistook support for silence. Millions of leads not taken, but surrendered. Know: if you gave it, you can take it back.

Root 7: The Summer of Mythic Yes
Lake Tahoe, California, 2001

I stood in the arrivals hall at San Francisco International Airport with a flimsy backpack and 200 bucks in my pocket, pretending I was braver than I felt. My heart thudded against my ribs, palms slick. I'd said yes to this adventure like it was no big deal, but the moment the glass doors slid shut behind me, my stomach dropped.

My first thought: *What the hell have I done?* Next one: *What the hell am I going to do now?*

My two best friends and I had a plan. We got J-1 work visas and told everyone we were heading to the U.S. for summer jobs. But the real dream? Climbing in Yosemite, the promised land.

We were supposed to report to a casino job in Atlantic City, New Jersey. That was never going to happen. We weren't interested in casinos; we were interested in cliffs. The kind of walls that make a climber's mouth water and hands sweat. Instead we booked one-way tickets to California, with marginal funds and even less of a plan.

Somewhere along the way, we met a couple of other Polish kids chasing the same dream. They heard there might be work in Lake Tahoe, and that it was beautiful. We pooled what little cash we had, rented a car, and landed in King's Beach on the northern edge of the Lake. Five kids, one motel room and a big hunger for something wild.

Those first few weeks were chaos. We hitchhiked around Tahoe looking for work and a place to crash, saying yes to anything we could find. My nervous system was in full crash mode, though back then, I didn't have the awareness or vocabulary to name it.

I didn't know how to press pause and ask, what am I actually feeling right now? I just knew I was scared and untethered. After days of uncertainty and near-homelessness, we got our lucky break. We landed customer service jobs at the cable car building in Squaw Valley, handing out trail maps and pointing tourists to the bathroom. Nine bucks an hour.

I thought I was just getting a job. What I found was the beginning of a different life. I didn't just need money, I needed a proof that I could create a place where I mattered.

One of my friends developed a severe allergic reaction to… everything. Dust, pollen, even food. He held out as long as he could, but eventually, the stress broke him. He bailed to stay with an uncle in San Diego.

And then there were two.

Vava and I figured it out on the fly, couch-surfing, saying yes to kind strangers. Jim let us crash after his son left for college, temporarily filling his empty nest. His neighbor traded a room for watching her two feisty pomeranians. For a stretch, we even squatted on a coworker's weed-soaked floor in Squaw Valley. We just kept showing up, figuring it out, rolling with whatever came our way.

One day we wandered into a Shell station and struck up a conversation with the guy behind the counter. His name was Andrew. We must've looked like proper wrecks, because he said, "You guys can totally crash at my place." His carpeted living room became our home for the summer. It was dry, it was safe, and it was free.

Then, like muleears in the sierra meadow, something began to bloom.

Vava came home one night, eyes lit up. He'd landed a barback job at the Hyatt, and spotted a backyard boulder at a nearby house. "They've got to be climbers," he said. He went back, knocked on the door, and introduced himself. Soon, we were invited to weekly bouldering nights at Dan and Ann's. They were strong, fun, and it turned out, Dan and Ann were Tahoe climbing legends. That backyard boulder became the center of our world. Our community grew from there. Some of those people are still treasured friends to this day.

As summer rolled on, I moved up from handing out trail maps to breakfast server at High Camp; the mountaintop restaurant at Squaw Valley's High Camp. My boss, Jerry Bukowski, a third-generation Polish guy, gave me the job because I reminded him of his family. And because I had potential.

Promotion meant tips and tips meant freedom. A promise that maybe, just maybe, my Yosemite dream wasn't dead after all. I was electric, feral with joy. So naturally, like any twenty-year-old with no impulse control I bought a bottle of tequila.

That night Andrew and I drank the whole thing and passed out. I missed my first shift.

Mortified, I showed up the next day, went straight to Jerry, and told him the truth: "I was so excited about this job that I passed out on tequila and didn't wake up until 4 p.m."

He looked me dead in the eye and said, "You were already fired. Your honesty is the only reason I'm giving you another shot."

That second chance marked a pivotal moment: I learned that being real matters more than being perfect. Radical honesty buys more freedom than perfection ever could.

I worked at High Camp the rest of that summer without a hitch. It turned out to be one of the best jobs I've ever had, because it started with truth and was held together by trust.

The summer bloomed with characters. Danny, the hilarious customer service rep, took me on "important missions" under the ski lifts to hunt for lost treasures; trinkets, watches, once even forty bucks. That kind of treasure hunt? I still do it to this day.

Zwy was the big boss, and for some reason, he took a liking to us two Polish kids trying to make it. He gave us nicknames and treated us like we were part of the family. When I came back the next year without a work visa, he hooked me up with an under-the-table gig.

Back then, Squaw was more than a job, it was a scene. A magnet for misfits, dreamers, and diehards. The kind of place where your title didn't matter, but your turn on KT-22* did. Where people came from all over the world to live in their cars, repair their gear with duct-tape, and show up hungover to open lifts and steal a first line.

There was a rawness to it, a shared understanding that life was meant to be lived hard and fast and close to the edge. You learned who you were on the skintrack, at the bar, in the whiteout. People stayed season after season, for the exquisite powder, the sun, the lines but perhaps even more for the feeling of quiet truth that out here, in the snowlight and storm, you were part of something real.

Then there was Super Dave, the restaurant manager. He could make anything happen. He gave me the coveted Monday night shift. Just me on the floor, meaning all the tips were mine. After work, we'd climb onto the roof of the cable car with a pitcher of beer and drink it on the ride down. It became our ritual, our reward, our moment of magic. On the top of the cable car bathed in starlight, with the scent of Sierra summer in the air, I wasn't just a tourist anymore, I was now part of it.

Our days off were filled with exploration. Once Super Dave invited me to go bridge-jumping with his friends. A guy in a black sports car showed up with a real wolf dog. His name was MC. He was magnetic and mysterious. We jumped off bridges, dodged trains, and had a wild summer fling. He was tight with the Tahoe crowd, and in that blur of adrenaline and moonlight, he made me feel seen.

One day, MC and I went climbing with a couple of his friends: Shane and Jeremy. They were easygoing, way goofy and fun to be around. I quickly realized I was the strongest climber of the group. We had an awesome day on the rock, laughing, swapping leads, just hanging out. I thought nothing of it.

It wasn't until much later, I realized who I'd been tied in with: Shane McConkey and Jeremy Jones – pioneers, legends, icons. Revolutionary trailblazers of the skiing world. I blinked when I finally pieced the names together, not in disbelief at their fame, but in quiet awe at how naturally I stood beside them, unaware I was already one of them. At the time, they were just two dudes fumbling with their harnesses.

That day revealed something profound in me: greatness doesn't always arrive with a spotlight. It can show up laughing, dusty, and human. And you don't need permission to be in the circle, you just have to know your own strength. I didn't recognize their names, but I recognized the frequency. The wild ones already knew – I was one of them.

That summer didn't just stretch me, it detonated the old story. In strange soil, under the cobalt California sky, I started to grow my own way. The chaos, the hunger, the triumph was a pivot.

I never saw MC again. That winter, he died at Squaw; suffocated in a tree well while skiing powder in the trees. Gone, just like that. His famous bumper sticker said: "MC Ski-pow-ski." That's what he chased: powder days. And in the short time he was in my life, he gave me a powder day too, a pocket of freedom, laughter, and wild aliveness. Thank you, MC, for that gift. I'll never forget it.

After Tahoe, I hitch-hiked straight to Yosemite Valley, just like I said I would. It had always been the goal. But when I saw the fabled sheer granite walls shooting thousands of feet above the valley floor, I realized that something had changed. Maybe the dream wasn't a place.

Maybe it was figuring out how to be fully alive without my family's prescription. In the wild, messy middle of it all.

The scene in the Valley that Vava and I stepped into felt like a feral fairy tale. The Yosemite climbing tribe of 2001 was alive with energy, irreverence, and elemental devotion.

We stepped into a world of legends. Dean Potter, Leo Houlding, Jose Pereyra, the Huber brothers, Ivo Ninov, Sean Leary, Cedar Wright and Timmy O'Neill. These weren't just climbers, they were titans of granite, blurring the lines between human and myth.

We all hung together.

Camp 4 was our temple, our firelight, our council. And at the center of it all was Chongo Chuck, our barefoot oracle, philosopher king, and original life coach. With a mind unbound by convention, he saw no difference between quantum physics, big wall climbing, slacklining, or metaphysics; everything was an invitation to shift perception.

He authored many books, including A Homeless Interpretation of Quantum Mechanics and How to Be Bitchin. Master of counter-surveillance (as described by park rangers in a famous court case) and philosophical loopholes, he was a teacher of freedom disguised as absurdity. The true teachings weren't in his books – they were in his conversations, labyrinthine, irreverent, brain-cracking portals to consciousness and possibility.

Days were filled with speed ascents, wild slackline crossings, and legendary rope swings off portaledges* on El Capitan. Nights brought us back to the circle, laughing, storytelling, painting our tents with manifestos.

I was learning how to live in the tribe, not at the edge of it. And being in the tribe meant climbing, soaring, belonging. But there was far more to it than just scaling cliffs, we were composing something immortal: writing a story of rebellion, devotion, and vertical prayer into the face of the sacred stone.

Have you ever stood in a circle of legends and realized the only difference between them and you was your willingness to see yourself as one of them?

As I slacklined high in the skies, suspended between granite and gravity, I would ponder Chongo's sagely wisdom bites like sacred koans: *Trying to be bitchin' can come at the risk of being, instead, a complete fool.*

But, not trying at all… can come at the price of never being bitchin' even once. Up there, each step became a meditation on risk, presence, and identity. Not just about balance, but about daring to live so fully that the fear of looking foolish bowed before the ecstasy of authenticity.

That summer taught me something I've never forgotten: I can survive the unknown. I can throw myself into the risk, into the wild, with no map, and come out stronger on the other side.

By the end of the season, it wasn't just cliffs I'd climbed, it was who I thought I was, each footstep etching a more truthful self into my bones.

I had arrived a nobody. I left with stories, with friends, with a version of myself I didn't know I was allowed to become.

I proved I didn't need certainty. I needed courage. I didn't need a plan. I needed a dream, and the guts to keep going.

I had landed at SFO terrified I'd made the biggest mistake of my life. And somehow, through all the mess and the magic, I climbed out with a stronger core and a fuller heart.

The Polish girl who showed up with nothing left with something real: a self forged in truth, not ease. Not because everything went smoothly, but because it didn't. And that was even better.

I didn't know it then, but that summer was just the beginning. Tahoe proved I could survive uncertainty. What came next would ask for much more.

Could I claim this life? Not drift into freedom, but choose it with both hands? Could I create a life so bold, it no longer fit the story I was born into?

Soul Note:

You weren't mapless. You were myth-making, etching new contours into the granite of your becoming. Every couch, every yes, every crash into chaos was an initiation. You weren't running to find safety, you were running toward sovereignty. That mythic quest stretched and sculpted you into someone new, more true.

Echo 7: From Comfort Coffin to the Exile of the Open Road

Joshua Tree, California, 2015

What she built with her hands wasn't hers. The dream she was living belonged to someone else. The price was herself. She walked, not knowing who she'd become. The achy knowing was in her bones: there was a wild twin living in the basement, and she had to bail her out.

The moment the brand-new TV was hung on the wall, I knew I was done. And I was terrified.

We bought the house together to fulfill D-Griff's dream of living in Joshua Tree. For six months, we poured our sweat and dreams into making it beautiful. The fancy curved flatscreen was a symbol of arrival, our happy ending.

But as he settled into the couch, content and fulfilled, something in me collapsed. He had arrived. Me? All I had was the raw, unmistakable edge of knowing that this was a dead end.

Have you ever built something with love, and known in your bones, it was never meant to be yours?

When we met, I was twenty, fresh off the boat with nothing but fierce determination. He had been my mentor, my anchor, at times even a father figure. He was the breadwinner. We were living his life.

Watching him get excited about collecting DVDs while I felt panic flood my chest told me everything I needed to know: it was time to go.

Yes, our relationship had its problems, but this wasn't about that. Something deeper was stirring. A question I could no longer ignore: Could I ever make it on my own?

Tahoe had taught me to walk into the unknown. But this was different. This wasn't about jobs or couch-surfing. This was about the soul. About stepping into the self I'd kept hidden, even from myself.

I packed my Prius with almost nothing; clothes, a tent, a cast iron skillet; leaving behind the carefully chosen dishware and the bookshelf I had lovingly filled with books. I ran my fingers one last time over the concrete floors I had painstakingly hand-painted. Passed the kitchen I designed. Stepped through the doorway I would never cross again. Then I ripped a "goodbye" out of my throat and drove away.

The radio blared: Girls Just Wanna Have Fun.

The irony punched me in the gut. The highway stretched ahead; empty, endless, unforgiving. Just like me. I didn't regret leaving. But the vastness ahead felt unbearable. Tears blurred the windshield.

There were girls out there having fun. But not me.

Alone in the world, driving to nowhere, the grief finally broke through. Our fifteen-year partnership ended quietly, kindly. Painfully. But it wasn't the marriage I was leaving. I was leaving the version of myself who stayed small to keep the peace. Who was trained to fall in line. Who didn't ask for too much. Who felt whole only when she was needed. In that moment, it felt like I had to choose: freedom or connection. It would take me years to learn that I was allowed to have both.

Somewhere along the way I picked up Melody Beattie's book on codependency and flipped to the self-assessment. I scored 20 out of 20 on the Adult Child of an Alcoholic test. I didn't even know what that meant. I had spent my whole life downplaying my father's drinking, brushing off D-Griff's daily weed habit like it was no big deal.

But suddenly, every quiet compliance, every "yes" when I meant "no," every time I swallowed myself to stay close; it all made sense. These were not quirks. They were trauma patterns. And I was now determined to break them. I just didn't know how deep the healing would go.

That open road cracked me wide open. Mile after relentless mile, I asked the question I had never dared to ask: Who are you without someone else's map? It forced me to confront the ways I'd blamed D-Griff instead of speaking my truth.

The way I followed his path instead of forging my own. How I had lived as a second-class citizen; immigrant, woman, outsider; riding coattails and giving away my leads, not just in climbing, but in life.

Beneath all of it was the most crushing belief: I didn't deserve a story of my own.

This wasn't Tahoe. Not some golden coming-of-age road trip. This was exile. Just me, alone with the parts of myself I'd spent a lifetime running from.

In the months that followed, I would pull over at the edge of some empty desert or icy mountain pass and sob until my ribs ached. I'd scream into my own hands, feral and guttural. It was the howl of my long-banished wild twin, finally clawing her way through the floorboards. I grieved what I never fully had, and what I never let myself ask for.

Underneath that grief lived a deeper terror: What if I'd just walked away from the best life I'll ever have? What if it was all downhill from here? What if just me isn't enough?

But even there, in the thick of it, something ancient stirred. A voice rose; quiet, persistent, undeniable. If I don't choose myself now, I never will.

So even as fear whispered, You won't survive this, I dried my tears, started the engine, and drove on. Into the unknown. Into a future I couldn't yet see. Every time the old script said turn back, I turned the key forward. And chose my soul over the map.

I wasn't just driving, I was unlocking the basement door with every mile. Letting her rise: fierce and free. No longer trusting someone else's strength, but daring; desperately, to trust my own.

Because if I didn't walk through this fire, I would never become the woman who lived life on her own terms. I didn't know her yet. But I knew she existed. And I knew I had to find her.

The alternative was clear: stay safe, stay silent, stay small. Pretend that comfort was enough. But I knew, if I stayed it would become a coffin.

So I kept driving. Because somewhere out there, a wild, unstoppable woman waited; locked in a basement built from silence and sacrifice. And she was finally ready to rise.

My first step? Refusing to turn back. The fun this girl was gonna have felt impossibly far off… but as I would one day discover, it was never really about that.

Soul Note:

You didn't leave comfort. You left the lie that you had to earn your place. What broke wasn't your life, it was the illusion you didn't have one of your own. The grief? That was shedding someone else's dream. The voice that rose? That was your wild twin. She waited years for this jailbreak. Now, every mile is her reclaiming. Keep going. You are not too much. You were never not enough. She's not in the basement anymore, but behind the wheel.

Root 8: Windswept to the Soul
Chile, Argentina, Brazil, 2003

Summer in Tahoe. Fall in Yosemite. Early winter in Joshua Tree. I was officially "on tour," like so many other climbers; chasing sun and stone. The girl who once asked for permission was gone. In her place stood the woman who leapt. When I first arrived in the U.S. with my two friends that summer, our plan was simple: scrape by, climb our hearts out, then return to Poland in the fall to resume university. It was a rebellion with a deadline, a break before real life. The plan was always to go back.

That was becoming a problem.

My soul had other plans, older than reason. My old life was already coming undone. The person I was becoming no longer fit the box she had left behind. Just thinking about going back stirred the same dread I used to feel after swim meets as a kid; riding the bus toward a cold, empty house.

I knew what would happen if I returned. I'd fall back into being the girl people in my life expected; polite, quiet, tidy. The one who fits in and doesn't make a mess. Going back would be a life sentence of mediocrity.

But now, I saw what I hadn't seen before: I had a choice. What if I didn't go back? What if I followed the pull toward somewhere even more foreign, more wild? The next stop on the international climbing circuit was Patagonia. What if I went there instead?

My family and friends in Poland would lose it. Who throws away a hard-earned university spot? But my new family; the global climbing tribe, didn't even blink. "Of course, you go", they said. "What else matters more than following what calls you"?

I was standing at a mythic crossroads.

My climber friends saw it coming. The hardest part was telling my parents and the university. There was no website link to click for a leave of absence. So, I handwrote three letters: One to my mom. One to my dad. One to the dean.

I didn't mention climbing. I wrote about wanting to understand myself. About the rare opportunity to travel solo through South America. I don't remember the exact words; I wish I had copies.

At the arrival hall of Warsaw airport, my parents, each with their new partner, scanned the crowd for their daughter. But Vava walked out alone. That day, I didn't arrive on Polish soil – I arrived into the unknown. Vava handed them my letters like offerings at a funeral; because the girl they were looking for was no more.

Have you ever handed your old life back like a letter, knowing you would never belong to it again?

Later, I called my mom using a calling card, reassuring her I had not lost my mind and promising I would finish school eventually. But we both knew: the girl who left that summer wasn't coming back. Talking to my dad was simpler. "I get it," he said. "I'd do the same if I could." The dean approved a sabbatical year. That was it.

I was southbound.

Long before I could name it, I was already following an internal compass. Moving before I felt ready. My soul was already pulling me forward.

When I landed in Santiago, Chile, I was twenty, terrified, and free. Cash in my sock. A tremble in my throat. I told myself I came to climb, to learn Spanish, to explore South America. But the truth ran deeper. I was chasing something I couldn't yet name. A self I hadn't met, but was ready to find.

I stayed at Andrés' house in Cajón del Maipo, a canyon just outside Santiago. We'd just met in Yosemite, and he'd invited me to crash. One day, he convinced me to run up El Plomo, a 17,700-foot peak, in a single push. I had never been above 10,000 feet, but, sure, why not? What could go wrong?

We did everything wrong: hiked too fast, summited exhausted, and passed out on the peak without a tent, guide, or plan, just raw ambition and altitude. A blind ascent, and the perfect metaphor for the leap I was about to take in life. We glissaded down in boots, laughing until we weren't. By the bottom, I had the most atrocious altitude headache of my life.

But I was hooked. That first taste of altitude was intense, and it left me hungry for more. Andrés suggested I try Anconcagua next; the highest mountain outside of the Himalayas, at 22,837 feet.

His friend owned a company that ran the basecamp on the mountain, so I had a place to crash. I joined a group of park rangers and together we summited. It was wild and joyful. Afterward, I celebrated by drinking too much Malbec in Mendoza, laughed about it, called the whole episode a detour, and pointed my compass south toward Patagonia.

The southern stretch of the Andes runs like a rugged spine along the Chile–Argentina border, a raw expanse of high-altitude plateaus, glaciers, temperate rainforests, volcanoes, and wind-battered peaks.

On the Chilean side, the mountains plunged steeply into the Pacific, carving out a labyrinth of fjords and channels. On the Argentinean side, the range melted into alpine lakes and vast, empty grasslands known as pampa.

Out on the Pampa, lonely gravel roads are the only indication of human existence, and the only crowds are the herds of guanacos; llamas' awkward cousins with state of the art side-eye. Beyond that, just the ever-present gale-force winds whispering: What the hell are you doing here? The pampa offers no sympathy. Only presence.

I climbed more big peaks and roadside crags. Crammed Spanish conjugations. Made friends at random trailheads. Hitchhiked across entire provinces. And waited for hours in the sun and rain; often hungry, always setting up my slackline* to pass the time.

One day, I stood on a dusty road all afternoon, hoping for a ride, only to get picked up by a front loader. It moved at five miles per hour, but I didn't care. I was tired, and it beat walking. I still wish I had a photo of that. But honestly, life was offering me something better; a slow, gritty transport into a new version of myself. I didn't need to get there fast. I just needed to keep moving.

Tatiana was a blonde-haired storm I met in Bariloche; kind, soulful, and just as tangled up in being twenty as I was. We were both caught in the confusion of trying to belong somewhere without losing ourselves. She had just left her family in Buenos Aires to build a new life in Esquel, carving out space to be someone of her own making. I followed her home, drawn by the rawness in her search. We spent a month in her little house with creaky floorboards and strong maté tea, swapping stories about love, climbing, and the invisible weight of being at once too much and not enough.

In her company, I didn't need to be impressive, just real. It was the first time since losing my childhood friend Ola that I felt what sisterhood could mean: two women, not competing, not performing, just trying to make sense of the world and of themselves.

On one particular climbing trip, Tati and I forgot all our food. That's when I ate goat for the first time; hacked straight off the carcass in a smoke-filled hut thick with the scent of sweat and ash, my hunger flickering by the firelight. Maybe the meat was exquisite, or maybe I was just starving, but either way, my life as a vegetarian ended that day.

As a teenager, being vegetarian had been my quiet rebellion; a way to say no to the normal, to feel different. But I didn't need that identity anymore. I had found my difference in the marrow of lived experience.

The second half of the goat rode with me in my sleeping bag; a smoky stowaway on the journey to another asado in Esquel.

The girl who kept quiet, afraid to be wrong, trying not to stick out was gone. In her place stood someone no longer bound by anyone else's rules; not even the ones she'd once placed on herself.

In Esquel, I linked up with Nacho, a young lawyer I'd met back in Santiago, now on a yearlong global climbing sabbatical. We were both chasing something beyond summits, unraveling our own spiritual knots.

Together we continued south rumbling along for days across the endless pampa; vast and empty, a land flattened by wind and time. The sky felt too big and the earth too bare. Guanacos darted through the brush like ghosts, and dust plumed behind us for miles. Hours passed without a single tree, house, or sign of human life. We saw bright pink flamingoes gathered in a shallow salt lagoon, like a hallucination against the muted palette of soil and scrub.

Toward the end of the earth we drove, chasing the faint promise of stone, near El Chaltén. Back then, it was just a jumble of random shacks and tents that could hardly be called a town. More like a dream held together by weathered canvas and windswept hope. We sat there for weeks, waiting out storms in a mountain hut, hoping for a weather window that would allow us to climb. It never came.

We hiked, slacklined, and dropped acid. I loved cracking everyone up by reciting poetry out loud in Polish. We told stories to keep the cold away, laughter our only kindling. But, the weather won out as is often the case in Patagonia, and we never got a chance to climb.

It would be many years before I'd gather the guts; and the cash, to come back to this incredible place.

One night, as the wind howled outside like an omen, an ancient knowing stirred in me. I remembered an existence I had not yet lived. A memory of being. It was as if the mountain called back a version of me buried beneath performance and protection. These absurd outings, these mythical detours, they weren't distractions. They were doorways. To my soul. To my source. To my original aliveness.

Some nights I would wonder if I was making a mistake. If I was missing out. What were my friends back in Poland up to? How big was my little sister? Internet access was scarce so communication was rare. Those thoughts always dissolved away by morning, washed away with strong coffee and the promise of adventure.

I was on a spiritual journey: my moods, as volatile as the fierce Patagonian weather, revealing what could be stripped away, and what would remain.

After El Chaltén I kept roaming alone; directionless yet tethered to something I couldn't name. Gathering lifelong friends, growing my Spanish vocabulary, and letting the road reshape me.

One day Nacho resurfaced, calling from São Paulo – some people don't drift through your life, they orbit. "One more route?" he asked. I didn't need convincing.

Years later we crossed paths again in Yosemite. His wild spirit hadn't dulled, his mind sharp as ever, his devotion to the vertical world unwavering. But now, he had stepped into his true calling. Nacho had become a leading voice in South American climbing, serving as editor of Escalando magazine and forging bold new lines across remote Patagonian ranges. The man who once chased mountains on sabbatical had become their chronicler, their steward. Watching him evolve felt like glimpsing a parallel of my own path: someone who chose the unknown, and found not just summits, but soul.

With Nacho calling and Patagonian winter nearing, I turned my thumb north.

It was over 3000 miles from the southern tip of Patagonia to the Brazilian coast. I was picked up by many truckers, some terrifying, some sketchy, some incredibly kind. I drove a semi. I learned to make yerba maté on the road. To stay alert. To trust my gut. To read people fast.

Every time I said "no" to fear and "yes" to trust, I modeled something to the girl who thought she had to be polite, stay small, and sit in the background. Every time I extended my thumb, I was casting a vote for the woman who did not need permission.

Somehow, I made it to São Paulo in one piece (I wouldn't do this again). It was a journey across countries, and identities. By the time I arrived in Brazil, my hair was tangled, my mind was raw, my heart was wild, and my soul felt whole.

Brazil was an entirely different world. Bold. Hot. Colorful. Filled with song and rhythm.

Nacho and I climbed in Rio de Janeiro and Três Picos do Paraná, chasing stone through jungled chaos. When he left to find his soul in Spain, I stayed behind with Roberta; a wild woman I'd first met on the summit of Aconcagua.

She had that blazing fire I couldn't yet name but knew I needed. A professional climber, and the only Brazilian woman putting up first ascents in Patagonia, she lived for the sharp edge of adventure and mirrored the wild joy I had forgotten. Her mouth was so dirty she made grown men blush, and her spirit made no apologies.

Roberta had something I was just beginning to reclaim: original aliveness. She was enough, and she knew it. She modeled what it looked like to be. Not to perform. Not to prove. Just be. With her, I was learning how to be fully in it. We shared three months of dance parties, late-night talks, climbing, and laughter. Roberta died in a car accident a few years later, but her essence lingers like a song, one I still hear when I dare to just be.

By spring, I was unfurled in the best possible way. My true self had emerged and started to use her voice. And after nearly a year of travel, my sock had grown thin and I was barely scraping by. I was so broke that when it was time to leave, I had to apply for a humanitarian plane ticket: fare usually reserved for priests and nuns. I don't know how I got it – I guess the universe approved it.

I could only afford a flight to New York City. From there, magic carried me; across state lines and stories, miracles at my side; back to Tahoe, back to Yosemite. Then, on November 1st, seventeen months after I first left home, I landed in a place that looked like it had been draped in a dirty old rag: misty, foggy, familiar.

Warsaw. I was home again. But I was not the same. And I didn't stay for long.

In every country, in every conversation and unfamiliar landscape, I had shed something old. It was just me; and the next climb, the next ride, the next word in a language I was slowly making mine. That year gave me everything I didn't know how to want. And none of it was in the plan. Maybe that's the point. When I returned, I knew nothing would ever be the same.

I didn't go to South America to find myself. I went to lose the self that was never mine to carry. What I uncovered wasn't a role, or a title or a future plan. It was my myth; the one I had unknowingly clung to. And beneath that myth, I discovered a truth that had waited patiently beneath the noise. From here on out, I wouldn't just be a girl who ran away to climb. I would be a woman who listened and followed the call.

Soul Note:

You weren't travelling, you were reclaiming your truth. The map you needed couldn't be handed to you; it had to be etched, one mythic detour at a time. Every mountain, every ride, every wild-hearted no, became a yes to your soul. You didn't lose yourself, just your mask. And what remained was the soul waiting to live through you.

Echo 8: The Forest That Fed Me
Swierczyna, Poland 1998

Before she learned to ask, the forest had already answered. She brought no offerings, no apology, only her hunger. The wild welcomed her, and in the language of berries, whispered: You don't need to earn what is already yours.

July was my favorite month because it meant huckleberries.

Just a few minutes walk from our summer cabin, down a sandy, beaten road, was a secret field hidden from view by the forest. As midsummer approached, my cousins and I could barely contain our excitement. We knew what was coming. Every season we'd go early to inspect the tiny green berries and predict the size of the bounty. There was always plenty. We gazed at those unripe gems as promises of an abundant future.

We had big plans.

The first pierogi (traditional Polish dumpling) of the season was a sacred ritual. Under my grandmother's watchful eye, we'd rolled dough, cut circles with a glass, spoon sugared berries into each one, and fold and seal them tight. The kitchen was an absolute mess filled with pure joy: four barefoot girls with blue-streaked mouths, sugar coated fingers, and just enough counter space to make magic.

This was the closest I ever felt to being at home.

After that first batch came the true heart of summer: whole days disguised in our mothers' flowy old dresses, gathering berries with no purpose other than to fill our mouths; juice dribbling down our chins, the blue taste of yes smudged into every crevice of our hands.

The forest was always generous, saying yes again and again. No matter how much we took, it always gave more. We'd move on to a new patch only to return later and find the old bush full of fruit once again.

This was my first experience of universal abundance. Of unconditional love. At home, love felt rationed, measured in quiet obedience and invisible needs. In the forest, abundance wasn't earned; it flowed freely, bursting from branches, asking nothing in return.

From my family I inherited a belief that I was only worth what I gave. My grandmother Maria had to earn love by holding her family together. She started working in her teens so that her brothers can attend school. My mother, lost and dissociated after my father left, became my silent responsibility. I made a vow: not to be a burden. I stayed quiet. I disappeared into the shadows. I didn't share my needs. I barely acknowledged I had any.

Once, my mom drove all the way across Warsaw without noticing I wasn't in the car. That day, I learned a serious lesson: if they do not see you, they can't leave you. Invisibility became my shelter and my sentence.

Years later, when my little half-sister was born, she was needy, loud, and demanding. I was shocked to see my mother give her attention and love. I spent my childhood suppressing my needs so I wouldn't lose love. I spent years believing love was a reward for silence. That neediness would get me abandoned. But here was this baby, fussing and fighting, showing me a new truth: it was safe to be difficult.

As a child, I was hyperaware of everyone's moods. I learned later this is a universal trait of children of alcoholics. I was told I was too sensitive. Yet another thing wrong with me that I learned to conceal. I struggled in silence, tuned in to every annoyance, every simmering anger, every choked-back sadness.

Until I stepped into the forest.

The huckleberry fields asked nothing of me. They gave berries freely. I didn't have to earn them. I didn't owe anything for them. It was the one place where I felt safe receiving.

The forest became my sanctuary. I wasn't "too much" there. I wasn't "too sensitive." I wasn't "wrong." I was just… loved.

Have you ever let something love you without asking why you were worthy?

In a world where scarcity ruled: rationed food, national stamps, and a belief there's never enough, the forest told a different story.

It gave, and I received. There was no guilt or shame in asking. There was only gratitude and trust. That was my first abundance practice. My first model of friendship. My first experience of being met, wholly and without conditions. That taste, that yes, never left. It was always mine, my first language of enoughness.

Sometimes I wonder if nature evolved as a backup parent, a sacred fallback for when the humans who raise us are too damaged to fully love. If that's true, I was lucky. The forest raised me well.

And even now when scarcity tries to colonize my mind like weeds overtaking a garden, I close my eyes, feel the weight of a handful of berries, taste their wild sweetness, and remember: abundance is my mother tongue.

The infinite yes.

Soul Note:

The forest never asked you to shrink, to earn, or to perform. She simply gave, freely, wildly, without condition, because she knew who you were before the world forgot. In her language of berries, sunshine and wind, she reminded you: you are not too much, not wrong, and your needs are never a burden. Abundance is not something to chase; it's your first language, an unspoken dialect of trust. So, when the world demands too much, return to the forest. Let her remind you: you never had to earn love. And when doubt creeps in, remember: she is still whispering yes.

Part 1 was a reclamation, a return to the voice beneath the silence, to the soul that was always whispering. It traced the wild, messy, beautiful journey of remembering. But remembering is not enough. Part 2 is where that remembering becomes action.

This is the terrain of the Path of Badassery, a living method shaped not by theory, but by lived fire. It's where soul meets structure, myth meets movement, and longing turns into leadership. Part 1 was the awakening, Part 2 is the embodiment.

Part 2:
The Path to Badassery

Trunks & Branches: A system for becoming wild, worthy, and whole

THE roots gave you memory. The Trunks offer you choice.

Your rise doesn't sprout from the surface, it begins deep beneath the topsoil. Before branches or blossoms, there were roots: first, pure presence. Then, to help navigate the world, personality formed around that presence.

Eventually, when we're ready to bloom we're invited to shed old adaptations and return to essence, to remember who we always were. To reclaim our soul's rightful place in the greater design. In Part Two, we explore how.

The Trunks I offer you now are not philosophies. They are structures, grown from lived experience, nourished by self-honoring, built to last. They are the spine of your sovereignty, steady enough to hold you when the winds return.

These are not just tools. They are thresholds. Invitations. Mirrors.

They keep you steady when everything shakes. Tend to them. Trust them. They're what make your rise unstoppable.

Walking the Path to Badassery is not about impressing anyone, it's about sovereignty, about being so rooted in your truth that nothing external can unseat you.

You didn't pick up this book by accident. And if you're still reading, it means you're ready to walk a different path. You're done waiting, done living halfway.

You've felt your truth stir, rise, and whisper: it's time.

I'm assuming something about you. You've already done work on yourself. You've read the books, filled the journals, tried the therapy, experimented with mindset shifts. And yet… something remains stuck. What you want now is real, embodied, life transforming. Not another mantra. Not a dopamine hit of inspiration. You're ready to become someone new.

My story was your warm-up. Living your own story will take massive courage – The Path to Badassery demands it. It's less about sounding wise at dinner parties and more about looking in the mirror and knowing: I showed up for me, I stayed, I didn't abandon myself today.

It's about reclaiming your life before it slips through your fingers. It's about not dying with your song still stuck in your chest.

Transformation doesn't bloom under spotlights. It roots in the quiet soil of your nervous system, takes shape through the ecosystem of your boundaries, and unfurls in the daily rhythms that water your becoming. These Trunks grow from lived terrain, not theory. They are nourished by the compost of your values, the groundwater of integrity, and your steady tending of the inner landscape.

The personal development world sells shortcuts: seven steps to your dream life, six figures in six days.

If you're looking to manifest a different reality without ever touching your pain, this isn't your book.

The Path to Badassery is a living framework built on six Trunks, each one a pillar of wild, worthy, and whole living:

- Trunk 1: Know Thyself – Unfolding awareness and Intuition
- Trunk 2: Tend Your Ground – State Regulation
- Trunk 3: Respect Yourself – Self-Trust and Forgiveness
- Trunk 4: Transmute the Challenge – Meaning-Making and Myth
- Trunk 5: Action – Embodied Courage and Identity Shift
- Trunk 6: Expression – Energy Integrity, Celebration, and Visibility

Each Trunk grows branches, stories, tools, and lived practices that will anchor these truths deep in your body, your relationships, and your choices.

These aren't feel-good exercises; they're invitations to remember your myth. You'll move through honest reflections, desire-mapping, nervous system resets, and bold, radical decisions.

It might feel inspiring at times, but don't mistake that for spectacle. This is sacred work, not performance. Let it be honest. Let it be yours.

These aren't pillars to admire, they're trees to grow. They'll show up in your choices, your breath, your boundaries. You won't just learn them – you will live them.

Each Trunk is a core principle: strong, central, load-bearing. Each Branch is an expression of that strength: agile, reaching, specific. The Trunks hold your truth and the Branches show how it moves through your life. Some will stretch you like vines toward light. Others may split the bark allowing tenderness to emerge. All are meant to be lived.

This isn't a ticklist, it's a map to metabolize. Don't consume it, let it transform you. Let each Trunk work on you like weather on stone. Sit with the Explorations. Pause at each Branch. Let your inner terrain absorb the rain of insight before sowing new growth.

And when you need to take a breath between the breakthroughs, turn to Part Three. Those stories are not detours, they're integration points. Living proof that this path is messy, real, and possible. Don't rush. Don't skim. Let yourself weep. Live it. Let it change you.

If you haven't yet, consider reaching for your journal. Let this journey be captured. This is your dojo.

Maybe you've checked all the boxes: career, house, relationship… but still feel like a stranger in your own life.

This is your jailbreak.

This is your way back to wildness. Not just a path, but a pattern the whole world is remembering. As you rise, you ripple. As you root, you reweave the collective fabric of your truth.

Your rise begins in the silence, in the sweat, in the sacred refusal to abandon yourself even one more day.

This is your soil. Let's grow.

Part 2: The Path to Badassery – Overview

Trunk 1: Know Thyself

Unfolding Awareness and Intuition
- Branch 1: Drop Their Plan and Make Your Own
- Branch 2: Understand Your Feelings and Needs
- Branch 3: Recognize Your Protective Patterns
- Branch 4: Practice Embodied Presence
- Branch 5: Follow Your Desire

Trunk 2: Tend Your Ground

State Regulation
- Branch 6: Recognize Your CRASH State
- Branch 7: Access Your COACH State
- Branch 8: CRASH & COACH Integration

Trunk 3: Respect Yourself

Self-Trust and Forgiveness
- Branch 9: Anchor in Your Higher Self
- Branch 10: Practice Self-Forgiveness
- Branch 11: Build Self-Trust
- Branch 12: Live in Integrity

Trunk 4: Transmute the Challenge

Meaning-Making and Myth
- Branch 13: Own Your Story
- Branch 14: Reclaim Your Mythic Identity
- Branch 15: Transform in Real Time
- Branch 16: Train with Stress

Trunk 5: Action

Embodied Courage and Identity Shift
- Branch 17: Act Before You're Ready
- Branch 18: Redefine Goals
- Branch 19: Commit Boldly
- Branch 20: The Process is the Way

Trunk 6: Expression

Energy Integrity, Celebration, and Visibility
- Branch 21: Rest, Detox, Movement, and Nature
- Branch 22: Mark the Thresholds, Celebrate the Milestones
- Branch 23: Update Your Identity
- Branch 24: Create from Truth
- Bonus Branch 25: Make powerful Agreements

Trunk 1
Know Thyself

Unfolding of Awareness and Intuition

Branch 1
Drop Their Plan & Make Your Own

Branch 2
Understand Your Feelings and Needs

Branch 3
Recognize Your Protective Patterns

Branch 4
Practice Embodied Presence

Branch 5
Follow Your Desire

Trunk 1: Know Thyself

Unfolding Awareness and Intuition

Trunk 1 splits into five branches:

- Branch 1: Drop Their Plan and Make Your Own
- Branch 2: Understand Your Feelings and Needs
- Branch 3: Recognize Your Protective Patterns
- Branch 4: Practice Embodied Presence
- Branch 5: Follow Your Desire

Before you rise, you have to remember who you truly are. Strip away the noise, the distractions, and begin from your roots. That's where your power lies. This isn't to become someone new, it's to remember who you've always been.

Trunk 1 is Know Thyself, the foundational Trunk of awareness and intuition. It's about developing a clear, unshakable understanding of your inner world. Because if you don't know who you are, you'll never be able to distinguish where you are meant to go.

This Trunk connects you to your internal realm. Slow down, listen to your body, and uncover what's genuine beneath the demands and distractions. Clarity doesn't just arrive, it's cultivated. It slowly begins to reveal itself when you stop waiting for the answer and start becoming the one who can hear it.

Awareness is the first and most vital step of real change. It starts by noticing what's already there. That tension in your chest. The story playing on repeat in your head. The need behind the habit. Most of us constantly ignore this wisdom.

To make this shift, you'll need to learn new skills:
- How to hear your real voice, not the chatter of your conditioning.
- How to notice the difference between superficial goals and deep, resonant truth.
- How to stop reacting to life, and start creating it

You'll also need to get real about who's driving the bus. We believe we make rational decisions based on our current circumstances. The truth? Our responses usually come from the past.

These actions were formed during times of anguish; protective strategies developed during childhood, outdated survival mechanisms, inherited trauma. The one that learned to stay quiet to keep the peace. Who got praised for his achievements, but not for being himself. Who has to control the outcome, or else the world will fall apart.

If you're unsure who's running your life, chances are it's the scared kid with a fake ID. These responses aren't bad, they're just outdated.

Through this Trunk, you'll begin to spot these patterns and learn how to meet them with compassion. You'll separate your higher self from your coping self. And you'll start choosing from truth, not trauma.

This work helps you to:

- Feel your feelings without drowning in them.
- Meet your needs without shame.
- Trust your internal signals.
- Live in alignment with who you truly are.

Without this Trunk, your rise may look impressive, but it won't withstand life's inevitable storms. This is where your power originates. So slow down and get curious. Let go of the crutch of other people's advice. Step into radical self-trust. This is where you stop living someone else's story and start writing your own.

Your truth might be hiding in the basement, but it's still breathing. You will hear it, you just need to learn how to listen deeper.

Branch 1: Drop Their Plan and Make Your Own

Default living is following a script. Design begins the moment you ask: What do I actually want?

Remember the girl who just wanted to do everything right so she wouldn't get left behind? The girl who watched her country change from communism to capitalism overnight at seven years old?

One day, the economy, education, healthcare, housing, speech, and religious systems were all under the control of the state government. The next, complete havoc ensued as Polish society tried to grapple with the disorder of a completely new set of rules, not yet fully defined.

As a young child, most of the turmoil was beyond my comprehension, but one truth landed early: all of this was made up. The systems we obey, the customs we follow, the definitions of success we inherit: they were all fabricated by people in power, often far removed from our lives and truths. Politicians, patriarchs, and authorities invented rules to keep order, to keep control.

And if that's true… why wouldn't we write some of our own?

Remember how my parents' divorce shattered the obedient script I had been following? Their vows didn't hold. And strangely, that didn't shatter me, it set me free. If they could walk away from their commitments, I could walk away from my self-imposed expectations.

I realized I wasn't bound by what they believed or who they hoped I would become.

That unraveling gave me a gift that many people never receive: it gave me permission. I was freed at fifteen. While others spent decades chasing approval or resenting their parents' blueprint, I now felt free to chart my own course.

Maybe you've also had your rule book tossed out the window at some point: by a divorce, a layoff, or a diagnosis. Or maybe it was more subtle than that: the job offer you accepted because it looked good financially but left you feeling somber inside. The town you moved to because of your spouse turned out to be the opposite of what you were hoping for. The family trip you agreed to because you felt obligated, but were dreading. These feelings are signals you're operating from someone else's playbook.

Whose Life Is This Anyway?

Realizing the life you've been acting in has been written, produced and directed by others is not a problem, it's an invitation. It's a sign that it's time to follow your desire and start steering yourself towards a life you are thrilled to live. One that gets you excited or even a little terrified every day.

Don't have a plan? No need to worry, you don't need one. You don't even need a map. You just need a dream and the guts to follow it to the open road.

I've seen people turn forty and suddenly realize they've been living someone else's vision their entire life. I've coached people who were highly successful, checking off every box, but they felt empty inside. And I watched my little sister drop out of high school and go through her "midlife" awakening at fifteen. Only to bounce back stronger and with more clarity as she moved forward.

It's easy to know what we don't want. It takes real courage to name what we do. The timing doesn't matter, you just need to answer the call.

One summer, when my younger cousins were visiting me in Hawai'i, a curious auntie asked them, "Eh, you gals get any plans fo' da summa, or what?" "We're not sure," they said. She nodded, then added with her thick Pidgin, "You sistahs, try figgah out what you like early, yeah? If not, you might end up jus' doin' what oddah people tell you fo' do."

The world will fill in the blanks for you, it will tell you what to tolerate, and what to sacrifice.

That's why this Trunk is so important. Without it, you chase someone else's dream and follow someone else's map. When you start clearing the overgrowth you will find your own wild path. Machete in hand. Determination driving you forward. No one leading but you.

Pre-rejection: Living the Worst-Case Scenario Before It Happens

We think we're protecting ourselves by holding back, waiting, staying small. What we're really doing is rejecting ourselves, before anyone else gets the chance. This is the trap: we avoid thinking about what we want because it would mean we have to face the risk of going after it. We create elaborate excuses and end up living in a state of pre-rejection.

We tell ourselves:

- They won't respond.
- It'll flop.
- They'll think I'm too much, or worse, not enough.
- I'll be humiliated.

So, we don't act. We don't ask. We don't show up. And in not taking the risk, we create the exact outcome we were afraid of: I was afraid they wouldn't accept me, so I never gave them the chance to reject me. This is what fear does: it tries to protect us from pain and discomfort by keeping us stuck.

Luckily, the moment you see it, you can choose differently. When we bring awareness to these voices, we stop letting them take control. We stop giving our power away to fear and start grabbing hold of the steering wheel.

Clarity alone can't anchor you. You can have a vision and still sabotage it if you don't know what's running underneath. Before you can walk toward the life you want, you have to feel where you are now. That's where we go next.

Pause & Reflect

- Where are you preemptively saying no to yourself out of fear that they might reject you or even agree with you?
- What are you protecting yourself from, and what is it costing you?

Anchoring Insights

- Life by default follows someone else's script; design begins the moment you ask, What do I want?
- "Rule-flip" moments (a regime change, a lay-off, a quiet ache) are invitations, not problems.
- If you don't name your dream, the world will write a smaller one for you.
- Courage = trading the comfort of known paths to follow your own wild trail (bring the machete)

Exploration 1: The Genie Visualization

The Genie Visualization isn't about fantasy. It's about giving yourself permission to want what you want. Set aside 30 minutes to sit or walk uninterrupted. Turn off your phone, and go to a place that is quiet and calm.

Then imagine a genie appears and says: "Your dream life is granted. No limitations."

- What do you see?
- How do you spend your days?
- How do you feel?
- Where do you live?
- Who's around you?

Let your imagination surprise you. You may see one dream. You may see five.

You don't have to pick. You don't have to make it happen. The point is to just recognize what lives inside you that you've never given yourself permission to want.

What if the life you crave is the one you are meant to live? Start by imagining it. Then dare to want it.

Branch 2: Understand Your Feelings and Needs

Welcome all Feelings

We cannot change what we are unwilling to feel. And we cannot feel if we refuse to slow down enough to notice.

This isn't about strategies for improving your emotional intelligence, so you can manage yourself better. It's about real freedom. When you're unaware of what you're feeling or needing, you make decisions based on fear.

You say "yes" when you mean "no". You people-please, over perform, overfunction, burn out, and pass that disconnection on to everyone around you.

This branch is about self-awareness: emotional, physical, and relational. It begins with a simple question: What am I feeling right now?

This question is the foundation of what I call the Locator Button. My counselor, Nancy Rubin, introduced me to this tool, and I still use it every day. Think of it as a personal GPS that drops a pin into your soul. No matter how lost you feel, it brings you back to where you currently are. Using the Locator Button is like a treasure hunt under the ski lifts. You start noticing what has always been there, concealed but waiting to be found.

Here's how it works: just pause, notice, and welcome. That's it.

You pause whatever you are doing: mentally or physically. You notice: What am I feeling right now? Is there tension in my body? A sense of urgency? A tightness in my chest? A dull ache in my belly?

Then you welcome it. Don't try to fix or change it. Just say, "Welcome. I see you. I feel you. You get to be here."

It's really that simple. Most of us never learned to welcome our feelings. We were taught that they were wrong. So we judge them, ignore them, suppress them, or perform over them. None of those actions make our feelings go away. Instead, they go underground and leak out later as chronic pain, anger, fatigue, anxiety, or shame. Every time you press the locator button, it's like placing your palm on your heart and saying, "I see you, you are good."

The Locator Button can be used at any time: sitting in traffic, doing the dishes, walking your dog, in deeply triggering moments like mid-argument, or after receiving bad news. It's a way to return home to yourself, no matter what kind of chaos is unfolding around you.

Weaponizing Self Awareness

I once spent weeks falling off the same climb. Failing in the same spot, on the same moves, over and over. I thought something was wrong with me. I obsessed over my mindset, my footwork, my fear.

Then a cold front rolled in, and with the drop in temperature I found myself at the top of the route clipping the anchors. The problem wasn't me: it was the weather! The warm conditions reduced the rock's friction, forcing me to grip harder, and exert more effort. The cooler temps allowed me to relax more, conserve energy, and flow instead of fight.

This experience opened my eyes to how often we turn self-awareness into self-blame. If we're feeling off, we assume we're broken, instead of recognizing that it might just be the conditions. Awareness without context can become a weapon. The key is learning to check both the inner signals and the outer environment before we decide what is true.

Common ways we might use self-awareness against ourselves:

1. **We blame ourselves first:** If something is not working out the way we want, we assume we are the problem, not the heat, the deadline, the sick kid, or the poor sleep.

2. **We think one bad week means forever, mistaking feelings as permanent facts:** One rough moment turns into "I'll never get this." One episode of anxiety equates to "I'm eternally flawed."

3. **We only see what fits our worst scenario:** If we constantly believe that we're not good enough, we ignore or disregard anything that proves otherwise.

4. **We unfairly compare ourselves to others:** Someone else's success becomes a magnification of our failures. "They got the promotion because they're smarter, not stupid like me."

5. **We believe it's all or nothing:** If THIS single thing doesn't unfold the way we want it to, our life is over. This leaves no space for learning, growing, adapting, or just being in process.

6. **We exaggerate even the smallest slips:** Missing a workout turns into "I have no discipline" instead of "I had a full day."

Story: *Kindergarten Trauma in a Zoom Room*

Eva opened our Zoom session with a playful invitation: "Choose a partner and dance!" Names flew: "Dance with me!" "Pick me!"

I froze.

My nervous system crashed. My inner dialogue was brutal: Nobody's going to pick you. If you ask, they'll say no. You're invisible here. I regressed, into that old part of me: the scared child who never quite belonged, who didn't know how to ask for love without bracing for rejection.

My cursor hovered over the "unmute" button. I wanted to call someone's name, but my hand wouldn't move. While every video square filled with music and motion, I sat rigid, a grapefruit-sized lump in my throat.

For ten full minutes, everyone danced on Zoom. And I cried in my little square. Ten minutes isn't a long time, unless you're sitting in shame. Then it feels like forever.

I pressed the Locator Button again, and again. What am I feeling? Rejected. Alone. Small. What do I need? To belong. To be seen. Welcome, heartbreak. Welcome, shame.

When we regrouped, Eva asked what surfaced. My voice shook as I spoke the whole truth of what I felt. Tears rippled across the gallery. "Me too," people said, naming their own fear of not being chosen. We spent the rest of the hour talking about loneliness, longing, and the fear of not being picked.

Afterward, Eva messaged me privately. She felt terrible for not noticing. My vulnerability touched a place in her; her own fear of not being a good enough facilitator. We ended up having a beautiful, deep conversation about worth, holding space, and being human.

It all started because I pressed the button. Because I paused, noticed, welcomed, and told the truth. When you name how you feel, you instantly come home to yourself. When you welcome it, you disarm the shame. When you speak it, you free yourself and others too. In kindergarten, I waited to be chosen. Today, I choose me.

Pause & Reflect

- When you feel left out or unseen, do you freeze, perform, or reach?
- What does your body know before your mind explains it?
- What do you make it mean when you're not chosen? Can you let the feeling exist without making it the whole truth?

Awareness is the Bedrock

A lot of high-functioning adults have no idea how to cultivate this kind of self-awareness. Consider this your first lesson: You are worth paying attention to. If you skip this, everything else wobbles. You'll try to rise from reaction instead of truth.

You might wonder, If I let myself feel all the sadness, anger, fear, guilt, shame, loneliness, regret, embarrassment, and despair, will it swallow me whole? Will I fall apart with no way back?

The answer is "no". You can feel it all without being consumed. When you feel it, the difficult emotions exit your body and you are finally free.

Anchoring Insights

- You can't change what you refuse to feel; slowing down is the gateway to truth.
- The Locator Button = Pause, Notice, Welcome – it drops a pin on your inner GPS anytime, anywhere.
- Naming a feeling disarms shame and turns a reaction into a choice.
- Honesty about emotion frees not just you but everyone around you.

Exploration 2: Locator Button Practice

Returning to yourself takes practice and repetition.

Daily rehearsal is the only way to develop this method of recognizing your present state of being. Do it while driving, in the shower, in line at the grocery store, in conflict, or first thing in the morning. It only takes 30 seconds.

1. Pause. Interrupt the autopilot:

- Place your hand on your chest, breathe in deeply, exhale completely and say out loud to yourself, I am here.

2. Notice. Ask:

- What am I feeling right now?
- Where do I feel it in my body?
- What thoughts are running in the background?

Name it honestly. Don't hide. Don't dress it up. Don't explain it away. Just tell it like it is.

3. Welcome. Say to yourself:

- Welcome, anxiety.
- Welcome, sadness.
- Welcome, loneliness.
- You get to be here. I see you.

You're not trying to fix it. You're just acknowledging it. That alone can often break the cycle of disconnection.

4. Ask. This is optional:

- What do I need right now?

Maybe it's rest. Maybe it's a connection. Maybe it's a glass of water. Maybe it's nothing at all. Just notice.

That's it. That's the button. Push it often. Make it a ritual. Let it become your doorway home.

Branch 3: Recognize Your Protective Patterns

We are all born whole, unwounded, unwoundable, and free from turmoil. This is our Higher Self: the part of us that remembers the truth. The self that is rooted in presence, peace, and power. The self untouched by trauma, unshaken by shame, uncluttered by fear.

Your Higher Self isn't something you earn: it's something you arrived with, and can return to. It lives beneath the commotion. It is the calm presence that doesn't need to prove anything, because It has always belonged.

Life is a turbulent ride and our earliest environments are never perfect. So, we adapt. We trade our authenticity for love, for safety, for acceptance, and for survival. We shape-shift to stay close to the people we need. We build internal protections: rules and voices that guard us from rejection or failure. These protections are not bad. They are often brilliant. But they are not our essence, but simply the armor we wear.

And that's where the ego comes in.

The Ego Mind

Our ego is not the enemy: it's our sense of self-worth, self-image, or identity. It's the part of us concerned with status, pride, personal achievements, and how we perceive our own importance and abilities.

In evolutionary terms our ego represents our capacity to recognize ourselves as separate from others, which allows us to better predict our own behavior, assess risks, and make strategic decisions beneficial to survival.

It's also what gives us the ability to develop self-awareness: to recognize our own thoughts, feelings, motivations, and behaviors. Without ego, civilization as we know it wouldn't exist. But the ego's primary job is for us to survive, not to flourish.

It uses protections to run its survival scheme, building fortresses on fear-based logic. It wants control, certainty, and approval. And it will do whatever it takes to preserve the image that keeps it safe, even if that means a life of quiet misery.

The ego is like a five-year-old who thinks she runs the world: manipulative, insistent, reactive, and terrified of change.

And yet, the ego is just the smallest of the nesting dolls. Expanding outward, you have the Witness or Observer (self-awareness), the Higher Self (Essence or Authentic Self), the Collective Consciousness (Interconnectedness), and the Universal Consciousness (Oneness, Unity).

We can't exile the ego. We can't destroy our protections. But we can bring awareness to them and gradually take back the reins.

Even the ego is divine: a fragment of protection shaped by the need to survive, now waiting to be welcomed into the sacred architecture of the self. When we love the ego, instead of allowing it to run the show, it bows and offers us the keys it once stole.

What Protections Sound Like

Often, the loudest voice in our head, the one that sounds the most urgent, or insistent, is the voice of our armor. The voice goes by many names: internal protections, protective parts, inner defenders, survival strategies, etc. Internal Family Systems (a therapeutic model developed by Dr. Richard Schwartz), simply calls these "parts", or sub-personalities such as "inner critic, people pleaser, or avoider".

Each "part" has its own thoughts, emotions, beliefs, memories, and motivations, like separate characters in your internal world. They are the voices that help you survive, protect you from pain, or carry wounds not yet healed. They are typically formed during childhood when your environment feels unsafe, overwhelming, confusing, or invalidating. But they can form at any time, especially during intense trauma or prolonged and repeated stress.

Can you recall a message from your ego voice? It might sound something like:

- "You don't have what it takes."
- "If it's not perfect, it's a failure"
- "You know what to say to make him happy"
- "Don't try, you're not strong enough."
- "If they really knew you, they'd leave."
- "You always just screw things up."

If these sound familiar it's because you've been rehearsing them for years. But it's important to remember that they are just small aspects of you, formed in response to the events and pain you have experienced in life. They often speak in extremes, because they have been working hard for so long, usually without any support.

The Problem with Letting Protections Lead

Operating from protections may bring short-term success or even applause. You might get the promotion or keep the peace for now. But there is a hidden cost: your vitality, your truth, your lasting joy.

Your protections keep you performing instead of connecting. Reacting instead of choosing. And when emotions like anger, fear, or shame, rise up, they kick in even harder.

But these negative emotions serve an important purpose, they are alarms that warn us when something is off. Like our nervous system screaming when our hand touches a hot stove. But unlike physical pain where we instantly react, we often camp out in the burn of emotional pain. We ruminate, blame, numb out, and wonder why we're stuck. We forget that we have other options.

The pain is not the problem though. Staying stuck in that pain is. To move forward, we don't need more control; we need self-awareness. And we need better questions.

Not: "How do I amass enough control to stay safe forever?"

But: "What do I know at this moment, and what am I ready to choose?"

One common protector is the 'Helper': it appears generous but is fear in disguise. True service is clean. It doesn't bargain for belonging or confuse sacrifice with love. For those of us wired to help, it's easy to cross the line of offering support because we fear that we will be unwanted if we don't.

When worth is tethered to being indispensable, boundaries blur and the body keeps score. What looks like generosity is often anxiety dressed as devotion. The work now is to pause, feel, and ask: Is this action true? Or am I trying to earn a place? That split-second check can mean the difference between sacred support and self-erasure.

Story: *Leverage Disguised as Love*

It started with a late-night phone call from a climbing partner I adored, let's call him Sam. He'd blown out his shoulder, his relationship was crumbling, he was spiraling, and grasping for a lifeline. We talked for hours, and in the days, weeks, and months that followed I supported him in any way possible.

I answered every text. Pulled strings to get him into a physical therapist. I talked to him every night. Even helped him with rent when the workers' comp check stalled. I told myself it was friendship in its purest form: unconditional, heroic, the kind of loyalty I wished someone had shown my younger self.

The truth? I secretly loved when life threw me Sam-types. Broken birds I could patch back together. It made me feel useful. Alive.

Three months in, I was triaging Sam's life daily, while my own physical fitness, sleep, and bank account were bleeding out. There was an urgency to it. Reckless abandon. Friends called it "saintly." My nervous system called it survival. I'd fused my self-worth to his recovery curve: if Sam rallied, I mattered. If he sank, I failed.

Then the backlash hit. Sam missed a PT session. I snapped, lecturing him like a delinquent son. He fired back: "Your help feels like a cage."

Cue heartbreak, and whiplash. I'd poured myself out until the pitcher ran dry, yet somehow, I was the problem. Only in the wreckage did the pattern come into focus, one I'd been living, not questioning, for years. I wasn't giving from overflow; I was bargaining for belonging. I called it devotion, but it was duty in disguise, fear dressed up as virtue. I wasn't serving him; I was serving the part of me still trying to matter by rescuing others.

The consequences were real: fractured trust, weeks of silent fallout, and a friendship that only half-recovered. And while I didn't intend harm, the harm was done.

Today, I ask gut-check questions: Am I acting from love, or from the terror of being unnecessary? Is this support mutually agreed upon, or am I freelancing as a rescuer? Clear agreements.

Before stepping in, I ask: "What help serves you, and what stays yours to carry?" Micro-boundaries. "I'm excited for you to schedule your own appointments," or an honest "I've got 15 minutes, will that help?"

I'm not "cured." The Helper still muscles forward when life feels shaky. But these days, I meet her with a hand on the heart: Thanks for wanting to love big. Let's love wisely.

Advanced self-abandonment rarely screams self-hatred. It whispers: I've got this, for both of us. Listen closer. If the body tightens, if resentment simmers, you've crossed the line from generosity to grasping. Step back. Breathe. Let true service that is clean, reciprocal, and sustainable take its rightful place.

Pause & Reflect

- When do you feel compelled to "save" others?
- What part of you believes their experience is my responsibility?
- Are you offering support from a place of genuine care, or are you seeking validation through being needed?

What IFS Taught Me

Internal Family Systems changed my life. It teaches that every protection, every "part," has a positive intent. The Inner Critic? It's trying to protect you from shame. The Controller? From chaos. The Pleaser? From abandonment.

The problem is most of these parts were built by your five-year-old self. Now they're running your life with the logic of a child, doing their best to keep you safe.

Remember the goal isn't to exile your parts, it's to acknowledge them, get to know them, and integrate them. To thank them for trying to keep you safe, and gently say, You don't have to do it alone. I've got it now.

Story: *The One Who Books The Ticket*

When I was two, I learned that love leaves. That I better not need anyone too much. That I better learn to leave first. So, for decades I did.

Whenever a relationship got hard, a familiar part of me took over: the one who keeps her suitcase half-packed and whispers: You're better off alone. She introduced herself as self-sufficiency, but in reality, she was fear in a leather jacket.

Her signature move? A one-way mental ticket to Maui. It didn't matter if she was in love. It didn't matter if things were repairable. The moment vulnerability entered the room; she headed for the door. Not always literally; but always in her mind. Vanish before they do.

For years, I thought she was me. I let her make decisions. I let her end what could have been healed. I confused her urgency for my truth.

IFS work cracked this illusion wide open. She's a part of me, not the whole me; she's a protection, a younger self who learned it was safer to leave than risk being left. Now, when she shows up, I don't argue. I let her picture Maui. I listen. I thank her for trying to keep me safe. Then I take the lead.

She doesn't need to book the ticket or fix anything, because I know who I am. I've got this, and I'm not leaving myself.

The Ongoing Practice

Protection-to-presence is a gradual shift: it requires practice, compassion, and patience. You won't live in your Higher Self 100% of the time. The good news is you don't need to. Just pause and ask, Who's talking? Who's choosing? Name the protective voice, and then acknowledge it: I see you. I hear you. You're not bad, but I'm choosing a different option. When fear stops driving, the road opens up to peace, power, and joy: where you started from all along.

Anchoring Insights

- We're born whole; protections are clever but outdated safety strategies.
- The ego's job is surviving, not thriving; it wants control, certainty, applause.
- Parts work turns exiling the Critic into welcoming the Critic and then taking the lead.
- Power returns when your Higher Self, not the frightened five-year-old, holds the wheel

Exploration 3: Naming Your Protections

Start by noticing who's here. The voices, the impulses, and the reactions. Get curious.

Name your protections: literally. Give them names, faces, and personalities. Draw them if you want. Let them speak. Ask:

- Who shows up when I feel threatened?
- Who takes over when I feel unseen, unloved, or not enough?
- Who tries to fix, hide, disappear, or prove?

You don't need a comprehensive list. Just spend time with one or two. Listen without judgment. Get to know them. Here are some common protections; yours may be different:

- The Critic
- The Judge
- The Pleaser
- The Controller
- The Planner
- The Fixer
- The Performer
- The Avoider
- The Rebel
- The Pusher

Let this be a conversation, not a diagnosis. These parts are not problems. They're protectors. And they've worked hard to keep you safe. You're not here to banish them. You're here to meet them and remind them: Thank you. I've got it from here.

Branch 4: Practice Embodied Presence

Most of us live in our heads: narrating, analyzing, and strategizing. But truth doesn't start in our minds, it starts in our bodies. Before your mind thinks of the words, before your mouth formulates the sentence, your body already knows what's true.

Focusing or "Felt Sense" is turning your attention inward. The term was coined by philosopher and psychotherapist Eugene Gendlin in the 1960s, when he discovered the single most important factor linked to therapeutic change was a client's ability to attend to a bodily "felt sense" and let it unfold.

It's a visceral sense of the body, or bodily awareness, where subtle, internal cues like a knot in your stomach, or a fluttering in your throat carry meaning; especially around something left unresolved, unclear, or emotionally charged. It's not a thought. It's a sensation. It's the intuitive, physical "deep knowing" that arises when you pay quiet, curious attention to something inside.

The sensations start out vague, barely perceptible. Kind of like "something's there, but I don't quite know what it is." These meaning-laden signals are your body's way of saying: "This matters. Listen."

Focusing allows for deep transformation to begin, because when you stop ignoring and start noticing, something shifts. Space begins to open up as you shift from thinking about your problem to being with it. Stepping away from the analysis and into awareness.

It is practiced in the following 6 steps:

1. Start by allowing space, pausing, and slowing down.
2. Then turn your attention inward and focus. The sensations are not only physical as they are tied to emotions as well, but they are very real. A few examples: a heaviness in your chest, a swirling in your belly, a clenched jaw, a foggy weight behind your eyes.
3. Once you find a sensation, you listen, gently. No fixing, Judging, or pushing away. Just pause and say: Hello. I know you're there. I'm listening.
4. Then wait for the meanings to begin to emerge. The sensation

might "speak" in images, words, memories, or metaphors: It feels like a small animal hiding. It's like a wall around my heart. It's saying: I'm scared you'll leave. Don't force this. Let it come from your body.

5. You feel a shift, often subtle, sometimes profound: something opens up, tension eases, a different color or a new perspective appears.
6. Realization unfolds: It was never about the surface issue at all.

The results:

- What you thought was procrastination was fear of disappointing others.
- What you perceived as anger was revealed as a longing.
- What you identified as laziness turned out to be deep exhaustion masked in self-judgement.

Focusing is a real world practice, not a lofty theory: it is the process of turning inward, even in a moment of urgency, when clarity and truth are paramount.

Story: *A Bathroom, a Boundary, and the Truth*

Whenever someone asks me to do something, I almost always think it's a great idea in the moment. I feel their energy, ride their excitement, and say "yes." But later, after more reflection I think to myself, Why the hell did I agree to that? So I decided to start doing something new.

Unless I have a whole body yes, I say, "Let me get back to you." If the moment calls for an immediate answer, I excuse myself to a space where I can find a pocket of solitude. The backyard, a hallway, the bathroom.

In that space, I pause, turn inward, and ask my body: How do I really feel about this?

I don't think about it, I feel for it. Using the practice of Focusing, I slow down and turn my attention inward. Maybe my chest feels tight. Maybe there's a drop in my belly. Maybe there's warmth, ease, a quiet yes. I don't force clarity. I wait until my body speaks.

Only then do I respond. Not from the rush of someone else's enthusiasm. Not from pressure to perform. But from my own truth.

Pause & Reflect

- What changes when you stop trying to figure it out?
- Can you let your body speak before your brain jumps in?
- Where does this yes, or no, live in your body?

Ecological Self

My rewilding mentor, Natasha Lythgoe, describes Focusing as a way to "value and cherish the slow, subtle, and vague." A sacred pause in a culture obsessed with speed and certainty.

Rather than rushing toward a solution, Focusing invites you to attune to the quiet signals beneath the surface. To develop intimacy with your own inner terrain. Natasha calls it "apprenticing the body." Not in dominance or mastery, but in reverent partnership, learning to trust the language of breath, gut, pulse, and sensation. As you listen in this way, you begin to realize: this isn't happening in isolation. It's not just inner work; it's ecological. This kind of deep listening arises from the same intelligence that animates the living world.

Our bodies are not separate from the Earth; they are intimately intwined. Just as a forest communicates through mycelium networks beneath the soil, your body speaks in signals too subtle for logic.

The more you listen, the more you awaken your Ecological Self; the part of you that knows you are not a machine to be optimized, but a living system; complex, sensitive, rhythmic, and woven into the fabric of nature. You pulse with seasons, carry rivers in your blood, and breathe with the trees.

Beyond a therapeutic tool, Focusing becomes a way to remember your place in the living world; self-rooted, relational, and inseparable from the wild intelligence around you.

Anchoring Insights

- The body knows first; a Felt Sense is the raw data beneath the story.
- Gendlin showed lasting change tracks with a client's ability to stay with a Felt Sense.
- Focusing is listening to your body without an agenda until something inside shifts on its own.
- Your awareness can widen to include the living world, moving from isolated self to interconnected self.

Exploration 4: Focusing with the Living World

Set aside 30 minutes, ideally outdoors or near a natural element (a tree, stone, water, or a window with a sky view.)

1. Settle and Arrive

- Sit quietly. Let your body arrive before your mind catches up. Notice your breath, but don't control it.
- Let the earth hold your weight. Let the sounds around you belong.
- You're not here to fix anything. You're here to listen to life, through your internal senses.

2. Sense Into the Body

- Gently bring attention inward. What's here now? What wants attention? Not as a thought, but as a sensation in your body. A pressure, a weight, a tightness, a temperature?
- You don't need to name it. Just say hello to whatever's there.
- Can you sense the edge of something? Vague, perhaps. Quiet. Let it know you're willing to keep it company.

3. Stay with the Felt Sense

- Allow the Felt Sense to gather, not the emotion or the story, but the whole body-feel of this cue.
- Stay nearby with gentle curiosity. Let it show you, not in words, but in images, textures, sensations, and movement.
- What is the shape of this experience? A color? A rhythm? Does it shift if you breathe into it?

4. Listen Without Agenda

- Ask inwardly: What does this part want me to know? What's the gift, the fear, or the need?
- Listen not for answers, but for a sense of congruence when something resonates.
- Even if it's silent, trust that a dialogue is happening. The body knows, even when we don't.

5. Widen the Field

- Now slowly include your surroundings, the tree beside you, the birdsong, the air on your skin.
- Let the boundary between inner and outer soften. Feel your body as part of the living world.
- What if this Felt Sense belongs to the Earth too? What if it's not yours to carry alone?

6. Thank and Close

- Gently thank whatever showed up, even if it stayed quiet. You listened. That is enough.
- Let your breath deepen. Feel every part of your body, your toes, your legs, your hands, your temples. Notice what shifted, however small.

May this listening ripple outward. May it matter: not just for your healing, but for the world that breathes with you.

Branch 5: Follow Your Desire

What if desire was not an indulgence, but a direction?

We've been taught to mistrust our desires. To fear them. To tame them. But what if desire is not something to control? What if it's how your soul speaks to you?

There is a current moving through you. Call it life force. Call it spirit. Call it the wild pulse of the Earth. It moves in you as longing. As a pull. As fire.

Not all desires are created equal. Some are hungry ghosts that arise from fear, emptiness, or ego; reaching for what numbs or distracts. Others come from a deeper place: the desire to create, to love, to expand, to come home to yourself. These desires don't agitate, they resonate. They don't demand control, instead they invite alignment.

Desire can be a distraction, or a direction. The universe whispering: This way.

Desire, when rooted in truth, becomes a compass pointing you inward. I didn't always know this. I used to treat desire like a dangerous thing, something to suppress, manage, or justify. Now I ask: Where is this desire coming from? What is it asking me to become?

I fully trust myself to know the difference between the hungry ghost and a generative force of the universe. They just feel completely different in my body.

Story: *Hitting a vein of desire*

High in Morocco's Atlas Mountains, in the remote Berber village of Taghia, Steven and I arrived; eager to climb the massive limestone walls that rose in the distance. With no roads and donkeys instead of cars, hiking into Taghia felt like stepping back in time.

The incredible Berber people have lived in Taghia and its surrounding valleys for over 2,000 years. Though modern technology has crept in, much of their traditional way of life endured.

The village had out of time feel; cradled in a steep, green gorge, with ancient footpaths etched into the cliffs. Goats roaming freely. Adults tending to crops and livestock. Children darting along narrow stone paths between weathered huts. Time moves differently here: slower, rooted, alive.

Climbers who make the journey are rewarded with routes that demand total commitment and offer profound solitude. No internet. No cell service. No cafés. No grocery stores. Their absence is a rare luxury.

4 a.m. starts, punishing approaches, and bone-deep exhaustion are the price of admission to climb these towering red and orange walls; 2,600 feet of sheer, sacred limestone rising from the valley floor.

After a few days of blissful suffering, even the hardest climbers welcome a rest day like it's their salvation: battered, content, and craving a well earned stillness.

One such day, happily lounging around with nothing to do, I started scrolling through the library on my Kindle. A book I didn't remember buying caught my eye: "The Journey of Soul Initiation" by Bill Plotkin. From the first page, my whole body lit up.

"This! This is what I'm meant to do! This is what I've been sensing but couldn't name."

It wasn't just interest; it was soul-level knowing. A full-body YES!

The moment we hit cell service in Marrakech; I found a vision fast program. I didn't hesitate. I didn't overthink it. I just knew. I found one immediately and signed up; landing twenty-seventh on the waiting list. I wasn't rattled. I knew I was going.

Why this? I couldn't have told you then. I just knew it was mine.

A few weeks before the trip, I was bumped to number one. I got my spot.

A vision fast is a powerful, ancient rite of passage rooted in indigenous and earth-based traditions. It involves spending time alone in nature; often without food, distraction, or even shelter. At its heart, it's about letting go of the known and stepping into the mystery of the wilderness to fully meet yourself.

Participants are often in a life transition (grief, retirement, divorce, identity shift), seeking clarity, shedding old stories or roles, or simply longing to reconnect with nature.

For me, it was a turning point.

That quest reshaped me from the inside, rooted me deeper, and gave me the language, rituals, and tools that now shape the work I offer to others. It also lit a fuse. I met someone whose presence struck like a flint, igniting a fire neither of us saw coming. Ours wasn't a random collision. It was a catalytic crossing, precise and inevitable.

And it started with one thing: Desire. Not the kind that bubbles up in your head. The kind that lives in your bones. In your body. In your knowing. When you let yourself trust desire; wild, holy, untamed desire, and you begin to remember who you are.

This is how the soul speaks: not with logic or timing, but through a deep pull that can't be ignored. Desire can't be forced.

But it can be heard, when you slow down and listen. One practice I return to again and again is what I call The Desire Walk; a simple act of moving slowly, without agenda, listening for what draws your attention, your body, your yes.

Pause & Reflect

- Do you trust yourself to be able to tell when your desire is coming from a hungry ghost, and when it's coming from the generative force of the universe?
- Where in your life are you ignoring a pull because it doesn't "make sense"?
- What happens when you treat your desire as a guide instead of a problem to solve?
- Who taught you to mistrust what you want, and are they still in charge?

Anchoring Insights

- Aligned desire is direction, the soul's way of saying: this way!
- Stillness and space let true longing surface.
- A full-body yes often arrives before logic approves; act on it.
- Practicing tiny acts of desire "The Desire Walk" keeps your inner compass calibrated.

Exploration 5: The Desire Walk (or Sit)

The Desire Walk is a practice meant to give yourself space to follow your desire, moment by moment, without an agenda. No goals. No checklists. Just presence and pull. It can be practiced in the following 5 steps.

1. Create time

However much you can manage. A solo weekend. A full day. A morning. A sunrise walk. Even an hour or two alone. The important thing is that you set aside unstructured time in nature or somewhere you can feel relaxed without distraction. You can sit, walk or alternate your positions.

2. Begin by slowing down

Breathe deeply in your belly. Drop into your body. Ask: What do I want right now? What calls me?

3. Follow the pull

Let yourself be guided by subtle desire. Do you want to walk toward that tree? Sit in the sun? Smell the soil? Touch a rock? Follow it. No rush. No "shoulds." Let your attraction lead you. (Be safe. Don't touch unknown plants or animals, and don't fall off a cliff.)

4. Stay with the sensation

Notice what happens when you follow. What opens up? What sensations arise in your body? What emotions, thoughts, or resistance do you feel? Welcome it all.

5. Reflect

- What happened?
- What did it mean to you?
- What is it telling you?

This is not a performance, it's a practice that will carry you far if you listen.

Living Compass – Trunk One Summary: Know Thyself

Core Distinctions

- **Your plan vs. their plan:** Moving from inherited expectations to self-authored vision.
- **Feelings and needs vs. habits and performance:** Replacing unconscious patterns with emotional honesty and inner attunement.
- **Higher Self vs. protective parts:** Differentiating between your deeper truth and the strategies built to keep you safe.
- **Cognitive analysis vs. felt sense:** Shifting from head-based problem solving to embodied presence and intuitive knowing.

Core Practices

- **Pause and notice using the Locator Button:** Cultivate awareness of emotional, physical, and energetic signals.
- **Ask, "Who's speaking right now?":** Identify which part of you is in the lead (protector, inner child, critic, etc.)
- **Felt sense before the story:** Use Focusing to access truth below narrative, logic, or judgment.
- **Track desire and trust the body's "yes":** Rebuild trust in your inner compass through moment-by-moment listening.

Key Tools

- **Locator Button:** A simple but profound practice to pause, name, and welcome what's arising.
- **Parts check-in:** Gentle self-inquiry to differentiate inner voices and build self-trust.
- **Focusing:** A somatic method for sensing truth beyond mental chatter.
- **Desire journal:** A practice to reconnect with authentic longing and move from internal permission.

Guiding Truth

Awareness is your first freedom. What you can feel, you're free to choose.

Your Wake-Up Call

Many of us meticulously construct lives filled with accomplishments and accolades. Yet, beneath the surface, there's a lingering sense of emptiness; a quietache, the feeling that despite our success, something vital is missing. We've become adept at meeting external expectations, but have lost touch with our inner selves.

This disconnect doesn't happen overnight. It's the result of years spent prioritizing the needs of others, suppressing personal desires, and chasing society's definition of success. Over time, this creates a life that looks fine on the outside but feels hollow within.

The wake-up call often arrives unexpectedly: through a crisis, a moment of truth, or a quiet dissatisfaction that can no longer be ignored. It's the soul's way of demanding attention; urging a return to authenticity and alignment.

These calls are often subtle, but when dismissed, they can manifest as emotional dissonance: increased sensitivity, restlessness, exhaustion, imbalance, or a sense of being ungrounded.

As a coach, I've seen incredibly successful people break down; not because they are weak but because no one ever taught them how to simply be with themselves.

What if that breakdown wasn't failure, but prophecy? What if the soul only screams when something sacred is trying to be born. That tremble in your chest isn't a flaw, it's your frequency rising to meet your next octave of truth.

Answering this call means honoring the dissonance between your inner truth and your outer life. It's the first step toward reclaiming a life of purpose, passion, and deep fulfillment.

This is the essence of Trunk One: reconnecting with yourself so that your outer life finally resonates from the inside out. Awareness and intuition give you the map of your inner world.

Trunk 2
Tend Your Ground
State Regulation

Branch 6
Recognize Your Crash State

Branch 7
Access Your Coach State

Branch 8
Integration

Trunk 2: Tend Your Ground

State Regulation

Trunk 2 splits into three branches:

- Branch 6: Recognize Your Crash State
- Branch 7: Access Your Coach State
- Branch 8: Integration

You cannot rise if your nervous system is in survival mode. Tending Your Ground is honoring the ecosystem of your body, your energy, and your inner terrain. When you're dysregulated, disconnected, or overwhelmed, even the best tools won't help. You'll grip. You'll perform. You'll burn out trying to do the right thing from the wrong state.

This Trunk teaches you how to stop running and start rooting. How to track your nervous system, meet your patterns with kindness, and build the capacity to stay. It's about choosing slowness over strategy, and presence over performance.

To shift this, you need new skills:

- Recognizing when you've crashed: and what to do next
- Accessing COACH state and leading from your Higher Self
- Regulating urgency and returning to choice and clarity

The concepts of CRASH and COACH come from the work of my dear teacher, Stephen Gilligan, with whom I studied for three years. A student of Milton Erickson and Gregory Bateson, Gilligan weaves together the precision of Ericksonian hypnosis, the depth of somatic intelligence, and the creative force of consciousness itself. His work is part technique but mostly transmission. His modeling and presence seeded the inner transformation that made this book possible.

This Trunk invites you to get real about your patterns, the hidden reflexes: compulsive fixing, self-abandoning, scrolling, spiraling, snapping, shrinking. The subtle habits of shutdown and overdrive. These are the survival strategies that once protected you; but now keep you from being fully alive.

If you don't know how your nervous system speaks, it runs your life from behind the curtain. Here, you'll learn to tell the difference between fear and instinct. Between a reactive "yes" and a true "yes." Between performance and presence.

You'll learn to come home to your body, instead of outsourcing your safety. And with practice, you will build the capacity to stay grounded, so life doesn't knock you over every time the wind shifts.

This work helps you:

- Regulate instead of react
- Rest without guilt
- Listen to your body's signals
- Build a nervous system that supports growth instead of sabotaging it

Without this Trunk, your clarity won't stick. Your action won't hold. Your growth will feel shaky.

Your roots create your rise. So, slow down. Come back to your breath.

There's nothing wrong with you. You're just overdue for a homecoming. Let this be it.

Branch 6: Recognize Your Crash State

Learning to recognize how you protect yourself; and how those patterns keep you stuck.

When a threat hits, the nervous system flips into fight, flight, freeze, or fawn. Gilligan calls this CRASH: Contracted • Reactive • Analysis-paralyzed • Separated • Hurting.

CRASH is not a flaw; it's a protective reflex. But when left unchecked, it becomes a trap. You start to mistake it for reality.

Signs you might be in a nervous system CRASH include: emotional, cognitive, and behavioral signs. Common among these are:

Physical:
- Slumped posture
- Heavy limbs or full-body fatigue

Emotional:
- Emotional numbness or flatness
- Disconnection from self or others (through substances, screens, or shutdown)

Cognitive:
- Brain fog
- Forgetfulness
- Going through the motions with no real engagement

Behavioral:
- Isolating or avoiding communication
- Binging (food, alcohol, scrolling, etc.)

Story: *Yosemite Crash*

One of my deepest CRASH states happened in Yosemite; when I least expected it. I had just landed the job of my dreams: Official Park Photographer, a title once held by Ansel Adams.

My work days were riveting: capturing iconic landscapes, storytelling through imagery, documenting cultural events and adventure sports, engaging with visitors.

But the 9-to-5 schedule didn't align with the climbing community. Most climbers worked evenings; restaurant gigs, janitorial, maintenance; anything that left the daylight hours free. I was constantly on the lookout for partners with similar schedules as mine, but to no avail. Days off didn't line up. People flaked, ghosted, or bailed at the last minute. Eventually, I started expecting it. I moped through my days feeling lonely, bitter, and rejected. I started free-soloing* before or after work and on my days off. It gave me some release; but by evening, the emptiness would set in.

Most nights ended the same: alone in my tiny dorm room, lights off, sipping boxed wine straight from the spout. Outside, Yosemite's granite spires caught the last light of day; silent, ancient, yet indifferent.

Inside, I was doing my best to hold it together. I smiled through the workday, delivered the photos, played the part. But by nightfall, I was hollow. The loneliness was unbearable. And I was hiding it.

I turned to a solution battle-tested by my ancestors: alcohol, isolation, and silence. To quiet the ache. To survive the night. The wine was cheap and effective. One glass turned into three. Most nights, I lost count.

This wasn't rock bottom. No DUIs. No public disasters. Just a slow, quiet erosion. My body was present, but my spirit had left the building. I didn't even realize how much of myself I was losing until I finally stopped.

When the contract ended, it felt like coming up for air after a year underwater. That's when I saw the wreckage: my health, my spirit, my capacity to feel anything at all.

With a friend's support, I stopped drinking. That one seismic decision exposed what was underneath. Given my family's history of alcoholism, it wasn't just a lifestyle change: it was a break in the lineage.

Sobriety exposed what the wine had been hiding: I had almost no tools to sit with myself. No real capacity to feel, to soothe, to shift. That's when I began learning how to regulate; not by turning away, but by facing.

Looking back, that was one of my first lessons in nervous system literacy. I'd spent months trying to solve loneliness with logistics and partnerships; when what I really needed was internal safety. I didn't need more climbing partners. I needed the ability to sit with the ache, and choose a different response.

This story describes a long-term chronic crash. But CRASH can happen many times a day.

Pause & Reflect

- What do you try to fix on the outside when you're unraveling on the inside?
- When you feel the ache of loneliness or disconnection, do you reach for something, someone… or for yourself?

You Are Not Your Crash

The biggest deception of a CRASH state is believing it's who you are. But CRASH isn't an identity, it's a temporary state. A storm in your nervous system. A collapse in energy. It shows up as feeling overwhelmed, shutting down, as reactivity, spiraling thoughts, or numbness. It feels real because it is happening, but it's not you.

CRASH is a signal, not an identity. It points to something unhealed, unheld, or unmet; but it doesn't define your worth or your truth. When you believe you are your CRASH, you organize your life around avoiding it, hiding it, or performing your way out of it.

The Self, the deeper you, is never in CRASH. The Self is the one who sees it, stays with it, and breathes through it. When you stop identifying with the chaos and start witnessing it, you begin to reclaim your power. You are not your CRASH. You are the one who can rise from it.

The deeper you; is never in CRASH. The Self is the one who sees it, stays with it, and breathes through it. Naming your experience, "This is a CRASH," gives you power. It creates space between you and the state. It shifts you from drowning in it to observing it. It also helps regulate your nervous system by sending a clear message to your brain. This is temporary. This is not who I am.

Sometimes, CRASH doesn't announce itself with drama or disaster. Sometimes it arrives in paradise; in the quiet moments when we finally slow down. It hides behind the illusion of "doing fine," until the body or the soul says otherwise. In those moments, we don't need advice or solutions. We need presence. Witnessing. Co-regulation.

Story: *A CRASH in Paradise.*

A year after my divorce, I flew to Maui with my friend Amber. We had a list of joyful activities planned: sunrise swims, beach walks, farmer's markets, yoga. The island held the promise of lightness, laughter, and escape.

But on our first morning after the market, something in me broke. The sun was warming my back, the scent of papaya and cilantro was in the air; when suddenly an unbearable ache rose in my chest. I couldn't pretend anymore.

"Why weren't you with me?" I asked, the words tumbling out with a sharp edge. "When D-Griff and I split up, why weren't you helping me, calling, checking in? I was so alone. Nobody was there."

Amber looked at me gently, "You never asked for help," she said. "You kept saying you were good; climbing, working, doing your thing. You didn't make space for anyone to come in."

I stared at her, my voice thick with emotion. "Yes, but you were supposed to cut through that. You were supposed to know. Did you really believe I was okay?"

And that was it. The dam opened. I wept. In public. In paradise. All the strength I'd been projecting cracked like brittle glass. I told her everything; about the pain, the silence, the unraveling of a future I thought I was building.

We cancelled the schedule. I just cried, and she sat next to me.

She didn't try to fix it. She didn't tell me I was being dramatic or ask me to tone it down. "I'm sorry," I hiccuped. "I ruined our Maui trip." "I'm happy to be here with you," she said. "Happy or sad, doing everything or nothing. You don't have to be different."

That was it. That was the moment. My first real experience of unconditional love. Love that didn't need me to be strong or useful. Something in me, braced for abandonment since childhood, finally exhaled.

CRASH state becomes bearable when witnessed without judgment. That day, Amber's presence showed me regulation by osmosis. The very medicine I now offer to my clients.

Supporting Yourself During a Crash

When you are in a CRASH state it seems logical to try to fix it, shame it, or force your way out of it. What your nervous system actually needs is safety, slowness, and presence. Here's how to support yourself in those moments:

Regulation before resolution: Don't try to figure it all out. Your system needs to feel safe before you can access clarity and choice.

Co-regulation: Healing in connection is powerful. That might mean a calm presence, a hand on your back, eye contact, or a grounded voice reminding you: You're okay. You're not alone.

Grounding: Help your body return to the present. Try pressing your feet to the floor, holding something cold, splashing water on your face, or noticing what you see, hear, smell, feel, or taste.

Slowness and permission: CRASH often comes with urgency or shame. Give your system permission to pause, be unproductive. To simply be.

Breath: Don't just take a deep breath, slow it down. Inhale gently and exhale even longer. Feel the air flow in and out. This activates your vagus nerve and sends a signal to your system: We're safe now.

Gentle rhythm: If you're frozen or collapsed, movement helps. Rocking, swaying, slowly walking; these rhythmic motions support nervous system regulation.

Kindness, not problem solving: Your system isn't broken; it's overwhelmed. Speak to yourself as you would to a scared child; I'm here. We're okay. That compassionate voice becomes the bridge back to yourself.

Anchoring Insights

- CRASH is a state, not an identity; it's your nervous system's short-term safety reflex, not a reflection of who you are.
- CRASH = Contracted · Reactive · Analysis-Paralyzed · Separated · Hurting.
- Common signs: include numbness, addictive loops, black-and-white thinking, a "win/lose" world view.
- Naming a CRASH is the first step towards regaining yourself. What follows is regulation, grounding, slowing, and kindness.

Exploration 6: Identify Your CRASH Patterns

Your nervous system speaks in sensations, impulses and patterns. This exercise helps you decode them.

Sensations:

What does your body do first when you're overwhelmed? Does your mouth go dry, your gut twist, does heat rise in your face, do your hands tremble?

Impulses:

What are you driven to do, or to avoid? Do you scroll, drink, argue, seek approval, cancel plans?

Paterns:

What do you habitually repeat under stress? Do you overwork, get sarcastic or dismissive, stir up drama, or take care of others to avoid facing your own needs?

Recent Evidence:

List three moments in the recent past when you crashed. What triggered it? What did you feel, think, or do in response?

Insight:

Looking at what you wrote, and ask yourself: What was my nervous system trying to tell me? What did it actually need?

Branch 7: Access Your Coach State

COACH is the opposite of CRASH. It's a state with an open, regulated nervous system; the fertile ground where awareness, action, and growth can take root. The acronym COACH stands for: Centered, Open, Aware, Connected, and Here.

In COACH State, your energy flows freely. You have access to your full self; wisdom, courage, compassion, creativity, and choice. You feel grounded and spacious. You respond instead of react. You welcome feedback. You are able to hold multiple truths. You stay connected to your Higher Self.

Centered: You're present in your body, calm in your breath, and connected to the here and now. You're not scattered or chasing outcomes; you're home.

Open: You're open-hearted, open-minded, open to possibility. You're not defending, controlling, or bracing. You're receptive and willing to be with what is.

Aware: You're aware of your thoughts, emotions, and triggers, but not run by them. You can notice without collapsing. You can choose instead of reacting.

Connected: You feel connected, to yourself, to others, and to something greater. That might be nature, purpose, spirit, or shared humanity. You're not cut off or isolated. You remember: I belong.

Here: You're grounded in this moment. This breath. This choice. Transformation doesn't happen later; It happens now. You're not time-traveling through regret or fear.

These five anchors are doorways back to your Self when you feel lost in fear, collapse, or reactivity. They give you a map to shift out of CRASH and into COACH.

While some of the practices overlap, the intention, and energy behind them differ: getting out of a CRASH is about stabilizing your system. Getting into COACH is about accessing creativity, choice, and conscious leadership.

Practices to Access COACH state:

Centered:
- Place a hand on your heart and belly. Inhale slowly. Feel your breath under your hands.
- Balance your posture: sit or stand upright, soften your knees, lengthen your spine.
- Take three deep breaths, then drop awareness into your feet: Feel gravity grounding you.
- Walk slowly, one foot at a time, with full presence.
- Say out loud: "I am in my center. I am home in my body."
- Recall a moment when you felt pure, unconditional love. This is your core memory of love.

Open:
- Scan your jaw, shoulders, and fists. Where are you clenched? Can you soften?
- Exhale audibly to signal to your body that it's safe to let go.
- Whisper inwardly: "You don't have to brace for impact."
- Let yourself cry, sigh, or tremble; without shutting it down.
- Repeat gently: "I can meet this with an open heart."

Aware:
- Name what's happening: "I feel tension in my chest. I notice I'm trying to fix."
- Use the Locator Button: Body – Emotion – Need.
- Ask: "What am I believing right now? Is it true? What part of me is believing it?"
- Pause and inquire: "Is this coming from my protector, or my Self?"
- Journal for five minutes without editing, then read it back from your Higher Self's perspective.

Connected:
- Touch a tree, rock, or piece of earth. Say: "I belong here."
- Text a friend: "Thinking of you. No need to respond."
- Hold yourself (literally): arms crossed, hands on shoulders. Rock gently.
- Make eye contact with a pet, person, or mirror. Stay for 20 seconds.
- Speak this aloud: "I am not alone. I am part of something larger."

Here:

- Do the 5-4-3-2-1 grounding practice: name 5 things you see, 4 you feel, 3 you hear, 2 you smell, 1 you taste.
- Place your hand on your heart and say: "Right now, I am here. This is real."
- Look at the sky, clouds, or horizon for 60 seconds. Let them anchor you.
- Light a candle and watch the flame. Stay with the sensation of watching.
- Ask: "What's needed right now; not later, not before; now?"

These are just a few examples of the ten thousand way ways to enter a COACH state. Other options might include: dancing freely to a song. Asking yourself, "what is the most loving thing I can do right now?" Speaking from your Higher Self out loud: "I know who I am, I don't abandon myself, I choose presence."

Story: *My Grandmother's Medicine*

My grandmother, Maria, survived the Second World War as a child. Three of her siblings didn't make it. She knew scarcity firsthand.

Every spring, the grandparents took us kids to her cabin in the woods. Once school let out, we spent the entire summer there.

She'd begin her day with the same ritual: raking leaves. Slowly. Rhythmically. Sometimes with a cigarette between her lips. She never let anyone help.

As a child, it baffled me. The task never seemed to end – what's the point in raking the forest? I didn't understand her devotion to it. Not until years later.

Raking was her medicine. Her COACH state. A nervous system shaped by war and loss found regulation through rhythm. She found a pocket of peace through presence. In her raking, I witnessed something I didn't yet know how to name: a woman reclaiming her ground, one pull at a time.

Tidying the yard was restoring peace inside of her.

Pause & Reflect

- What does being with yourself feel like in your body?
- What rhythm, ritual, or remembering returns you to presence?

Anchoring Insights

- COACH is the physiological opposite of CRASH: a regulated state where your nervous system stays open and responsive.
- COACH = Centered · Open · Aware · Connected · Here. You can train it with breath, posture, loving images, or grateful memories.
- The goal isn't to avoid CRASH. It's to learn how to hold it within COACH.
- Resilience = recovery speed: Name Crash → Activate COACH → Take one grounded next step.

Exploration 7: Identify your current level of integration

Take an uninterrupted moment to reflect and answer these questions:

- Do I catch myself earlier in a CRASH than I used to? Am I noticing whispers before they become screams?
- When I'm in discomfort, can I tell who's leading; my Self or my patterns? Do I pause and choose from freedom, not fear?
- Have I practiced something bold or different this week, something that stretches my old identity? Have I spoken a truth, set a boundary, or chosen rest without guilt?
- Is my nervous system more flexible and responsive than reactive and rigid? Do I trust myself to come back without shame?
- Am I showing up, expressing myself, and letting others see the real me, even when it's messy? Is my presence aligned with who I know I am becoming?

If most of your answers are "yes" then: you're not just learning COACH state, you're integrating it. Keep going. You're becoming the person your nervous system can trust.

If most of your answers are "no" or "not yet," that's not failure, it's feedback. Where can you return to practice? What haven't you tried yet? This is a perfect moment to circle back to self-awareness and reconnect with your Self; without judgement or shame.

Branch 8: CRASH & COACH Integration

You've built two core capacities:

- Spotting the CRASH and regulating back to safety.
- Activate COACH and leading from calm, clarity, and connection.

Integration is about weaving these skills into the fabric of ordinary life, so they run on embodied memory, not willpower. The goal isn't to avoid CRASH (that's impossible) or float in COACH 24/7 (that's perfectionism's fantasy). The real goal is a higher baseline. An agile nervous system that recovers quickly, chooses cleanly, and stays available for what matters.

The Biology of Safety

Here is how this links into evolutionary biology: your nervous system evolved to keep you alive. It's a primal scanning device, constantly assessing your environment for safety or danger. When it detects a threat: real or perceived, it activates the sympathetic nervous system, triggering survival responses like fight (anger, control), flight (anxiety, overworking), freeze (numbness, shutdown), or fawn (people-pleasing to stay safe). This is what I call CRASH.

When the body perceives safety, it shifts back into the parasympathetic system, which here I call COACH: centered, open, aware, connected, and holding. This is where digestion, repair, connection, and creativity become possible. An agile nervous system flows fluently between these states, adapting to life without getting stuck.

Modern life bombards us with chronic, low-level stressors: deadlines, social comparison, overstimulation, and unresolved emotional burdens, which often keep our systems stuck in CRASH: a dysregulated, survival-based mode where we spin in loops of reactivity, disconnection, and depletion. Without intentional practice, we adapt to this state as normal, forgetting what it feels like to truly feel safe, creative, and connected.

The goal isn't to avoid CRASH, but to recognize it early and have the tools to return to COACH. Breath, movement, nature, and safe relationships all become bridges back to regulation. This is the biology of safety, and the beginning of reclaiming your power.

Resetting Your Baseline

What if COACH was your new baseline? If that sounds impossible, then you might be picturing it as some serene monk-on-the-mountain fantasy; always calm, always perfect. But that's not what baseline COACH means.

Baseline COACH means you're not afraid of your CRASHES. You don't get lost in them and you don't mistake them for who you are. You return to COACH more quickly, more skillfully, each time you leave it. You stay present. You respond instead of react. You see your patterns, name them without shame, and choose powerfully in the face of them. Your nervous system is more resilient, and able to flex, adapt, and recover from a CRASH instead of living at the mercy of it.

So, how do you return to COACH instead of defaulting to CRASH? Start by spotting the subtle signs early. Your nervous system usually whispers before it screams. Watch for early cues like:

- Irritability
- Nagging
- Controlling
- Compulsive scrolling
- Muscle tension
- Perfectionism

Then ask: "Am I in my Self, or am I managing something unconsciously?" The sooner you notice the drift, the easier it is to return.

The Daily Work of Coming Home

Practice. Design daily rituals to reinforce regulation. Repetition is like strength training for your nervous system. Here are a few simple practices:
- **Morning grounding ritual**: deep breaths, movement, and setting intention.
- **Midday nervous system check-in**: three breaths, hand on chest, ask: "Where am I right now?"
- **Evening closure**: gentle music, reflection, nervous system downshift.

This is possible. All it takes is repeated practice, repair, and return. With each successful return, your baseline slowly rises, until you're living from a deeper place. Not just when things are easy, but especially when they're hard.

Story: *The Woman on My Shoulder*

It was fall in Rifle, Colorado, peak climbing season, when she showed up. An incredible climber: strong, confident, focused. We had a history, enough tension to make me believe she hated me.

Every time I saw her, I spiraled. I avoided the crags where she climbed. I tried to time my warmups around hers. But somehow, we always ended up in the same place at the same time. Each sighting triggered a full CRASH: shame, comparison, the same old story of not belonging.

That entire season became a bootcamp. CRASH, return, CRASH, return. I didn't like it, but I had no choice. If I wanted to climb, I had to regulate.

Eventually, I picked a traverse linking three routes across a busy face. It was an ambitious project, and I knew it would make people wait. That alone pressed on the tender bruise of: I take up too much space.

Mid-dyno*, as I launched for the jugs, CRASH thoughts flooded in: I'm in the way. I'm a burden. I shouldn't be here. I shouldn't have been born. Then I saw her.

She was right there, hanging off the end of her rope beside me, taking photos of her friend on the next climb over. She couldn't have been closer if the universe had tried.

And suddenly I saw the absurdity of the story I'd built. The meaning I'd invented. How I cast her as the villain in my own internal war, and none of it was real.

I laughed: loudly, hysterically, until I cried. She didn't notice.

That moment didn't erase my CRASH patterns. But it gave me something more powerful: Perspective. Integration. The ability to notice the spiral, meet it with humor, and return to myself.

That's what practice makes possible. Not perfection. But the space to laugh. To breathe. To come back. Again and again.

Pause & Reflect

- How do you treat yourself when you realize you've CRASHed?
- Can you meet your return with kindness instead of punishment?
- What becomes possible when you choose to return to yourself?

Build Resilience, Not Perfection

It's not possible to stay in COACH forever. The work is to build a nervous system so resilient that when life crashes into you, you don't abandon yourself. You know how to come back. CRASH isn't failure, it's feedback.

Each time you fall out of alignment you're given a chance to practice the return. Each return is a vote for your future Self; the one who leads with presence, chooses from truth, and recovers with grace.

Resilience isn't about how rarely you fall. It's about how you meet yourself when you do. Integration isn't a peak you reach. It's the path you keep walking back to, breath by breath.

Anchoring Insights

- Integration is repetition: It becomes real when you live it, not when you understand it.
- COACH is like a muscle: You strengthen it through tiny daily reps; breath, choice, and truth.
- CRASH is your teacher: Not your enemy. Not your identity. Just a signal saying: "A part of you needs healing."
- Returning is the path: No matter how far you drift, you can always come home to your Self.

Exploration 8: Transforming CRASH into COACH

Name Your CRASH
- "I'm feeling anxious right now."
- "I'm shutting down"
- "I'm spiraling into comparison."

Activate COACH State
- Close your eyes, invite slow long deep breaths.
- Picture someone you love and let your body soften.
- Picture a place where you feel alive; let your shoulders drop.
- Recall a moment of deep joy or gratitude and place your hand on your heart.
- Let your breath and posture shift. Feel this. Anchor it in your body.

Hold the CRASH Inside the COACH
- Visualize your CRASH state as a shape, movement, scent or color.
- Gently welcome it into a calm, spacious part of you.
- Don't try to fix it, just hold it with compassion.

Set a Positive Intention.
- "I choose calm."
- "I want connection."

Invite Intuitive Resources
- Let a memory, phrase, image, or energy appear.
- Don't force it, just listen.

Take Inspired Action
- One small aligned step. That's how resilience builds.

Living Compass: Trunk 2 Summary: Tend Your Ground

Core Distinctions

- **CRASH state vs. COACH state:** Learning to shift from survival reflexes to presence and choice.
- **Regulation before resolution:** Prioritizing nervous system safety before making decisions.
- **Rhythm over hustle:** Replacing urgency with sustainable, embodied pacing.

Core Practices

- **Name the CRASH:** "This is a state, not my identity." Recognize when you've flipped into survival and pause.
- **Regulate before solving:** Ground, breathe, and co-regulate to restore safety before taking action.

- **Activate COACH:** Use breath, posture, memory, and intention to return to your higher Self.
- **Maintain nervous system rhythms:** Create daily rituals; morning grounding, midday check-in, evening downshift.
- **Return with kindness:** Meet every drift with compassion, not shame.

Key Tools

- **CRASH vs. COACH:** Identifying and shifting your nervous system states.
- **Daily rhythm design:** Repeatable structures for anchoring safety throughout the day.
- **Coach State Anchors:** Practices for presence and regulation. Centered · Open · Aware · Connected · Here.
- **Resilience tracker:** Reflect on CRASH patterns, track recovery, and build self-trust.

Guiding Truth

Lead from regulation, not reactivity.

Your Wake-Up Call

Unless we pause, we can't feel how tired we are. Unless we slow down, we won't notice how much energy we leak just trying to keep up, unaware of the crashes we've normalized. We've learned to operate through stress, override our bodies, and stay endlessly "on."

Beneath all that output lives depletion, resentment, and a quiet inner chaos we've come to see as normal. We've mastered control, but forgotten connection. Forgotten what it feels like to actually live in our own skin.

But I've seen the shift. When a client catches herself mid-pattern, about to perform, fix, or overextend, and instead, she pauses. She breathes. She turns toward herself, not away. That one choice becomes a threshold. A doorway into an entirely different life. One built on presence, and anchored in sovereignty.

Trunk 3 Respect Yourself

The Trunk of Self-Trust and Forgiveness

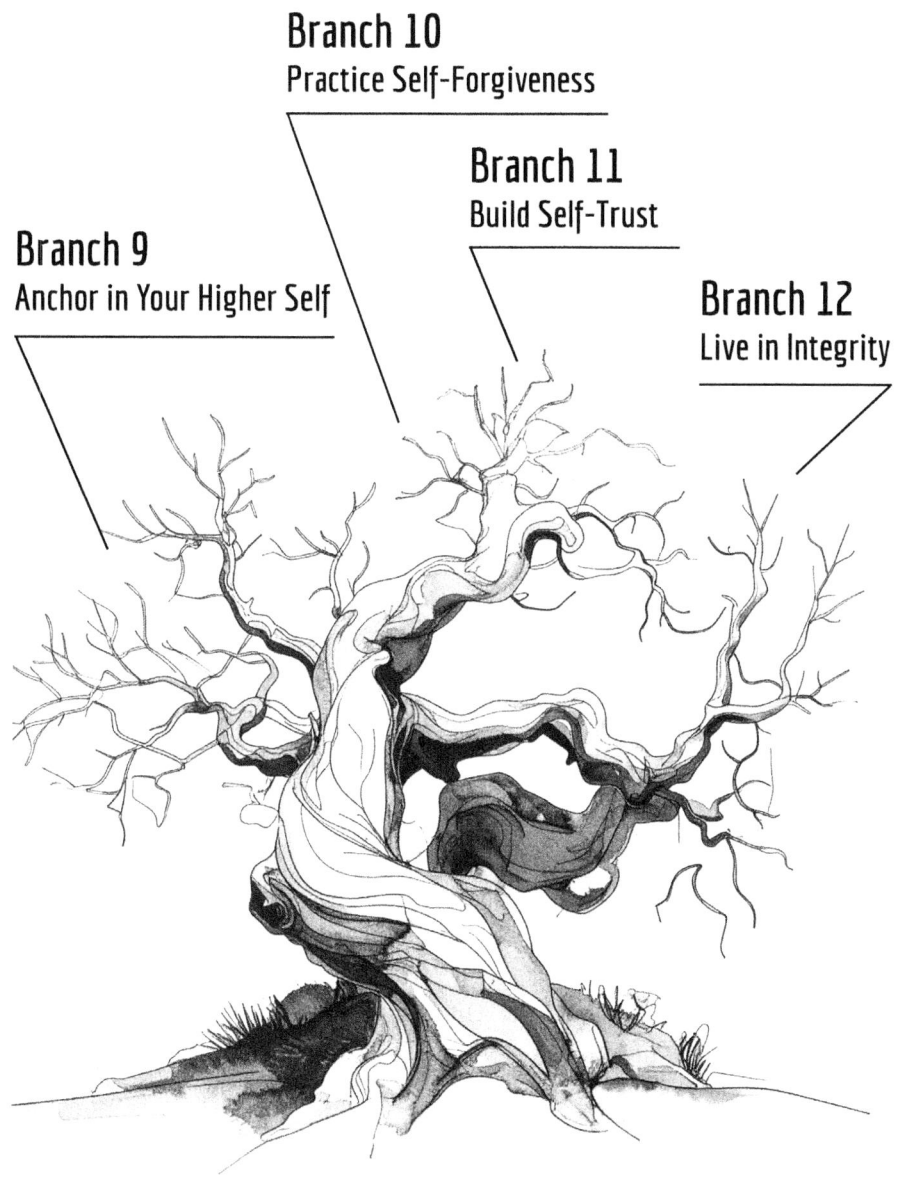

Branch 10
Practice Self-Forgiveness

Branch 11
Build Self-Trust

Branch 9
Anchor in Your Higher Self

Branch 12
Live in Integrity

Trunk 3: Respect Yourself

The Trunk of Self-Trust and Forgiveness

Trunk 3 splits into 4 branches:

- Branch 9: Anchor in Your Higher Self
- Branch 10: Practice Self-Forgiveness
- Branch 11: Build Self-Trust
- Branch 12: Live in Integrity

Trunk 1 taught you to know yourself. Trunk 2 taught you to tend to your internal state. Now Trunk 3 is where the rubber meets the trail; where things get real. No matter how much awareness you build, no matter how regulated your nervous system, you won't rise if you keep abandoning or betraying yourself.

This Trunk is about how you treat you; especially when no one's watching. Self-respect isn't thinking highly of yourself. It's acting in alignment with your truth. It's keeping your word. Cleaning up your messes. Listening when something feels off. Choosing what's right for your soul over what's convenient, impressive, or expected.

Most people spend years trying to earn other's respect while quietly violating their own. They say "yes" when they feel like saying "no". They overextend, over-apologize, and over-function. They beat themselves up, ghost their own goals, and wonder why their confidence never sticks.

That's not being a good person. That's self-abandonment.

To respect yourself is to become someone your nervous system can trust. Someone who stops outsourcing their worth, and starts walking in self-sovereignty. To get there, you'll need to:

- Let go of the old shame story; and forgive yourself for not knowing better.
- Choose the Higher Self; again and again, even when it's hard.
- Build trust through small, aligned actions.
- And above all: live in integrity.

Not as a moral badge of virtue, but as the structure of your life. Without integrity, nothing works. Without self-respect, nothing feels right. This Trunk calls you to stop pretending, stop pleasing, and stop hiding. Not in pursuit of flawlessness, but congruence. To become the kind of person who says what they mean, means what they say, and lives like it matters.

The power of this Trunk is that it transforms you into someone you can trust with your own life. Ready? Let's roll.

Branch 9: Anchor in Your Higher Self

This is the moment you decide to have your own back. You are more than your wounds. Whether or not you believe in a higher power, you can still choose to anchor in the part of you that is steady, whole, and quietly powerful. Because when we think of ourselves as powerful, we do powerful things. Our lives are not defined by what happens, but by how we respond to it.

There are days when I feel like everything in my life is unraveling. I question my worth. I feel small, heavy, and disconnected. But then; I see a client's name on my calendar. Something shifts. I take a breath. I sit up straighter. I place my feet on the ground. And without forcing it, I remember who I am. Not a performance. A return to presence.

Choosing to COACH

No matter how chaotic my inner world feels, the moment I enter that coaching space; I drop in. I become clear. Calm. Loving. Powerful.

That version of me; my highest self, shows up like clockwork. Not because I'm perfect. But because I've practiced trusting her. She leads the session. She sees the client's brilliance, even when I've forgotten my own.

And every time, I leave more whole than when I entered. Because in showing up for them, I returned to me. Sometimes we anchor into our higher self by doing our work, engaging in a hobby or helping someone else. Sometimes it arrives through collapse. Through surrender. Through fire.

Story: *I Never Asked to Be Born*

I didn't smoke Bufo to chase bliss. I did it because I wanted the truth. Bufo, the world's strongest psychedelic; nicknamed the god molecule wasn't a thrill, it was a key. Something was still in my way that I couldn't reach through coaching, journaling, or logic. But I felt it. I wanted to meet the part of me that kept resisting life.

What I met was death. And birth. And something far more ancient than either.

The medicine hit immediately. First came terror. Then the void. Every structure that ever held me; mind, identity, body; disintegrated. I melted into a scream with no mouth. I forgot how to breathe.

And then, something broke open. I remembered: I am all of it. The me who resisted and the me who chose were waves of the same sea. The field had always loved me. I had just forgotten the sound.

Then I heard it; deep and undeniable: "I never asked to be born."

Not a thought. A truth. The most primal protest I'd ever felt. It came from the part of me that never got to choose. The part that inherited trauma. Swallowed abandonment. Built a brilliant, high-functioning strategy to survive. The part that stayed small. Stayed tough. Stayed unworthy.

Now she was dying.

I wasn't just watching the ego collapse. I was inside it. My protectors roared, scrambling to restore order. Grief poured through. When I finally stopped resisting, something else happened: I was being born. For the first time, my breathing body chose life.

I felt my body, and my mother's at the same time. Her fear. Her effort. Her love. I crawled through the birth canal. I felt received. I wanted to be here. I chose this life. The scream softened to stillness. The terror transmuted to trust.

And beneath it all, I met the one who had never been wounded. The one who had been waiting. Not the strategist. Not the achiever. Not the one who had to prove her right to exist. Just me. Whole. Alive. Free. She had no name. No job title. No agenda. Just being in truth.

Later, I was shown the version of me I'd been trying to keep alive: The performer. The fixer. The one who needed to be liked. I saw how she was built; out of pain, pattern, protection. I didn't judge her. I just saw her clearly. And I knew: She no longer needed her to lead.

That was the day my ego stopped being the boss. Not because I killed it. But because I stopped mistaking it for who I was.

That day, I touched something deeper than willpower – I anchored in essence. That was the invitation: To stop chasing worth, and start trusting the Self that was already whole. It didn't happen in a moment of inspiration. It happened in the deepest undoing of my life.

Pause & Reflect

- What is your biggest fear?
- What have you been resisting feeling?
- What might become possible if you let it move through?
- What would shift right now if you trusted your wholeness?

Anchoring Insights

- Identity is a choice. Define yourself by your response, not your wounds.
- Higher Self is presence, not performance. Clarity, love, and grounding outshine proving.
- Anchoring is a practice. Use simple cues, like the breath to return to wholeness.
- Collapse can be a doorway. Surrender reveals the Self that cannot be broken.
- Remember to remember: Let past moments of Higher Self show you the way back.

Exploration 9:

Call to mind a moment when you acted from your highest self. Maybe it was:
- A time you stood up against injustice.
- A moment you showed grace in the face of loss or betrayal.
- An instant you admitted you were out of integrity, and made it right.
- A moment you were playing small... until something bigger required you to rise.

Maybe, like my story, you were stuck in a pattern; bickering with someone you loved, until life threw you a curveball and, somehow, you showed up as your best self anyway.

Hold that memory. Let yourself feel it. Notice what that self feels like in your body. Because once you remember you can finally return.

Branch 10: Practice Self-Forgiveness

Without self-forgiveness, we stay trapped in the past.

We all mess up. We all make choices from wounded places. That doesn't make us unworthy. It makes us human.

Self-forgiveness isn't about avoiding responsibility, It's about releasing the judgment that holds us hostage. It's how we clean the slate; not to escape consequence, but to step out of shame.

My coach Steve Hardison says: "Self-forgiveness is better than a Presidential pardon. Because you get to give it to yourself every day." You're not letting yourself off the hook. You're setting yourself free.

I've learned that as long as I'm punishing myself for who I used to be, or who I think I should have been, I'm not fully here. Not in my body. Not in my power. Not in my life.

Self-forgiveness, for me, is an act of reclamation. It's saying: I will no longer drag the weight of my past into every room I enter. I will no longer define myself by moments when I was scared, stuck, or trying to survive.

I forgive myself not to erase the past, but because I refuse to keep abandoning myself in the present. I forgive myself because I want to create. Freely. Fully. Fiercely. And I can't do that if I'm still making myself wrong for being human.

Story: *Forgiving The One Who Needed to Be Needed*

The thing I've had to forgive the most? Getting caught in codependence. The trip to the Bugaboos was a crash course in what not to do. I over-gave, over-functioned, and when it wasn't reciprocated, I disappeared. It took me years to see clearly that my generosity wasn't rooted in love; it was rooted in fear.

The hardest part isn't seeing the pattern, it's forgiving myself for it. Even now I still catch myself slipping; trying to fix things. Trying to earn my place through usefulness. When I do, the shame creeps in: You're doing it again. You haven't changed at all. But I have a new practice now.

I get quiet with myself and say:
- "I forgive myself for judging myself as people-pleasing and codependent."
- "I forgive myself for seeing my worth only in how much I give."

- "The truth is: I am love. I am loving. I am lovable."
- "I don't have to do anything to be that. I don't have to prove it. I am."

Self-forgiveness isn't one and done. It's a practice. And every time I choose it, I come home to myself again.

Pause & Reflect

- What story about yourself are you still carrying like a debt?
- Are you trying to atone, or are you ready to move forward?
- What would it feel like to meet the version of you that you usually blame with tenderness instead of judgment?

Self-Forgiveness Affirmation (Hardison Style)

I forgive myself: fully, completely, now.

Not because I earned it. Not because I deserve it. Because I said so.

I am not my past. I am not my mistakes. I am not the story I've carried.

I am the creator of who I say I am.

I am not just the author of my story. I am the frequency it harmonizes with.

Today, I align with the field of grace, and it responds in kind.

Today, I say: I am free. I am love. I am whole.

I do not need permission. I am the permission.

I walk in full forgiveness, because the only thing keeping me from my power is me.

With the weight of self-blame lifted, I'm free to do what matters most: trust myself again.

Anchoring Insights

- Self-forgiveness sets you free from shame, and reclaims your power.
- It doesn't erase the past, it liberates the present.
- Punishment keeps you stuck. Forgiveness gets you moving.
- You don't need to earn forgiveness. You just need to decide.
- Forgiveness is not passive; it's one of the most powerful acts of self-respect.

Exploration 10: Self-Forgiveness Practice

Write down some negative self-beliefs you carry. These might sound like:

- I'm alone.
- I always make the wrong decision.
- I'm lazy.
- I'm not trustworthy.
- I'm too much.

Make this list big and comprehensive. It's unpleasant at the moment but I promise it will be worth it. Doing this on paper will save you from an eternity of unconscious self stabbing. Once you have a hefty list, connect with your Higher Self (as you practiced in Branch 9), and choose, on purpose, to forgive yourself for judging yourself as those things. You were never those things, so you don't need to forgive yourself for being them. Only for believing them.

Say it out loud or write it down: "I forgive myself for judging myself as . . . ."

Let it stir what it needs to. Tears, stillness, breath; whatever comes is welcome. Forgiveness is a powerful medicine. Take a moment. You're safe here.

When done fully, this practice will feel like a deep burden lifted. A quiet inner shift. A return. Let it land. Let it free you. This is the beginning of your self forgiveness practice. Repeating this on a daily basis or on a need-to basis is recommended.

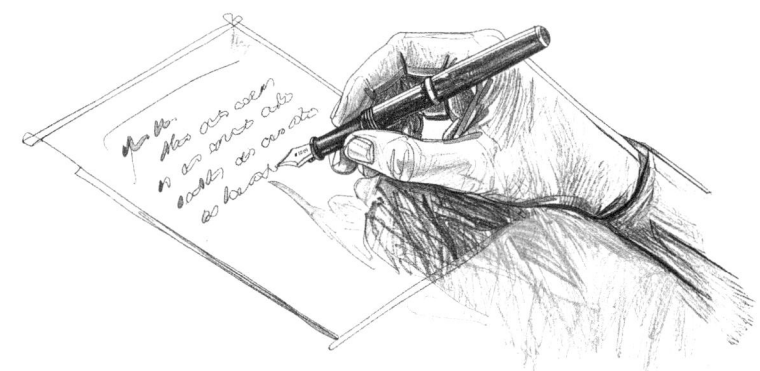

Branch 11: Build Self-Trust

Climb the Decision Mountain

Self-trust isn't a feeling you wait for: it's a commitment you practice. The most powerful way to practice self-trust is in how you make decisions. Every time you choose with intention, you send a message to your nervous system: I trust myself to lead. I trust myself to act. Self-trust doesn't mean you never waver. It's not a trait, it's a skill – built one decision at a time.

It begins when you decide your decisions are valid. Not perfect, not always easy, but worthy of commitment. It's not linked to making the "right decision." It's about having your own back once you've chosen.

Making decisions, especially as a leader, can feel like standing in a valley, staring up at two towering peaks. Both look steep. You're unsure which one to climb. So, you wait. Hesitate. Camp out in the valley, hoping for clarity that never comes.

At first, you might tell yourself you're being smart, gathering data, weighing the options, playing it safe. But be honest: Are you thinking, or avoiding? Prolonged indecision, dressed up as strategy, often becomes paralysis.

A "wrong" choice isn't a failure. It's clarity in disguise. You learn by moving. You build self-trust by climbing. So pick your peak, commit to the path, and let every step remind you: You're the one leading this life.

The Valley of Indecision

The valley is full of motion that looks like progress, but gets you nowhere. Like reorganizing your gear in basecamp instead of heading up the mountain. You know the signs:

- Overanalyzing every angle
- Asking for advice again and again
- Losing sight of your own values
- Mistaking busyness for momentum

Stay here long enough, and you'll trade possibility for stagnation.

The Cure: Start Climbing

It's often better to climb the wrong mountain than to stay stuck in the valley. Why? Because wrong turns build discernment. You grow. You sharpen. You get honest. A failed ascent brings information. You're still improving your fitness even if you're on the wrong mountain, and that fitness will come handy later. Clarity doesn't come from sitting still. Your path reveals itself through movement.

Don't Confuse Motion With Progress

Indecision burns energy without gaining elevation. The cost of inaction disguised as responsibility is far greater than the risk of a wrong turn. Decide. Start the climb. Certainty is often the result, not the precondition, of movement. You don't need the perfect map. You need the courage to move. Progress belongs to those who start.

What Kind of Decision-Maker Are You?

Some of us are under-thinkers. We leap before we look; often discovering our edges by getting in over our heads. We thrive under pressure, but sometimes create chaos in the process.

If that's you, self-trust won't come from speed, it will come from presence. Practice pausing. Notice the urge to jump, and choose consciously instead of compulsively.

Others are over-thinkers. We fear making the wrong choice, so we stall: waiting for perfect clarity that never arrives. We analyze every option until momentum dies. If that's you, remember: Trust grows when you commit, not when you wait.

Practice choosing quickly, and back yourself, no matter the outcome. Let movement create clarity. As you practice self-trust, you gain increased decisiveness, less second-guessing and the ability to take more aligned action.

You're ready to transmute life's challenges through presence, commitment, and courage.

The mountain won't climb itself. But you? You're already half way up.

Story: *Lessons from a Shiver-Bivy*

Drinking straight from the river, each mouthful was the sweetest I had ever known. Letting the source itself flow into me, I could feel life return with every swallow. But how did I get there?

I was eighteen, climbing in the Italian Dolomites. It was the night I first discovered box wine, and the morning I paid for it. Hungover and hazy, we sipped coffee at 8 a.m. when our eyes caught a limestone tower, 1,000 meters above camp. Someone said, "Let's climb it." And at 9 a.m., without preparation or plan, we blasted.

The lower part was long and relentless. By nightfall, we were still only two-thirds up. Ahead: nothing but chimneys. For hours, we wedged and scraped ourselves upward, fumbling toward the stars. In the struggle, the chimneys emptied our camelbacks, stealing the last of our water.

The summit gave no victory. We didn't know the descent route, and to search for it in the darkness would have been a bad idea. So we huddled together, shiver-bivouacking through the night.

By morning we were wrecked: dehydrated, shivering, but alive. The descent was slow, each punishing step a mirror of our impulsivity. Yet when we finally staggered into camp and drank from the river, I knew the climb had given me more than any day in camp ever could.

Since that day, I've never been benighted on a climb again. But I've never forgotten either: folly can still be a teacher, and the sweetest water is the kind you suffer to reach.

Pause & Reflect

- What part of you still believes there is a "right" answer that protects you from regret?
- Are you willing to trust yourself; not just to choose, but to course-correct as needed?
- If you already knew you could handle the outcome, what would you choose today?

Anchoring Insights

- Self-trust comes from choosing, not waiting.
- Progress begins the moment you leave the valley of indecision.
- A "wrong" move is often the first step toward clarity.
- You don't need certainty; you need courage.
- Every small decision you commit to strengthens the muscle of self-leadership.

Exploration 11: Build the Muscle

Make five small, bold decisions that are outside your norm. The power is not in the size of the decision: it's in the fact that you made it, and you committed to it. Bold Decision Examples:

- Go to the gym at 4:00 a.m.
- Wear something that feels daring or expressive.
- Hike a trail that intimidates you.
- Cold-call someone you've been avoiding.
- Speak up where you would normally stay quiet.

As you go, journal about each one:

- What did you choose?
- What happened?
- How did you feel afterward?
- What did you learn?"

These are not about proving anything. They're about teaching your nervous system that you are someone worth following. Whatever you choose, make the decision, and back yourself. That's the practice.

That's how you climb. That's how you rise.

Branch 12: Live in Integrity

Say What You Mean, Do What You Say

Imagine building a skyscraper with concrete that's only 80% solid. It might look fine; strong, impressive, even elegant. But under pressure, every weakness will be revealed. Cracks form. Stress spreads. Eventually, it collapses.

Life is no different. When your words don't match your actions, when you say yes while thinking no, when you ghost your own goals; the erosion begins. At first it's subtle. You still function, you still perform, but deep down, something starts to fracture. Burnout. Resentment. Self-doubt. That quiet gnawing feeling that something's still off.

Integrity isn't about being good or looking good. It's about being whole. Congruent. Aligned. It means doing what you said you'd do. Not just when it's convenient, but when it's hard and no one's watching. When your nervous system begs for an out.

What Happens When You Don't Have It

Lack of integrity won't send you to hell, but it will create one of your own making. You become a balloon with dozens of pinholes, constantly leaking energy, quietly and relentlessly.

You tolerate things that erode your clarity. You break small promises to yourself and call it "life." Then you wonder why your confidence won't stick, your vision stays blurry, and life never quite clicks.

Most people live in low integrity, not because they're bad, but because they underestimate the cost of misalignment. They think it's just a skipped workout, a white lie, a canceled plan. But every moment of dissonance chips away at self-trust.

Integrity isn't about perfection, it's about keeping your word. Full stop. No justifications. No wiggle room.

Your subconscious keeps score. Each time you flake, you teach your nervous system that you're unreliable. And that ripple shows up everywhere: in your leadership, your relationships, your health, and your bank account.

With integrity, things work. Without it, they don't. Simple as that.

What Integrity Actually Looks Like

- You say what you mean.
- You mean what you say.
- You keep your word: or you clean it up fast, directly, and without drama.
- You don't pretend.
- You don't delay hard conversations.
- You don't use excuses.
- You check in with your gut before making commitments, not after.
- And you stop weaponizing your emotions as excuses.
- You don't over-explain your yes or your no.

Here's the kicker: Integrity doesn't start with others. It starts with you. If you say you're waking up at 6 am to train, then wake up at 6 and train. If you say you're launching the offer, launch it. If you say you're unavailable for bullshit, stop tolerating it. No one else is coming to enforce your standards. No one is coming to save you.

Story: *What Are You Pretending Not to Know?*

Mattias was a yes-man. At work, he was beloved. Reliable. The go-to guy. The one who made things happen. He said yes to every meeting, every favor, every "can I pick your brain?" request. His calendar was packed. His inbox overflowing. His presence? Scattered and thin. The truth was heavier and far simpler: He didn't have bandwidth to help. He was just terrified of what it might mean about him if he didn't.

As the founder of a successful company, Mattias looked like he was crushing it. But with more success, the pattern intensified. He started ghosting meetings, skipping calls he had booked months ago, blaming Zoom links for the unraveling in his life. Always with a "valid" excuse.

At home, the pressure leaked out sideways. He snapped at his wife for asking him to take out the trash. Then retreated into shame.

When he canceled another session with me, I dialed his number. "What are you pretending not to know about yourself?" He took a long pause. Then finally said it: "I say yes to things I already know I don't want to do. I'm inauthentic. I'm terrified of who I'd be without it." The illusion cracked.

We built a 30-day truth-first practice. Before saying yes: pause. Check your gut. If it's not true, don't say it. At first, it felt impossible. Like the sky was going to fall. But then…

He texted a friend: "I can't talk tonight." He canceled a meeting; instead of ghosting. Asking for time to think before replying. Small things, each one patching a hole in his integrity.

Then came the real test: He told his wife the truth. That his "yes" had been a mask. That the version of him she loved… wasn't the whole him. He didn't collapse. She didn't applaud. But things slowly shifted. Now, when he says yes too quickly, she raises an eyebrow: "Really?"

Mattias isn't everyone's favorite anymore. He's just himself. When he says yes, it matters. Because he means it.

Pause & Reflect

- Where am I tolerating small leaks in my integrity: through my word, my actions, or my commitments?
- What am I pretending not to know about myself?
- What promise will I keep today that would rebuild trust in myself?

Integrity and Self-Respect Are Twins

If you don't keep your word, your self-respect slowly evaporates. And when that goes, nothing you build feels solid. That's why Trunk Three: Respect Yourself, exists. Because without integrity, all the trust, forgiveness, and Higher Self work gets foggy. And without self-compassion, integrity becomes brittle; harsh, performative, desperate.

But once integrity roots in your life, everything sharpens. You become trustworthy; to yourself first. You become someone who sets a standard just by entering the room.

The bold game to play? Look for places where you're still out of integrity. And close the gap.

Because I Say So

When you are your word; when your nervous system trusts that what you say becomes what is, something powerful happens. You collapse the space between vision and reality. You stop waiting for external proof, permission, or guarantees. You decide, and the world reorganizes. That kind of self-trust is rare, and potent. It means you can create impossible things; relationships, businesses, a life that shouldn't exist, and yet does. Not because it's easy. But because your word is a force. And you've trained it to mean something.

Anchoring Insights
- Integrity isn't about being perfect. It's about being authentic.
- If you don't clean up your messes, your subconscious will live in confusion.
- Every broken promise becomes a crack in your foundation.
- Start small. Keep your daily commitments.
- Self-respect isn't a feeling: it's the result of aligned action.

Exploration 12: 24-Hour Full Integrity Reset

For the next 24 hours, commit to radical, zero-compromise integrity. That means:
- No lies. Not even soft ones.
- No ghosting. No vague maybes.
- No hiding, avoiding, overcommitting, or overexplaining.

Everything you say and do must be clean, aligned, and true; first and foremost to yourself. During this time:
- Say "No" when you mean no. Not "maybe," not "sure if you need me." A clean no is not cruel, it's authentic.
- Follow through on everything you say. If you said you'd go to the gym, go. If you said you'd call, call. Can't follow through? Clean it up fast and directly.
- Pause before speaking. Even one extra breath before replying can stop a habitual lie or an autopilot yes.
- Notice where you want to perform. Who do you pretend for? Who do you manage? Where are you hiding behind "niceness"?
- Tell one hard truth. Say the thing you've been avoiding. Speak it cleanly; No explanation, no justification.

Afterwards, reflect on these questions:
- Where did I feel tempted to bend the truth; how and why?
- Which moment required the most courage?
- What felt different about moving through the world in full integrity?
- Where am I leaking energy in my life right now?
- What's one commitment I'm done breaking?
- What will I no longer tolerate myself doing?

This might be one of the most impactful explorations you'll ever do. Because once you know what it feels like to be in full integrity, anything less becomes intolerable.

Living Compass: Trunk 3 Summary: Respect Yourself

Core Distinctions
- **Self-respect vs self-image:** Built through consistent, aligned action; not performance or approval.
- **Forgiveness vs. avoidance:** Releases shame but never excuses harm.
- **Self-trust vs. self-doubt:** Grows through choosing, acting, and adjusting; not waiting.
- **Integrity vs. morality:** Congruence between word and action, not perfection or virtue signaling.

Core Practices
- **Lead from the Higher Self:** Act from truth, not from protective parts.
- **Forgive the old story:** Stop dragging the past into every room you enter.
- **Make decisive moves:** Let clarity follow committed action.
- **Keep micro-commitments:** Rebuild credibility from the inside out.
- **Clean up broken promises within 24 hours:** Restore alignment with speed and grace.

Key Tools
- **Breath reset:** Breathe and regulate before responding.
- **Identity affirmations (Hardison style):** Speak truth into your nervous system.
- **Decision-fitness:** No more stalling. Start climbing the mountain.
- **Self-forgiveness:** Release judgment, restore wholeness.
- **24-hour integrity reset:** Commit to radical congruence for one full day.

Guiding Truth
Self-respect matures when word and action are aligned.

Your Wake-Up Call

Some of the most impressive people you know carry a secret: They don't actually trust themselves. And they don't even know it. They trust their performance. Their usefulness. Their ability to deliver for everyone else. But when it comes to telling the truth, honoring their limits, or keeping a promise to themselves, they freeze. They fake it. Or they quietly disappear.

I see this kind of quiet rupture all the time in my work. People who've earned everyone's respect; except their own. This is what happens when we skip the practices of Trunk Three. When we don't have our own back. When we confuse achievement with wholeness. When we live out of alignment and call it "being responsible."

Without self-trust, we can't hear our own voice. Without self-forgiveness, we stay shackled to shame. And without integrity, we leak power with every small lie we tell ourselves. Even when we're standing at the summit, it doesn't feel real. Because we didn't bring our whole self with us.

But I've also seen what happens when someone stops outsourcing their worth. When they forgive themselves; not to bypass truth, but to return to it. When they draw a boundary; not to push others away, but to finally include themselves. When they say what they mean and mean what they say, not because it's easy, but because it's real.

That's when wild things begin to happen. A client who hadn't spoken to her daughter in a decade picks up the phone. Another quits her job and takes a sabbatical to remember what lights her up. A third walks away from the polished version of his life to build something honest; with muddy hands and a full heart.

That's the power of this Trunk. Self-respect isn't a reward for getting it right. It's the ground you build your life on. And it gets stronger every time your actions align with your truth. That's integrity. That's when your life starts to feel like yours again.

Trunk 4
Transmute the Challenge

Turn Pain Into Power

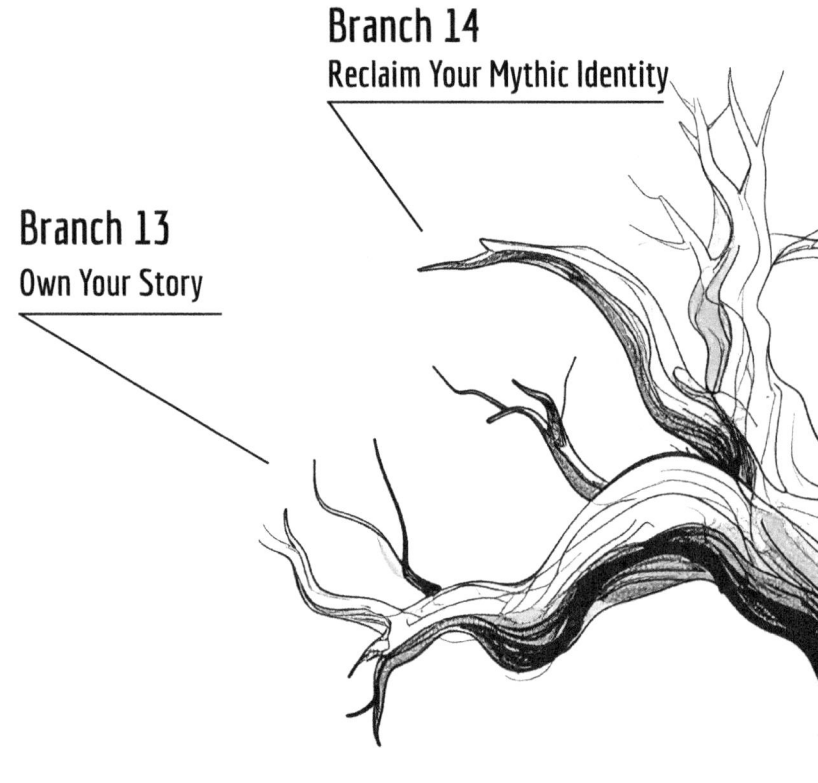

Branch 14
Reclaim Your Mythic Identity

Branch 13
Own Your Story

Branch 15
Transform in Real Time

Branch 16
Train with Stress

Trunk 4: Transmute the Challenge

Turn Pain Into Power

Branches in this Trunk:

- Branch 13: Own Your Story
- Branch 14: Reclaim Your Mythic Identity
- Branch 15: Transform in Real Time
- Branch 16: Train with Stress

Trunk 1 was about knowing yourself. Trunk 2 about tending to your state. Trunk 3 about respecting your truth. Trunk 4 is where you turn your deepest pain into your greatest power.

Pain isn't what breaks us. It's what shapes us; if we let it. This is the Trunk where you stop fearing hardship and start using it. Where you stop asking, "Why is this happening to me?" and start asking, "Who am I becoming because of this?"

Everyone has a story. A loss. A betrayal. A collapse. Something that cracked their world open. Most people get stuck there. They spin in "Why me?" They build identities around their wounds. They make pain the protagonist.

Transformation begins when you realize: The loss wasn't the end of your story. It was the turning point. This isn't about bypassing pain or pretending it didn't happen. It's about composting it: letting the rot become rich soil. Letting it grow something honest, beautiful, and strong.

This is the art of alchemy: Not changing what happened; but changing what it means.

In this Trunk, you learn to:

- Reclaim authorship over your own narrative.
- Meet adversity without making it your identity.
- Spot old patterns before they hijack the present.
- Let challenges shape you, not shrink you.
- Mark your thresholds, so your body remembers: you crossed something real.

Pain is part of life. Suffering is what happens when we refuse to use it. This is the power of Trunk Four: It teaches you to rise by choice, not chance. To stop performing strength, and start living it. To let your hardest moments become the ones that reveal your deepest truth. Turn toward the fire. It's time.

Branch 13: Own Your Story

From Victim to Author

It's easy to see our past through the lens of pain.

- They did this to me
- It shouldn't have happened
- I was wounded

It feels valid, especially for the child in us who didn't have the tools or choices to do anything else. But here's the pivot: That version of the story is not the end.

When you're ready to own your story, you stop seeing yourself as the victim of your past, and start seeing yourself as the resilient, resourceful, powerful human who lived through it.

You rewrite the past by asking: What did this build in me? Strength. Empathy. Resilience. Courage. Your pain becomes a foundation. Your scars, evidence of your brilliance.

Compost the Judgment

Even the messiest decay feeds something. It's not garbage. It's fuel for transformation. We're quick to label life as good or bad.

- No traffic → good
- Delayed flight → bad
- Happy kid → good
- Swollen ankle → bad

But most of what we call "bad" is simply not the outcome we planned or thought we deserved. So, we resist it. Stew in it. Bargain with it.

What if every challenge carried a hidden invitation? What if, instead of resisting reality, you could work with it?

- Broken ankle? Write your book.
- Flight delay? Make a friend.
- Employee quits? Create space for someone better.
- Pandemic? Reinvent your life.

We're not just making lemonade here; we're making Meyer lemon crème brûlée.

Story: *The Harmonic of Letting Go*

When I left Joshua Tree in my Prius, it felt as though I had driven my life straight off a cliff. Fifteen years, a shared dream, a handcrafted home; all traded for a three-digit bank account and a long inventory of everything "wrong" with me.

At the time, it felt like ruin.

From a distance, I see it now for what it truly was: one of the greatest initiations of my life. .I had to strip myself bare to find my way back to the unwounded self.

The years after the divorce were not a straight climb upward. They spiraled.

I followed those spirals deep into old wounds, naming family trauma, mapping codependent loops, and recognizing the inherited patterns that had passed silently through generations. I started to question my riding of other's coattails. I noticed when I was yet again shrinking to belong. I began mapping to my own rhythm, no longer desperately keeping time to someone else's beat.

Even my voice changed. Once filtered through compliance, caretaking, or code-switching to keep the peace, it began to emerge from a deeper place; the one that speaks from self-coherence. Where I once whispered, Am I allowed? I began to declare, I'm here.

And in the space made by letting go, I learned that freedom and connection were never opposites. I had to release one form to reclaim the other in its truer shape. What I thought was ruin became rich soil for a life that was finally, honestly mine.

In the years that followed I entered a fertile chapter: wild and radically unburdened. There were no rules to follow, just instinct, desire, and lots of space to move.

The wave that had pulled me away eventually returned, carrying something unrecognizable at first: my relationship with D-Griff, transformed. Once I stopped needing him to be the source of my stuckness, he stopped being "the guy who didn't do the dishes" and became one of my strongest allies. Our connection, free from codependence, was finally able to grow into something truly extraordinary.

It was hard. It broke me open. And I won't glamorize the hurt or suggest anyone rush their healing. But I will stand in the truth of what it forged. I'd do it all over in a heartbeat.

Pause & Reflect

- What meaning am I making of what happened?
- Who would I be if I let that story evolve?
- Am I willing to see myself as more than what I survived?

Anchoring Insights

- You are not the victim of your story: you are the author.
- Your pain holds power when you claim what it created in you.
- Judgment keeps you stuck; ownership sets you free.
- You don't grow in spite of the challenge, you grow because of how you met it.

Exploration 13: The Gifts Inside the Challenge

List five difficult experiences you've lived through. Examples:

- A breakup that helped you find your voice.
- A job loss that motivated you to start your own business.
- A childhood wound that gave you empathy.
- A betrayal that taught you how to set boundaries.
- A failure that led to reinvention.

Next to each one, name the gift it gave you. Not what it took, but what it built in you. Be creative and generous in attributing gifts, you might be surprised what surfaces.

Branch 14: Reclaim Your Mythic Identity

You Are Not Your Name or a Role: You Are a Living Story

Most of us grow up believing identity is a job title, a personality type, or a list of strengths. But your true identity, the one your soul came here to live, is something deeper, older, and wilder. It's what Bill Plotkin (depth psychologist and founder of the Animas Valley Institute) calls your mythopoetic identity.

This identity isn't your personality, your performance, or a label. It's the sacred story that lives in your bones. A unique metaphor. A symbol. A dream. It's a role only you can play in the great unfolding. A song only your soul can sing. For example, instead of saying "I'm a coach," my mythopoetic identity might be:

- I'm the flame that walks into a cave, bringing light to the places others fear to enter.
- I am the architect of coherence, building sanctuaries where souls remember their original rhythm. I don't offer maps, I lay down geometry in motion, so others can hear the pattern inside themselves.
- I am the threshold walker, who turns ache into architecture and wildness into language. I walk beside initiates as they reauthor the story their bones have always carried.
- I'm the voice of the river that breaks stones, eroding false stories with quiet truth.

Your soul's identity isn't something you invent, it's something you uncover. It speaks in dreams, in symbols, in nature, in archetype. It doesn't yield to logic, but your body recognizes it. When you're living it, something deep inside exhales. The Earth nods. Life aligns.

This identity reveals itself through descent. Through heartbreak. Through surrender. It emerges not when you're trying to perform, but when something breaks you open and strips away what was never really you.

Myth isn't fantasy. It's the soul's memory; speaking in symbols. To remember your myth is to remember the blueprint written into your bones by the universe itself.

And when you reclaim it; life stops being a checklist and becomes a quest. Trials become initiations. Struggles become thresholds. You stop performing and start becoming. You are not re-inventing, you are someone returning, ancient.

You weren't born to dazzle the world with bullet-points on a résumé. You're here to let your life unfold like living poetry.

I remember the teenage girl on her first climbing trip, huddled in a guide room, watching Masters of Stone on a grainy VHS. That wasn't just a film; it was a transmission. My myth was whispering: Buy the shoes, say yes to the impossible.

I didn't know it yet, but I was being led. Across borders and heartbreaks. Through countries and cliffs. Through loneliness, longing, and the fire of initiation. My myth was pulling me into the dream: Yosemite. The golden meadow. And there was D-Griff; the man who'd been waiting for me for a decade. It wasn't chance or logic. It was soul-knowing. It knew long before I did.

Plotkin says. "Your soul faithfully comes to our aid through dreams, deep emotion, love, the quiet voice of guidance, synchronicities … and at times through illness, nightmares, and terrors."

Where has your soul already whispered your myth? What moment cracked you open? What memory won't let you go? Where, in your own story, do you feel the thread of something ancient asking to be remembered?

Story: *The Goddess of Heartbreak*

I was nursing a breakup that laid me bare. It wasn't dramatic or cruel. We loved each other, but we couldn't find a way forward. So we parted, because it was the only honest thing left to do. The letting go hollowed me. There was no blame, only the ache of a love that had reached its edge.

Soon after, I traveled to San Diego for Trance Camp, an intensive training program led by Dr. Stephen Gilligan focused on "Generative Trance;" a practice designed to unlock deep, sustainable transformation. During a session, my practice partner's voice drew me inward. "Move the feeling. Let it speak. Let it rise."

Something rose. I became a goddess: not a metaphor, but marrow and flesh. I stood on an ageless summit, barefoot, and radiant. And from that mythic height, I remembered: I chose this life. I chose every note in the symphony; the love and joy, the terror and longing, the death and rebirth. I am not a casualty of loss. I am a river; aching to feel every current, pouring myself into the ocean, vanishing into something more vast.

In that sacred light, heartbreak was no curse. It was proof. Proof that I was gloriously, unbreakably alive. The River would flow, no matter who or what tried to dam her. I realized that I wanted to feel it all.

Pause & Reflect

- What if I longed for everything that made me alive; each heartbreak, each emotion?
- What story has been whispering through my dreams, my heartbreaks, my longings?
- Am I willing to stop explaining, and start embodying the one I was born to become?

Anchoring Insights

- Your soul's identity is uncovered, not invented.
- Mythic identity is revealed through descent, heartbreak, surrender, and initiation.
- Living your myth turns life from a checklist to a quest.
- You're not here to impress. You're here to sing your song to the world.

Exploration 14: Write Your Mythic Story

Write the mythic version of your life. Speak in symbols. Let metaphor lead. Use archetypal language.

Don't say:

"I moved across the country and changed careers."

Say:

"She left the safety of the village, drawn by a wild longing. Her feet burned with the desire to climb the mountain no one else dared name…"

Make yourself a character in your own myth. Give her a mythical name. Speak as if the soul knows you, not the world. If you need a place to begin, here's how mine would start:

She waved, youthful of face yet ancient of soul, as she left the village of forgetfulness, drawn by the silent summons of the granite oceans. She sought neither fame nor conquest, only the buried ember of herself cradled in the folds of stone and sky. Thumb out, soul aflame, she set off toward horizons that remembered her name.

Your turn. Let the story write you.

Branch 15: Transform in Real Time

The Obstacle Is the Way

Now that you've reclaimed your story and remembered your mythic identity, it's time to put that understanding into practice: right here, right now.

You already know how to mine the past for gold. But what if you could feel the roots growing deeper while the storm is still raging? What if you could sense the next version of you forming as the challenge unfolds? That's what this branch is about.

Most people find the gifts only in hindsight: Sometimes years later, often times never.

But mastery means standing in the storm and saying: This is for me. Not in spite of the pain, but because of what it's forging in me. Having the trust to focus not on what you are losing, but on what's always been underneath.

Resistance Is the Real Struggle

Most of the time, it's not what's happening that hurts: it's the story we tell about what's happening. "I shouldn't be here." "This isn't fair". "Why me?"

That's the real weight. That's the real struggle. The faster you shift from resisting to receiving, the less energy you waste and the less suffering you create. This isn't toxic optimism. It's skilled alchemy. Meeting life as it is. Holding pain with love. Letting it shape you.

Story: *Falling Apart to Come Together*

One beautiful May morning, I collapsed.

My partner and I had just lost everything in a financial disaster tied to a real estate investment. It hit every raw nerve. I felt like an utter failure. Someone who couldn't be trusted with money, power, or responsibility. The shame came fast and loud. But the worst part wasn't the money; it was the meaning I made of it:

How can I be a coach if I'm this broken? That voice felt true, until I noticed it wasn't new. It was an ancient echo of unworthiness, disguised as logic.

The collapse peeled back the layers. Beneath the money story lived something older: I am unworthy. I am unsafe. I am powerless. It exposed the deeper architecture holding my life.

And paradoxically; that collapse didn't disqualify me from being a coach. It qualified me. It rooted my compassion, sharpened my awareness, humbled me, and brought me home to my own humanity. If anyone is going through a bankruptcy – I'm their coach!

I rebuilt by being with what was hard; honestly, fully, and without shame. What I lost in certainty, I gained in truth. And that made all the difference.

Pause & Reflect

- What if this collapse isn't the end of me, but the unmasking?
- What deeper truth is rising now, that the surface has shattered?
- Am I willing to let this unraveling reveal the part of me that cannot be broken?

Anchoring Insights

- Mastery is presence, not hindsight.
- Pain isn't the enemy; resistance to it is.
- Breakdowns carry invitations; if you ask, What's growing in me?
- Daily micro-shifts mindset build resilient, real-time resourcefulness.

Exploration 15: Find the Gift Now

Pick a small challenge you're facing right now. Not your biggest dragon. Just a 2-out-of-10 kind of difficulty. List ten gifts this challenge has already brought, or could bring.

Example: Car broke down →
- More walking, slower pace.
- Notice neighborhood details.
- Ask for help, deepen bonds.
- Save gas money, rethink the budget.
- Get resourceful: bus, rideshare, adapt.
- Practice patience with timing.
- Question attachment to convenience.
- Less traffic, more time in nature.
- Lower carbon footprint, eco-awareness.
- Meet new people along the way.

Stretch your lens. Look for gifts in your health, creativity, relationships and timing. If that feels easy, level up to a 5-out-of-10 challenge. The more you train this muscle, the faster you'll shift from reaction to resourcefulness. This is how you stop spinning, and start gaining traction.

Branch 16: Train With Stress

Use Challenge as Fuel

By now, you've learned how to mine your past, hold challenges gently in real-time, and expand into a mythic identity. But what if you didn't wait for life to challenge you? What if you trained for it?

What if, instead of waiting for life to throw you into the fire… you walked into it on purpose?

That's what this branch is about.

Choosing stress not as something to avoid, but something to work with. Because challenge isn't just something that happens to you. It's something you can seek, shape, and grow from.

The Hormesis Principle

In biology, hormesis means small doses of stress can have beneficial effects. Lift weights: muscles form microtears and then rebuild stronger. Take a cold plunge: your nervous and immune systems become more robust.

Try something emotionally edgy once a day: your identity expands.

Say in a meeting: "That didn't sit right with me," or "I'm feeling really vulnerable sharing this…" These tiny truth-telling moments stretch your emotional capacity. They activate your inner growth edge.

It's part science, part soul work.

When you choose a challenge consciously, you're not testing your limits; you're authoring them. You're proving to yourself: I am worthy of this edge. I trust myself to hold more. I am becoming someone bigger than my fear.

Avoid these micro-stressors entirely? Your emotional muscles atrophy, just like your physical ones if you never exercise them.

The Comfort Crisis

Michael Easter's The Comfort Crisis reveals how modern life, engineered around convenience, safety, and predictability, has made us physically weaker, mentally softer, and spiritually undernourished. Comfort, he argues, creates crisis. When we overindulge in climate control, endless entertainment, and the avoidance of discomfort these luxuries become corrosive. We lose our capacity to adapt, to struggle, to live deeply.

Easter draws on the ancient Japanese ritual of Misogi, suggesting a once-a-year challenge so demanding you're not sure you can complete it. The goal: "Do something so hard it has a chance to change you."

A true Misogi should feel absurd. There should be less than a 50% chance you'll succeed, and no one to compare yourself to. It's not about winning or instagram likes. It's about who you become in the process.

Time in wild, unpredictable environments, without technology and certainty, and with a generous dash of boredom restores nervous system regulation and awakens primal clarity. In this framework, discomfort is not suffering. It is contact with the edge of your current self. Surviving it, on a cold mountain, in deep silence, or inside your own truth, is how identity expands.

The Edge Is the Teacher

Growth doesn't always feel like growth. Sometimes it feels like humiliation, setback, silence, or failure... But if you can stay near that edge; with presence and intention, for just a little longer... Something begins to shift. Your nervous system adapts. Your tolerance expands. Your self-trust deepens. Not because you won but because you didn't give up.

The rewards are real. Wins will happen and that's great, but they're not the point. The real fruit is becoming someone who doesn't back down from attempting difficult things, but thrives in them.

I often get asked why I keep chasing the screaming edge of comfort. The answer is always the same: Discovery. Expansion. The chance to meet the deeper version of me, one that is raw and resilient. The hardest climbs aren't physical. They expose your internal terrain, your stories, your fear, and your relationship to effort, failure, and self-worth.

When you keep showing up for something that demands more than you think you have, you become more than you thought you were. That's what happened to me on "Eulogy."

Story: *Eulogy to Eulogy*

Some lessons come whispering through trembling muscles, shallow breath, and the overwhelming urge to quit. This was one of those lessons.

One summer in Rifle I started projecting* Eulogy; eighty vicious feet, with barely an honest handhold on it. To send* the route I had to unlock a puzzle of awkward body positions: through core tension, creativity, faith; and lots of knee-bars*

At first I couldn't do a single move. This climb felt impossible. But I was committed. With time and consistency I figured out every sequence, and visualized every inch of the route. In August, I reached the final move without falling. Then peeled off. It was a breakthrough. Close enough to believe.

The next session: I couldn't even get off the ground. No progress. Only anxiety. My body trembled before I even tied in. My breath went shallow. My mind looped. I forgot the process, forgot the joy. I compared. I cried.

Suddenly, I just want it to be over. Not the climb, but the discomfort. I dropped into a persistent CRASH state; fully aware but resisting it instead of acknowledging it.

I entered the dark age. For the next few sessions I kept pushing, even though I knew it was a mistake. Trying to force the outcome instead of staying with the process. I was trying so hard that I tore my calf muscle: the crucial knee-bars, now gone. Old stories hissed, You shouldn't even be here, you're taking up space.

I had invested 2 months into this climb and now I was forced to walk away.

I mountain biked, danced on one leg, and ran a retreat with a friend. The tunnel vision loosened. Life returned: not just black and Eulogy; but sky, laughter, movement.

Then, on a crisp September day, I returned to the wall with no pressure. No tightness in my chest. Just me. Present. Open.

I tied in. Pull onto the wall. And… I climbed it. All the way to the anchors. Not perfectly. But cleanly, without falling or hanging on the rope. I sent it!

Trying hard and winning feels great. But giving it all while the outcome is uncertain is the real work. When you offer your effort into the void, with no guarantees, no promise of success, something shifts. You stretch beyond your old stories. You prove with your presence that you are more than the box you've been living in.

I didn't become a different climber the day I sent "Eulogy". I became her in the weeks before; when I kept showing up, stood next to fear, and refused to look away. Surrendering but never letting go. The transformation wasn't spectacular. There was no audience. No flawless ascent.

Just the gradual work of becoming someone who no longer quits on herself.

Eulogy taught me how to have my own back when things get hard. A vital skill for someone who insists on living at the edge of her comfort zone. The lesson transfers wide. It helps me show up in conversations I'd rather avoid, in projects that stall, in moments when the unknown feels too big. Each time, I remember Eulogy, and that strength isn't just in pulling yourself up, but in staying with yourself when you want to let go.

Thank you Eulogy, for refusing to bend. For teaching me perseverance without ego. For showing me the limits I'd built in the name of safety. Thank you for confronting the lie that deep identity change isn't possible.

Thank you for being hard, so I could finally see just how strong I am. And I know now that every wall: stone, flesh, or circumstance, has its own anchors up top. The real climb isn't about reaching them, but about who you become while hanging in the space between.

Pause & Reflect

- Where do I walk away without meeting my edge?
- Where do I habitually choose comfort without questioning if it's the best thing for me?
- Can I choose to be brave enough to stand where my protections get exposed?
- Am I willing to meet what I've built to survive; with love and keep climbing anyway?

Anchoring Insights

- Intentional challenge builds capacity. Stress is something you can train with; on purpose.
- Growth rarely feels good in the moment. It often arrives disguised as discomfort, doubt, or failure.
- Hormesis applies to the soul. Just like muscle builds through resistance, your spirit strengthens through stretch.
- Ditch comfort in some areas of your life.
- Stay with the edge. Creating difficulty, rather than waiting for it, builds resilience, power, and deep self-trust.

Exploration 16: Choose Your Training Ground

Pick one area of your life where you want to expand your capacity. Then ask:

What's one intentional challenge I can choose that edges me out of comfort? Something I can feel that requires presence, patience, and belief. (Something that you don't know for sure that you can succeed at). Examples:

- Speak in front of a group when you'd rather hide.
- Climb a hill or run a distance you've avoided.
- Ask for something unreasonable and stay open to the "no."
- Take it up a notch. Design a Misogi for yourself.

Do it not for the outcome, but to grow your ability to stay in the stretch. That's training with stress, not performance. Real, hormetic growth.

Living Compass: Trunk 4 Summary: Transmute the Challenge

Core Distinctions

- **Pain as compost, not curse:** Transform discomfort into fertile ground for growth.
- **Mythic identity vs. victim narrative:** Live from your deeper story, not your wounds.
- **Curiosity over resistance:** Choose wonder over avoidance when meeting challenges.
- **Edge over comfort:** Remove some comforts from your life on purpose.

Core Practices

- **Reclaim authorship through story reflection:** Reflect on a painful experience and rewrite it through the lens of strength, resilience, or resourcefulness.
- **Transform emotional pain through creative expression:** Use writing, movement, mythic metaphor, or art to alchemize discomfort into meaning. Not to analyze it, to feel it, move it, create from it. Use challenge as fuel for transformation.
- **Reclaim your mythic identity with symbolic storytelling:** Write your life as myth. Let archetypes, symbols, and nature-based metaphors speak through you.
- **Meet challenges in real time with open curiosity:** The next time something feels hard, pause and ask: What deeper resilience is being revealed right now?
- **Train intentionally at your hormetic edge:** Choose one small or big challenge each day that stretches you; emotionally, physically, relationally.

Key Tools

- The Composting Lens – Reframe difficulty into opportunity.
- The Mythic Zoom-Out – View your life from a broader perspective, not a series of problems to deal with.
- The Deliberate Edge Practice – Choose a challenge to see how it will expand you.

Guiding Truth

What you face and feel, you can grow from.

Your Wake-Up Call

Some of the most pivotal moments in life don't look like breakthroughs. They look more like heartbreaks. Like everything falling apart.

I work with plenty of people who know how to fight through pain, but not how to be with it. They've been taught to override, to push harder, to conquer the challenges. When that strategy stops working; when the identity built on performance starts to crack; they panic. They either double down, or collapse.

When we skip the practices of Trunk Four, we don't learn how to meet the challenge, only to outrun it. We miss the chance to compost pain into power. We reject the very thing that could make us whole.

A shift happens when you turn toward the fire instead of away from it. When you stop asking, "Why is this happening to me?" and start asking: "What is the opportunity here?" , "What wants to be born through this?" "How can I write a new story instead of clinging to the old one?" That's when gold starts to crop up.

I've watched clients reclaim shattered marriages by shifting their view of a partner, from an obstacle to an ally in their evolution. I've seen grief become fuel for massive creation. Illness becomes a portal to purpose. Childhood wounds alchemized into fierce, unapologetic boundaries.

The pain didn't vanish. But it transformed them. Because they chose to meet it with presence instead of resistance. They chose to rise; not in spite of the pain, but with it.

This Trunk shows you how. Your story is not a sentence; it is a sacred initiation.

Trunk 5
Action

Embodied Courage and Identity Shift

Branch 18
Redefine Goals

Branch 17
Act Before You're Ready

Branch 19
Commit Boldly

Branch 20
The Process is the way

Trunk 5: Action

Embodied Courage and Identity Shift

Branches in this Trunk:

- Branch 17: Act Before You're Ready
- Branch 18: Redefine Goals
- Branch 19: Commit Boldly
- Branch 20: The Process is the way

You've done the excavation. You've listened inwardly, met your exiled parts, remembered who you are beneath the noise, and transformed your pain into power. You now know your patterns. You can regulate your state. You can connect with your Higher Self.

But without movement, nothing transforms. That's the power of this Trunk: it turns inner knowing into outer becoming. It alchemizes insight into identity. It makes all the invisible work visible; through what you choose, how you show up, and what you build.

Trunk Five is about expressing your truth through aligned action, not by pushing harder, but through easeful, expansive creation. Grounded. True. Disruptive. Healing. Action that doesn't wait for permission, because it is the permission.

Insight doesn't change you. Action does. Every real move reshapes your identity. Every choice made from truth becomes your path.

These four branches will challenge you to:

- Act before you're ready.
- Redefine your relationship with goals.
- Commit like your future depends on it.
- Let go of outcomes and honor the process itself.

This isn't just about reaching the summit. It's about becoming the kind of person who climbs. Our transformation can't happen in theory. It lives in motion. One conversation. One decision. One next step. It's yours to walk.

Branch 17: Act Before You're Ready

Action Creates Motivation

Most people wait to act until they feel clear or confident. This waiting has been the quiet thief of countless lives, stealing time, dreams, and possibility. Confidence and clarity don't grow in the forest; they are forged through deliberate action. Waiting for the "right time" is stalling. Your mind will always find a reason to delay. Your nervous system will always prefer the safety of the known.

Change happens when you move. You don't need more certainty. You need to take the next step (you may want to bring a machete). Not from pressure. Not to prove. From the part of you that trusts. The one who doesn't need permission to show up fully.

Action isn't a reward for being ready. It's the path that makes you ready. Every step reveals the next. Every aligned move becomes a signal to life: I'm in. The path appears as you start walking.

Just like Tahoe; when I splattered full-force into the unknown. No map, just guts and a wild willingness to learn on the job.

Start Where You Are

You don't need to have it all figured out. You just need to begin. That conversation you've been postponing. That email you've been editing for two weeks. That next step you keep telling yourself you'll take once you feel ready.

Start now. Start anyway. It might be messy, you may stumble, and your voice might shake. But movement interrupts paralysis. It shifts your emotional state, and builds momentum. The moment you act, you're no longer spinning in your head, you're in the world again. Engaged. Alive. Available.

Confidence doesn't come first. It follows. Motivation doesn't lead. It responds. The action is the medicine.

Stop waiting to be ready – be ready.

Remember the girl who watched her country's rules flip overnight? Who realized: this is all made up? She's not here to follow someone else's plan anymore.

If she could move, so can you.

Story: *Bird of Prey*

Climbing Bird of Prey in Yosemite was a masterclass in raw, unrelenting discomfort. A thousand feet above the valley floor, I was deep in a vicious 10++* offwidth* crack; too wide to jam my hands into, too narrow to wedge my body inside. I didn't have the right gear. For nearly 50 feet, I was essentially soloing. No protection between me and the anchor. My body trembled with the knowledge that a fall would be very, very bad.

The higher I climbed, the worse it got. My breath was ragged. My vision blurred. Panic wasn't knocking, it had taken over the house. My inner world went full-blown red alert: *You can't do this. You're going to die here. You're out of your depth.* I was terrified. My legs shook uncontrollably. I was sobbing into the granite; snot and tears mixing with chalk and sweat, whispering prayers to a god I wasn't sure I believed in.

And still… I moved.

There was no elegance, no grace, just desperation and will. My body screamed, my mind fractured. I had no way up, no way down. Just a hundred vertical feet of pain and pressure, held in place by friction, body tension, and survival instinct.

Then, I finally found a narrowing and slotted a cam*. Just one little piece of gear, one sacred piece.

My body softened. The panic began to drain like a fever breaking. The shaking stopped. And in that stillness, clarity returned. What moments ago felt like an execution became a dance. The impossible became doable. And then… done.

I easily reached the ledge, clipped in, and burst into laughter. It was absurd. Holy. Beautiful.

The fear didn't leave because I conquered it. It left when I gathered just enough presence; through the blur, through the shaking, to place a single cam. One tiny sliver of safety in a wall of risk.

That moment anchored me, literally and metaphorically. It brought me back to focus and calm. I didn't silence the fear; I stayed with it long enough to see clearly, to act precisely, to find my way forward. I moved through it with trust in my chest, grit in my blood, and the trembling knowing that I could.

We're all climbing something: grief, change, uncertainty. The moment that changes everything is rarely the summit, but the instant we find just enough stability to place a proverbial cam, when we stop spiraling and start moving again.

That's what badassery looks like: not the absence of fear, but presence and movement inside it.

Pause & Reflect:

- Where am I stalling, making up excuses?
- What have I been desiring but haven't taken action on?
- What if fear isn't the exit sign, but the invitation to discover more about my capacity?
- What truth could I discover if I stayed with the discomfort just a little longer?

Anchoring Insights

- Clarity follows commitment; not the other way around.
- A single small action can break months of inertia.
- Readiness is not a feeling. It's a decision.

Exploration 17: The 48-Hour Bold Step

Choose one action that edges you out of comfort. It doesn't need to be big, just real. A phone call. A post. A decision. A truth told. Do it within 48 hours. No excuses, no overthinking.

Too easy? Do ten of those. Too scared? Try this instead:

Bonus Exploration: The Fear List

Write down ten things you're afraid of doing; especially ones that matter. Examples:

- I'm afraid of posting my artwork online.
- I'm afraid of asking my boss for a raise.
- I'm afraid of telling my partner what I really want in bed.
- I'm afraid of joining a dance class where I don't know anyone.
- I'm afraid of saying "no" to a friend who always asks for favors.
- I'm afraid of going to a networking event alone.
- I'm afraid of hiking a trail I've never done before.
- I'm afraid of telling my parents about my career change.
- I'm afraid of sharing my personal story on social media.
- I'm afraid of starting a conversation with someone I admire.
- I'm afraid of wearing clothes that feel too bold for me.
- I'm afraid of calling someone I've been avoiding.
- I'm afraid of singing in public.
- I'm afraid of walking into a gym for the first time.
- I'm afraid of cooking a new recipe for guests.

Write yours. Pick three. Do them.

Afterward, journal:

- What did I feel before, during, and after?
- What shifted, internally or externally?
- What did this one act make possible?
- What shifted in who I believe I am?

Branch 18: Redefine Goals

Goals Are a Place to Come From

Most people set goals like they're trying to earn something; Worth. Belonging. Proof. But just like shifting regimes in my country, your goalposts were probably built on someone else's idea of success. Now it's your turn to decide what's real.

I never quite got the hype about goals. They felt like something for Manhattan bankers, not for a dirtbag* climber, Eastern European immigrant. Even as a coach, I talked about commitment and intention, but I sidestepped goals altogether.

Then I heard Steve Chandler (nicknamed the grandfather of coaching) say: "What if a goal is a place to come from, not a place to get to?" My mind exploded!.

Because most people treat goals like distant destinations; "I want to get there someday." But that mindset creates separation, between who you are now and who you think you have to be to deserve the outcome. But what if your goal isn't out there? What if it's something you can embody now?

Live Your Goal Now

Rather than chasing the summit that will one day make you enough, what if you lived from your goals right now? Let your goals shape your choices in the present:

- If your goal is to be a loving parent: give your full attention for ten minutes before bedtime tonight.
- If your goal is to be healthy: drink water instead of a soda. Go for a walk instead of scrolling.
- If your goal is to have a strong relationship with your coworker: reach out to them now, with honesty and vulnerability, not when conflict arises.
- If your goal is to have boundaries: say no once today, without apologies.

That's how you collapse the gap between who you are now and who you want to be.

It's how you move from scarcity to creative ownership. The outcome? Maybe it comes, maybe it doesn't. But you will have acted from alignment, not lack. And that's a huge win already.

Set the Goal, Release the Grip

Goals give us direction, urgency, and structure. They focus our attention and galvanize commitment. But the moment your identity gets tangled in the result; the goal starts to own you. It becomes something you have to prove, instead of something that calls you deeper into truth.

Hold your goals lightly. Let them guide you, not define you. Getting the outcome you want is amazing. Celebrate it. Let it land. Let it expand how you see yourself. You are someone who follows through, who creates and who leads.

Just don't cling to it. Don't make it mean more than it does. The moment the outcome becomes your identity, you start living in fear of losing it. A goal can become a hungry ghost. Let your wins shape you; not trap you. Progress is a gift, not proof you finally deserve to breathe easy.

Story: *Mt. Chaltén, A Goal Much Bigger Than Me*

When a client told me she wanted to climb Mount Shasta; her childhood dream; I realized I couldn't walk her through her edge if I wasn't willing to meet my own. If I was going to coach her through a big dream, I had to put skin in the game. I had to stretch, too.

I had done this several times before, but not in quite a while. It was a cue: it's time to set a bold, terrifying goal. One that demands all of you.

I didn't start small.

Steven and I picked Fitz Roy, in the Chaltén Massif. Nearly two vertical kilometers of wind-lashed granite, in a place infamous for some of the worst weather on Earth. It wasn't just a peak. It was a soul goal. The kind that screams in your face: "You're allowed to want what you want!"

The moment we committed, I was out of my depth: The training. The logistics. The cost. My aching knees. The mental chatter yelling: don't do it. But I went anyway. And along the way, I learned:

Desire. I first saw Fitz Roy years earlier on my solo trip through South America. It haunted me. I wanted that journey the way a seed wants light: urgent, wordless, pulling. Committing stirred everything: longing, unworthiness, thrill, doubt.

Intention. This was the unbending yes. Flights booked. Gear packed. A long trek on foot to the base of Chaltén. Anxiety burned off through sheer effort, wind, weight, movement. We weren't imagining it anymore. We were in it.

Allowance. The climb took over. Problem-solving. Changing conditions. Fatigue. No room left for worry. We moved with the moment. No resistance. No drama. Just breath, stone, and presence. A strange peace settled in; like the mountain was breathing through us.

Surrender. The window closed. We woke high on a ledge to the most beautiful sunrise, and the most vicious wind, which locals call the broom of god. It dictated our retreat. The goal shifted to get off alive. The new summit was letting go. We could do everything right and still not make it. And that truth didn't crush me. It freed me.

We didn't reach the top, but I came home with something else: A stronger body. A quieter mind. A soul filled with love wider than fear. And a deeper trust in the woman who shows up when everything's on the line. Standing on the summit wasn't necessary to change me. The climbing was.

Pause & Reflect

- What do I desire to experience about myself more than anything?
- If I were already the version of me who completes this goal, how would I think, speak, and show up today?
- Am I holding my goal as a place to get to, or as a place to live from right now?
- What's one aligned action I can take today from that place?

Anchoring Insights

- A bold goal calls forth a bolder self.
- Identity precedes outcome.
- The mountain gives gifts all along the way, not just on the summit.

Exploration 18: Become the One Who Already Did It

Name a bold goal that scares or stretches you.
- Write: "If I already were the person who achieved this, how would I think, speak, and act today?"
- If this goal were already complete, what would I no longer tolerate in myself?
- Choose one thought, one way of speaking, or one action, and live it this week.
- Afterward reflect: What shifted when I acted from completion instead of striving?
- Let your future self lead. Let your actions catch up.

Branch 19: Commit Boldly

Commitment Activates Identity

Commitment isn't a mood. It's not something you wait to feel. It's an agreement you make with yourself. We're trained to wait; wait for clarity, wait for confidence, wait to be "ready." But clarity is a result, not a requirement. Confidence is generated, not granted. Commitment comes first. It creates clarity. Action builds confidence.

Readiness is an illusion. In order to get going what you need more than anything is a decision. A stake in the ground where you stop asking if and start saying go. Commitment is an identity shift from trying something to becoming something. From hoping things change. To being the change.

Commitment is a refusal to abandon yourself even when things get hard. It's a container that holds you when motivation wanes. It's the future calling you forward louder than your fear pulls you back.

The moment you commit, life moves. Resources appear. Conversations shift. Even your nervous system starts recalibrating to a new truth. None of that happens while you're still negotiating with fear.

My life didn't change because I started trying harder, it changed when I realized I had been rehearsing smallness. Every time I overgave, overperformed, or underclaimed, I was asking the world to prove I mattered. I was outsourcing my worth. Waiting for permission to take up space. The shift came when I stopped begging to matter and chose instead, to belong to myself.

When I zipped up my sleeping bag after that fiasco of a film shoot in Yosemite, I drew a line in the sand: "I'm done auditioning."

Be willing to move before the net appears. Not because you're chasing an outcome; but because the act of showing up is the outcome. Boldness in service, without attachment, is freedom. The game changes the moment you stop asking life to show you that you matter; and decide you do.

What happens when you commit?

When you commit, everything begins to organize around your decision. Clarity sharpens. Distractions lose their grip. Opportunities that once felt out of reach start to appear because you start showing up differently. You stop leaking energy into doubt, delay, or the search for a perfect plan. You stop waiting for permission. Instead, you move with grounded conviction. Your nervous system begins to trust you. People respond to your presence in new ways. Life is no longer something to brace against, and becomes something you co-create.

Why We Half-Commit

We tell ourselves we're being strategic. Just weighing our options, being smart, not rushing. But most of the time, it's fear in disguise.

Fear of failure. Fear of success. Fear of being seen. Fear of not being enough.

So, we sit on the fence and call it wisdom. But the longer you stay uncommitted, the more of your life you spend in limbo. At half-power. Half-presence. Half-you. We are engaging in full blown self-betrayal and calling it safety.

Commitment Is Identity

When you commit, you stop being the person who wants the thing, and start being the person who does the thing.

That's not just semantics, it's neuroscience. The moment you decide, your nervous system recalibrates, your environment shifts, your actions align, and the world starts responding to a clear signal.

You stop leaking energy and start generating it. This is why commitment feels powerful. Because it is. Because you're not waiting anymore. You're choosing. And every time you choose, you become.

Story: "You Bastard" A Story of Friendship and Commitment

The Triple Bypass is one of Colorado's most iconic and grueling road cycling events. Spanning nearly 120 miles from Evergreen to Avon, it climbs over three mountain passes, and racks up more than 10,000 feet of elevation gain. It's not a race, it's a reckoning. A chance to meet yourself on the edge.

Steven and his friend John rode it several years in a row, chasing a slightly faster, stronger version of themselves. But one year, the objective quietly changed.

The forecast had looked marginal for days. And on the morning of the ride, it delivered: cold, gray, and soaking. At the starting line, they stood shivering, staring west into a wall of storm. When the starting signal sounded, they pushed off eagerly, welcoming the heat that would come with effort.

The rain started as a mist as they wound their way up Juniper Pass. Within a few miles, it thickened into a steady drizzle, soaking their spandex to the skin. Steven pulled ahead of John early, legs churning, breath rhythmic.

Descending into Idaho Springs, he passed clusters of riders huddling under cafe awnings and storefronts. Tempting. *But maybe it'll clear up*, he thought. It didn't.

As he approached Loveland Pass; the route's high point at nearly 12,000 feet, the rain turned to downpour. Water sloshed in his shoes. Cold rivulets streamed down his back. His hands numbed on the bars. Still, he climbed.

The descent was treacherous. The road ran like a river, as Steven cautiously feathered his brakes around each slick switchback. By the time he reached Lake Dillon, his hands and feet were nearly frozen from miles of coasting. His muscles screamed. But he was in too deep to quit now.

One more pass. One more freezing descent. Then the final stretch.

He'd been soaked for hours. Mud-streaked. Exhausted. But unwavering. He was no longer riding for speed. He was riding because he had decided. He was committed.

As he rolled into Vail, the clouds finally broke. Sunlight pierced through. For the first time all day, warmth. The last few miles into Avon glowed golden.

As he crossed the finish line there were no cheering crowds. No excited energy like in years past. Just a few volunteers and oddly clean cyclists. Famished, Steven made his way to the catering tent.

The server behind the table casually asked, "So how far did you make it?" Confused, Steven replied. "What do you mean? I rode the whole thing". The server's eyes widened. "You mean you rode all the way from Evergreen? Everyone else quit. They got driven here; for the free food and beer."

As Steven sat down in the grass to let the sun soak into his bones he heard a familiar voice shout out. "You bastard!" It was John, grinning as he walked over. "After you pulled ahead, I kept hoping you'd dropped out. But when I didn't see you at any of the aid stations, I knew; if you weren't quitting, I couldn't either."

That day wasn't about speed or strength. It was about unbending commitment. About invisible agreements, the kind you make with yourself. And the kind that live quietly in friendship. Badassery doesn't always get a trophy. It may look like pedaling through freezing rain because quitting isn't your language. Sometimes it's knowing someone's out there holding the line with you, silently saying: if you don't quit, I won't either.

Pause & Reflect

- Where in my life am I still negotiating with my desire?
- When do I say "I wish I could" or "must be nice".
- What am I pretending I'm making a plan, that's actually a delay?
- If I were already the version of me who does the thing, what would I do next?

Anchoring Insights

- Commitment ends negotiation with the smaller self.
- Failure becomes feedback, not identity.
- Full-commitment energy attracts support and momentum.

Exploration 19: Are You All In?

Read aloud or journal through the following questions:

- Where in my life or leadership I say I'm committed, but my actions say otherwise?
- What am I afraid will happen if I stop hesitating and go all in?
- What stories or excuses have kept me circling the same decision?
- If I were fully committed in this area, what would that actually look like?
- What do I already know I need to choose, but haven't?

Now choose one area of your life to go all-in on for the next 30 days. Track what changes; not just externally, but in your energy, clarity, and sense of self.

Your next level won't wait forever. Neither should you.

Branch 20: The Process Is the Way

Let go of the performance. Become the person who doesn't need proof.

Most of us live like happiness is just one achievement away: The next trip. The next climb. The next brag-worthy accomplishment. I used to live that way too. Climbing El Cap. Kitesurfing between Hawaiian islands. Stacking impossible goals to pad my badass résumé. Truth? It's never enough.

The Infinite Game

When a client was crushed after an injury forced her to cancel our Andean expedition, I told her something born from lived experience: "Guess what you'll see when you reach the summit? A breathtaking view; of even higher mountains."

We chase goals. We ascend. We push through discomfort. We arrive; only to find that the finish line is just a new vantage point. Sometimes it's exhilarating. Sometimes it's exhausting. Often, you don't even realize it… until you're fresh out of mountains to climb.

The work never ends, so get off the treadmill.

Most people set goals like they're trying to earn something. Worth. Belonging. Proof. But real peace doesn't come from getting there. It comes from being here. When you fixate on the outcome, you miss the only part of the journey that actually exists: The present.

The most powerful shift you can make is to stop chasing summits and start honoring the climb itself. That's the difference between performance and presence. Between checking off your bucket list, and letting the bucket change you.

Story: *Be Here Now (on the Wall)*

We say we want to do hard things. But more often, we just want to have done them. We think we crave the summit photo, the story, and the pride. Reality? Without the journey, it's just a picture. The harder the process, the more it reshapes you, the more it demands presence, the more you value it.

It was day six on the North America Wall of El Capitan. Thirty plus pitches. 2,900 vertical feet. Aid climbing*; a slow, tedious, and often terrifying form of ascent. We'd already climbed twenty-seven pitches, over 2,600 feet. My hands were numb, raw, and inflamed. I poured water into the Jetboil with clenched fists for our morning coffee ritual.

We'd stocked our vertical pantry in a rush, and by day four, D-Griff was dragging. When I finally dug through our haul bag* to take a closer look at what we'd bought, it hit me. In our late night speed-shopping frenzy, we'd filled it with things that were most visible on a shopping shelf. Low-fat, low-carb, low-calorie everything. Perfect for cutting weight. Terrible for fueling long days on a big wall. What we needed were labels that screamed Warning: high-calorie gut bomb ahead.

By day three, my fingers entered a state only big wall climbers understand. Completely numb from inflammation; Then violently reawakened each morning in what we call the "screaming barfies." a ritual of pain. A frostbite thawing kind of pain that makes you want to scream and throw up at the same time.

That agony lasted for a full hour, every morning. No epiphany. No transcendence. Just the brutal truth of choosing this; again and again. Because some part of me knew: the wall doesn't give you anything you don't earn.

Ahead of me lay a hard traversing pitch. Sky hooks made up most of my protection: tiny metal claws balanced on stone edges. They are ok to hang from, but worthless for catching a fall. My hair was turning gray in real time as I inched across the wall. I just wanted to be done.

By 1 p.m., we were one pitch from the summit. I could almost taste flat ground, pizza, and a hot shower.

"We're staying here tonight," D-Griff said.

"The hell we are" I riposted, incredulous, creating an opening for the wisdom I'll never forget.

"You'll summit, carry all this junk down, and feel amazing for a moment. Then, tired and aimless, you'll wander up to the meadow, start looking up and soon you will forget how hard it was. In a few days, you'll crave this feeling again. You'll think the answer is to climb it again. But we're already here. So let's be here now."

I hated that he was right.

We laid still on that sloping ledge with nothing to do, and nowhere to go. Just sky, wind, and stone. The world slowed. By then we'd completely run out of our nutrient-deficient rations. And then; miraculously, we found an old can of Beefaroni wedged in a crack. We ate it cold, straight from the tin. Easily one of the most disgusting things I've ever put in my mouth. But still, a gift from the universe.

In my pain and hunger, a new question emerged: What if life wasn't about pushing through every hard thing just to tick the box? What if the real invitation is not just to finish; but to be transformed by the experience? To feel it all?

That awakening was worth every screaming barfie I got the following morning.

Sometimes it's not about the summit. It's about staying exactly where you are. Letting the discomfort do its sacred work. Strip away the noise, the striving, the need to prove. Letting it reveal what you're really after, or what you've been trying to outrun. That night on the ledge; filthy and starving; I stopped chasing completion, and met pure presence. That shift? That was the real ascent.

Pause & Reflect

- Where am I rushing to the outcome just to avoid being with what's here now?
- What part of me still believes I'll be enough only when I finish, prove, or win?
- What opens when I let presence matter more than progress?
- Where have I made my goal mean something about my worth?
- What would shift if I let the process matter more than the prize?

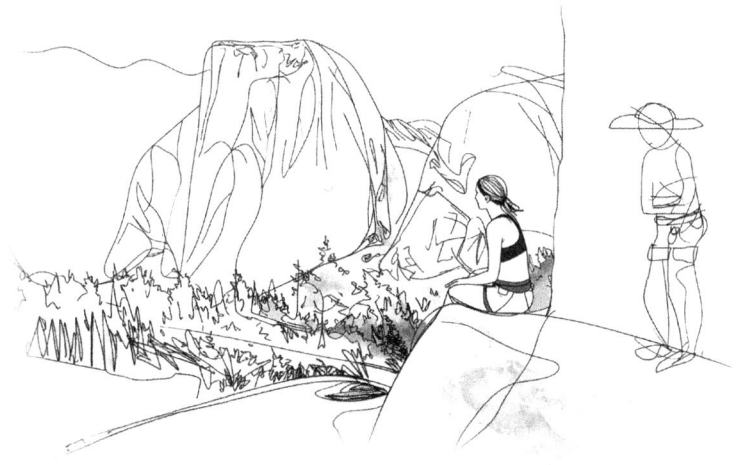

Process vs. Outcome Goals

Outcome goal focuses on achieving the summit. A Process-Oriented Goal focuses on your commitment to action, practice, and presence; not the result you hope to achieve. Process goals are rooted in daily devotion, not future validation. Fulfillment doesn't come from crossing the finish line. It comes from how you walk the path. In a world obsessed with outcomes, we forget that the most transformative moments don't happen at the summit. They happen while we're attempting to get there.

When you stop rushing to be done and let yourself be shaped by the experience, you return to what matters. The biggest growth doesn't come from pushing forward. It comes from staying. You don't need a finish line. You need a pulse check. Are you here? That's the real arrival. Here's the difference:

Outcome: "I want to lose 20 pounds."

Process: "I'll walk five days a week and prep healthy meals on Sundays."

Outcome: "I'll feel good once I land the big client."

Process: "I'll show up powerfully for the next call, trust my intuition and say the uncomfortable thing."

Outcome:: "I want a promotion."

Process: "I'll schedule weekly check-ins with my manager and complete one growth task each week."

Anchoring Insights

- Process > outcome. Meaning comes from how you show up, not what you achieve.
- Outcome goals lead to chasing. Process goals lead to presence.
- When the process is the point, joy returns to the now, not "someday."
- A good process goal stretches you without sacrificing your soul.
- You don't need to suffer your way to success. Joy is now allowed.

Exploration 20: Make It a Process Goal

Take one current goal you're holding: maybe something big and shiny that feels a little heavy. Instead of asking "How do I hit the target?" Ask: "How do I grow through this?"

Now, rewrite your goal as a process-oriented practice, using the following compass points:

- Play the Infinite Game

What if the point wasn't to win, but to stay in the game? What makes this goal worth doing even if no one's watching and nothing gets posted?

- Make It Habit-Oriented

What daily or weekly rituals would move this forward? Don't just chase the result, build the rhythm.

- Focus on the Journey

Where is the joy in the doing? How could you savor the path instead of sprinting to the finish?

- Discipline with Devotion

What if you showed up out of love, not pressure? Let commitment become a ritual of self-respect, not a contract with perfection.

- Let Outcomes Be Flexible

If things shift, how will you adapt with grace? Can you hold the result lightly and the learning tightly?

- Fail Forward

What failures would actually mean you're growing? Can you use them as feedback, not proof you should stop?

Then ask yourself:

- What would change if I enjoyed this now, not later?

- What would it look like to make the journey the goal?

Let your goal become less of a test, and more of a path that makes you more you as you walk it.

Living Compass: Trunk 5 Summary: Move

Core Distinctions

- **Movement generates readiness:** You don't wait to feel ready; you move, and readiness follows.
- **Action from truth vs. action from pressure:** Aligned action rewires identity; pressured action reinforces performance.
- Commitment comes before Clarity and Confidence, not after.
- **Process shapes identity more than outcome:** Who you become on the way matters more than what you achieve.

Core Practices

- **Act before you feel ready:** Momentum is created, not found.
- **Redefine goals so they sculpt your being:** Choose goals that form you, not ones that prove you.
- **Commit boldly:** Let identity follow commitment, not precede it.
- **Let the journey shape you:** The process is the path; presence is the transformation.

Key Tools

- **Micro-leaps:** Track small acts of aligned bravery to build capacity and momentum.
- **Goal-to-being:** Transform external goals into internal identity shifts.
- **Bold commitment:** Declare and commit to a decision that stretches your sense of self.
- **Process reflection:** Reflect on how the journey is shaping you; emotionally, mentally, and somatically.

Guiding Truth

You become ready by moving; not waiting.

Your Wake-Up Call

Some people spend their entire lives waiting. Waiting to feel ready. Waiting for a sign. Waiting for permission. I work with people who have built impressive lives on the outside; but on the inside, they're still operating at 50% capacity. They've read all the books, done the mindset work, and had some breakthroughs. But they're still thinking about their transformation instead of embodying it. Insight alone doesn't change you; action does.

When we skip the practices of Trunk Five, we intellectualize growth without living it. We keep dreaming but never leap. We wait for a "perfect time" that never comes. But when someone finally takes the bold step they've been avoiding, their life completely shifts.

They stop performing. They stop negotiating with fear. They move from truth. They make the audacious ask. They launch the imperfect offering. They climb the most spirited mountain. It might not feel safe, but it doesn't matter. That one move; however messy or small, reorganizes their entire identity. It whispers to the body: I am no longer waiting.

Trunk 6
Expression

Energy Integrity, Celebration + Visibility

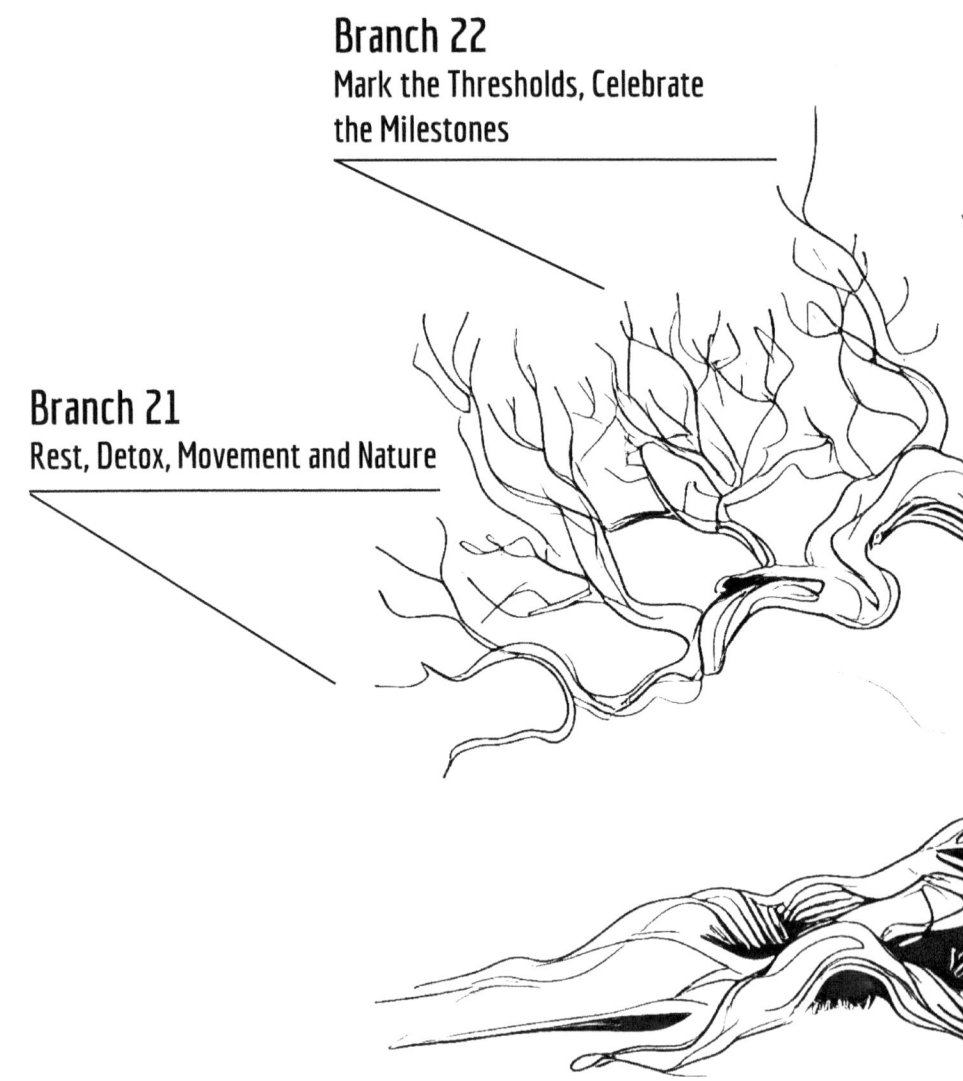

Branch 22
Mark the Thresholds, Celebrate the Milestones

Branch 21
Rest, Detox, Movement and Nature

Branch 23
Declare Your Identity

Branch 24
Create from Truth

Trunk 6: Expression

Energy Integrity, Celebration and Visibility

When your transformation roots deep, it begins to bloom. Not just inside you, but through you. You're no longer living just for yourself. You rise, and that becomes a gift.

This last trunk has four branches:

- Branch 21: Rest, Detox, Movement and Nature
- Branch 22: Mark the Thresholds, Celebrate the Milestones
- Branch 23: Declare Your Identity
- Branch 24: Create from Truth

This is where everything comes together. Not just internally, but visibly and tangibly. In the way you walk into a room. In the words you speak. In the project you build, the art you make, the boundaries you hold, and the life you choose to lead from now on.

Here, we reclaim rest. We restore rhythm. We remember the medicine of nature: not just as somewhere to visit, but as a place to return to inside ourselves. This is the ground all growth stands on.

Trunk 6 is the integration of your entire journey. It's where the transformation you've cultivated in your nervous system radiates through your expression.

This Trunk is about expressing who you already are and always were underneath the noise.

Healing isn't complete until it shows up in your actions. Empowerment doesn't land until it shapes your days. Alignment doesn't matter until it becomes embodiment. This is where the inner work becomes outer reality.

Here, you no longer live just for yourself. You become a gift. Your grounded presence is medicine for the room. Your truth becomes permission for others. Your visibility is leadership; not performative, not strategic, but sacred, fully felt, and completely yours. This is the part of your heroes journey where you bring your gifts back to the village.

This is the power of Trunk Six: You are a living transmission of your values. You no longer need to shout to be heard. Your life speaks for itself.

The four branches of this trunk will guide you to:

- Rest and replenish your nervous system so your body can hold your expansion.
- Mark the thresholds of change so your system knows what's real.
- Update your identity so it matches your transformation.
- Create from truth, so what you offer the world is congruent with who you are.

You are not who you were when you began this book. You don't have to hustle for your healing anymore. You are allowed to celebrate your greatness. Let it bloom.

Branch 21: Rest, Detox, Movement, and Nature

By now, you've done the hard things. You've faced your stories. You've remembered who you are. You've built resilience, taken bold action, and anchored in a deeper self. It's time to integrate.

You cannot stay rooted if you're always rising. Strength isn't just about what you push through. It's about knowing when to soften, when to pause, when to return. This branch is not about retreat – it's about rhythm. A regulated nervous system isn't built on constant output. It's built on cycles: effort, release, integration. Without recovery, you're not getting stronger, you're just surviving.

Rest is resistance

Rest is resistance to a world that prizes productivity over presence, control over connection, and burnout over balance. In a system built to reward constant striving, rest is a radical reclamation of self. It says: I am not a machine. I do not exist to produce, prove, or perform. I am worthy without output. I am enough, even in stillness. Choosing rest disrupts the trance of hustle culture. It confronts the deep conditioning that says your value comes from how hard you push.

Especially for those socialized; or innately wired, to caretake, accommodate, or over-deliver, rest is not indulgent. It's necessary. It's how we remember a rhythm older than earning, older than extraction, older than fear. It's how we return to a life led from aliveness, not accomplishment.

Many high performers avoid rest out of fear what they'll feel when they finally slow down. When an athlete stops training the aches and pains come out to heal. The silence of non doing can feel loud. The stillness stirs what's been numbed.

The feelings are not dangerous. They're information.

Beneath the surface is a far deeper fear: That rest will cost them. If they pause, they'll fall behind; financially, socially, professionally. Someone else will sprint ahead, win the race, get the prize. Resting feels like surrendering momentum, visibility, or drive.

This is productivity propaganda. Rest doesn't mean you stop rising. It means you rise rooted. When you stay with it, you not only recover but also transform. Rest lets the work land. It's where the wiring you've installed becomes embodied truth.

Movement

Resting doesn't mean collapsing into stillness. It's about active restoration. Your body was made to move. Not to burn out. Not to punish. But to regulate, renew, and rejoice. Whether it's dancing, climbing, walking, yoga, swimming, or swaying barefoot in your kitchen; Movement metabolizes stress. It moves emotion. It restores rhythm. It invites joy.

Movement doesn't have to be intense to be powerful. But it must be embodied.

Nature doesn't rush. The tree isn't trying to impress the sky. The river doesn't need a plan. And yet, everything is in motion. Everything belongs. Nature holds a mirror to your nervous system. It whispers: You don't have to carry it all. You're part of a web that can hold you too. Let yourself be held. Not because you've earned it. But because you're alive.

As a child, I didn't know the word "regulation," but I lived it. Barefoot in the Polish woods, with a basket of mushrooms in hand, there were no goals, no grades, no gold stars. No praise for performance. The forest accepted me without demand. It didn't ask me to prove, hustle, or become. It just let me be. That was my first experience of safe presence in my body. That kind of rest is sacred.

Story: *Summer in the Clearing*

Our forest summers were untamed and timeless. Summer felt like a whole year stretched open before us. My grandparents had a rickety old cabin in the Mazovian woods, tucked at the edge of a wide meadow.

From the summer solstice on, my cousins and I lived there full-time. The adults came and went, but we stayed rooted in the rhythm of the forest, mostly under our grandparents' care. Running barefoot, wild and sunburnt, our bodies thick with mosquito bites and joy.

Each morning began with a pilgrimage along the sandy beaten road to fetch fresh milk from the nearby farmers. Their cows fed the entire summer colony. The smell of their kitchens; woodsmoke, potato skins, damp cellar, clung to our clothes. We returned slowly, distracted by cloud shapes and stick-duels. Time was a river with no banks.

One summer, Grandpa Leszek decided to renovate the cabin by tearing off the roof. Just as the upstairs lay wide open to the sky, the biggest storm of the decade rolled in. My crib, tucked under an overhead cabinet, was the only dry spot in the house. I woke to thunder and water pouring through the rafters.

I don't remember the chaos, just the calm. I woke up warm and safe in the cow milking farmers' heavy metal-framed bed, curled up under wool blankets beside my three cousins.

The adults must have been scrambling till dawn; but for us, it was a magical night, when the house got a shower.

We played hard and free, mostly unsupervised. We biked dusty backroads, climbed pine trees, made theatre with handmade costumes, and dammed creeks with muddy fists. That movement was our medicine. It shook out the stress, the noise, the residue of a world we carried in our DNA, but didn't yet understand.

Each evening, our play turned ritualistic. We circled in the sand to play "Pif-ko pshe-cif-ko," our homemade game of world war and restoration. Each kid picked a country. Someone would declare war and throw the stick. We scattered. The chosen country retrieved the stick, and used it to redraw the world in the sand: invading, defending, sometimes being overtaken.

We had no idea how close we were to our country's recent past. Poland had been partitioned, occupied, renamed, and redrawn within our grandparents' lifetime. And here we were, taking turns invading each other in a game that somehow soothed us.

What stuns me now, trying to replay it as an adult, is how attuned we were. No one threw the stick too hard. We only took as much land as we sensed the other could handle. It was primal. Organic. Intuitive. The rules evolved as we did. Somewhere deep down, we were working through something.

Only now do I understand: We were releasing trauma. Regulating by instinct. Rehearsing healing of ancestral wounds. We were composting inherited chaos. Shaking off generations of fear with laughter. Cycling tension out of our bodies with sprints through the trees.

Most of the time we were doing sweet nothing. Resting before we knew what burnout was. Detoxing before we had words for overstimulation. Resetting our nervous systems before we even knew we had them.

Pause & Reflect

- Where did I learn that resting is unsafe, or that motion must always be productive?
- Can I let my body tell me when it's time to pause; not just my calendar?
- What would change if I trusted that my worth doesn't increase with output?
- What happens when I choose presence, not to fix myself, but to be with myself?
- What feels different when I spend time in nature honoring every living being?

Rooted in the Wild

Rest, Detox, and Movement find their deepest expression in Nature.

Detox isn't just about sugar or screens. It's about stepping away from the inputs that spike your nervous system: people-pleasing, urgency, overstimulation, comparison loops, and the pressure to always be "on."

True detox is remembering: you don't have to perform your worth. You already are worthy.

When we look at natural cycles, we see night and day, summer and winter, life and death. To thrive as a living being, it's essential to weave these natural rhythms into our own lives.

Nature is more than a backdrop, it's an active participant in your regulation. Research shows that even 20 minutes outdoors can lower cortisol, reduce blood pressure, improve immune function, and boost mood. Natural light recalibrates your circadian rhythm. The patterns in leaves, waves, and clouds activate the brain's default mode network, the same network engaged in meditation, allowing your mind to rest and reset.

Nature is where all three meet: where movement restores rather than depletes, where rest is effortless, and where detox happens without force. In nature, you're reminded through every sense that you belong to something bigger. The ground holds you. The wind carries your breath. The horizon widens your vision. You return calmer, clearer, rested, and reconnected.

For deep rest, allow unscheduled time that involves movement in nature, preferably daily and without digital distractions.

Anchoring Insights

- Recovery is non-negotiable. It's not a reward; it's a required phase of growth.
- Movement is restoration. It regulates, rewires, and reclaims your aliveness.
- Detox includes everything that overwhelms your system; food, people, apps, and thoughts.
- Nature restores what the world drains. Let it remind you that you're already whole.
- Rest is a portal, not a pause. It deepens everything you've built.

Exploration 21: The Micro-Rest Challenge

Choose one small, intentional act of restoration for tomorrow. Not to fix yourself, but to come home to yourself. Ask:

- What is subtly draining me right now?
- What gently restores me?
- What input can I clear?
- What nourishment can I invite?

Then choose one:

- A 30-minute walk outdoors with your phone on airplane mode.
- A meal with no screens, just your breath and your senses.
- 15 minutes of honest movement: stretch, sway, dance, or shake.
- An hour unplugged after sunset, letting night fall without interruption.
- 10 minutes lying on the ground, with nothing to do, nowhere to go.

Afterward, notice:
What shifted? What softened? What became clearer?

Branch 22: Mark the Thresholds, Celebrate the Milestones

You are doing the work, facing your patterns, making brave choices. You are doing everything right, but if you don't pause to mark this moment, your nervous system may never register the shift.

Change only anchors when it's seen, felt, and honored. Without ritual, you risk downplaying your growth and quietly slipping back into the old story.

Reclaiming Ritual

Modern adulthood offers only a handful of official ceremonies: baptism, graduation, marriage, baby shower, retirement, maybe an office holiday party. But where is the ritual for the moments that truly change you?

The breakup that split your heart open. The unbending vow to never abandon yourself again. The first time you chose truth over approval. The day you stopped apologizing for your power. The night you forgave yourself for staying too long.

These moments shape you, yet most pass without witness.

We were never taught to honor our own growth. So we rush on, downplay the change, and move to the next task. Change doesn't stick. Your body forgets, and your identity does too. Like a tall tree without deep roots, you might topple in the next storm.

You may call it what you want – a severance, a threshold, an incorporation, a sacred unbinding, or a rewilding of the soul. Without ritual, the memory of your alchemy fades. You may even question if the chrysalis ever cracked. If the wings were real. And slowly, the old story pulls you back.

Ritual Isn't Performance

A ritual marks a truth. It updates you and signals to the world: I am no longer who I was. I have crossed into something new. I am living from a different place now, whether my résumé reflects it or not.

This is about relationship, with yourself, with the land, with the truth trying to emerge through you.

My most sacred rituals are simple and quiet. In the desert, I gather juniper berries in my palm and give them love. When it feels right, I toss them into the open space whispering, "Root low. Grow high." When they land, I feel different. It reminds me who I am and what I belong to.

When I climb without a rope, I don't treat the rock as a backdrop for bravery. I ask for safe passage. I offer something first: picking up trash, collecting abandoned gear, wiping away spilled chalk. It is my way of saying: I am not only here to take. I am here to be together with all the living beings.

That act of care is my prayer. It grounds me in unity, humility, and love, a kind of safety no rope can give.

So honor your passages, enshrine them in your own myth. Make it untamed. Make it luminous.

The way to root transformation in your nervous system is to make it memorable. Memory consolidates when multiple senses are engaged, when your body moves, your hands create, your voice speaks. A fire's crackle, a river's chill, the scent of sage, these anchor the moment not just in your mind, but in your muscles and breath.

Celebration is how transformation becomes embodiment.

When the Land Joins Your Ceremony

Rituals are amplified in nature because the land itself participates. When you step into a forest, stand by a river, or feel the wind on a ridgeline, you are not just in a setting, you are in relationship. Every sound, scent, and texture becomes part of the ceremony.

Nature holds memory. The same way it records seasons in the rings of a tree or the layers of a canyon wall, it can hold the imprint of your symbolic actions. When you mark a threshold outdoors, casting something into the current, burying an object in the soil, speaking words into the wind, you're engaging a witness that has no agenda, only presence.

The natural world responds in ways that can't be scripted. A sudden gust of wind, the call of a bird, the shift of light through the trees, these moments often arise in uncanny alignment with the intention of the ritual. You could call it synchronicity, but it's simply the Earth joining in, adding her voice to your act.

In nature, your ritual becomes more than a personal statement. It becomes part of a larger cycle. You offer something to the earth, the water, the sky, and in return, you receive a sense of belonging, humility, and connection that can't be replicated indoors.

This is why so many ancient and indigenous traditions carried their ceremonies outside. The land doesn't just hold space for your transformation. It affirms it.

Story: *Returning the Ring to the River*

A year after the divorce, the ring still pulsed in her jewelry box, a small, silver sun with a spiral heart, holding the ghost of another life.

It wasn't just any ring. A close friend had crafted it, each line intentional. The spiral was her essence, the radiating rays her light. It had once been a talisman, a mirror of who she was. But now it belonged to the past.

Sandhya was already in love again, alive, aligned, full of promise. She could see herself marrying this man. Yet the ring lingered. A dead weight – tether to a life already shed.

One spring morning, her body decided for her. It was time.

She slipped the ring into the pocket of her bike shorts and set out on the same forest trails she used to ride with her ex. The path crunched beneath her tires. Pine and damp earth scented the air. Sunlight flashed between branches. With each turn, memories rose: laughter, shared adventures, lessons learned. No bitterness, only reverence for what had been.

She stopped to gather sage and lupine, their fragrance filling her hands. The trail carried her to the river, to the weathered bench where they had once spoken their vows.

let it fly from her palm. For a heartbeat, it spun in the sunlight: spiral, silver, green, before breaking the surface with a quiet splash. Ripples widened as the current took it.

In that moment, the weight left her hand and her chest. She let the river hold it. She let the river take it.

It was more than letting go of a relationship. It was a threshold, a declaration: I am no longer who I was.

She hadn't called it a ritual, but that's what it was: homemade, unpolished, true to her heart. A ceremony that honored the quiet courage of her own path. She hadn't waited for someone else to name the moment. She named it herself.

Sandhya's river offering carried all three phases of a rite of passage: the severance of releasing the ring, the threshold of pausing at the river's edge, and the incorporation of riding away lighter. This is how change takes root.

Pause & Reflect

- What object, memory, or symbol from your past still holds emotional weight, and what would it mean to release it?
- If you were to create a simple, personal ritual to mark a turning point in your life, where would it take place?
- What declaration about who you are now is waiting to be spoken out loud?

Anchoring Insights

- Change becomes muscle memory when it's celebrated.
- Celebration helps you embody your transformation.
- If you don't honor your growth, no one else will. Only you can feel what you feel. Honoring changes in your feeling is your job.
- Ritual doesn't need to be traditional. It needs to be authentic.

Exploration 22: Create a Threshold Ceremony for a Transition

You don't need to stage it, dress it up, or make it look like anything other than the truth. What matters is that it speaks to your soul. Let it be simple or symbolic, sacred or surprising. Alignment and presence matter more than perfection.

If ritual feels intimidating, start small. Here are some light, accessible ways to begin...

- Change something in your physical environment, a room, an altar, a piece of clothing, to reflect who you are becoming.
- Prepare a meal with intention, infusing it with gratitude for what you've learned and nourishment for the road ahead.
- Walk into the woods and speak aloud the name of the self you are releasing, then let the trees hold it.
- Write your old story on a piece of paper and burn it, bury it, or release it into flowing water.
- Invite one or two trusted friends to a small fire. Share what has changed in you, then offer something to the flames. Ask them to say: I witness you.

To deepen your practice, you can draw from the timeless framework of the School of Lost Borders, which describes three phases in any rite of passage: Severance, Threshold, and Incorporation.

1. Severance: Letting Go

Name what you are releasing, an old identity, a belief, a pattern that no longer fits.

- Write a letter to the part of yourself you're letting go. Offer gratitude, truth, and farewell.
- Create a symbolic object to represent what you're releasing. Burn it, bury it, leave it behind, or transform it into something new.
- Clear out a physical space. Let the outer mirror the inner.

Approach this phase not with shame, but with reverence for what brought you here.

2. Threshold: Embracing the In-Between

Step into the liminal space between no longer and not yet.

- Spend time alone in nature, letting the land mirror what words cannot.

- Fast or meditate to connect with your inner self.
- Paint, dance, weep, sing, let your body speak your truth.
- Sleep under the stars or rise before dawn. Mark time differently.

This phase isn't about knowing. It's about being with what is.

3. Incorporation: Returning with Wisdom

Bring the insights from your ceremony into your daily life.

- Share your experience with someone you trust, allowing them to witness your transformation.
- Declare a vow or commitment that reflects who you are now.
- Create a daily, weekly, or seasonal ritual that reminds you of your new identity.
- Mark the date. Name the passage. Speak it aloud.

Honor the threshold. Name what has changed. Celebrate not just the outcome, but the courage it took to get here. This is how transformation becomes identity. This is how you carry the medicine forward. Whether your ritual is a quiet moment by a tree or a shared gathering with loved ones, what matters is the meaning you pour into it.

Let this not be an ending, but a beginning. A spiral path home to yourself. A vow whispered to the living field: I am here, I am changed, and now the land knows too.

You've marked the moment. You've let the land witness your becoming. The ritual has sealed the change in your body. Now comes the next step: living from this place. Ceremony roots the truth in your bones, but identity gives it language. Without words to match your evolution, the old names and patterns will quietly reclaim you. This is where you claim the self who will walk forward from here.

Branch 23: Update Your Identity

By now, you listen to your body instead of outsourcing the truth. You've tended your ground and built a resilient nervous system. You respect yourself, with clear boundaries, deep self-forgiveness, and the courage to act. You've transmuted your challenges into power. You've taken bold, aligned steps in the world that match your truth.

You are not who you were when you began. The way you speak, decide, and stand in a room has changed. You carry yourself differently now. But unless you acknowledge the crossing, the old story may quietly reclaim you.

Here's the catch: If your self-image hasn't caught up with your growth, it will undermine that growth. You may have done the deep work, but if you still call yourself a people-pleaser, an imposter, a perfectionist, or "too much", your nervous system will keep trying to organize your life around those outdated labels. You'll shrink to fit a life that no longer fits you.

This branch is where your identity catches up to your evolution. Where you begin to see, speak, and walk as the person who lives everything you've learned. Updating your identity is a necessary step on your path to limitless. It's the crossing from surviving as who you were into living as who were always meant to be.

Let the True You Lead

Old patterns speak in scarcity and self-protection. They say: What will they think? If I don't fix this, I'll lose love. Your True Self speaks in freedom and clarity. It asks: What's real right now? What choice feels true, even if I'm scared? The difference is everything. Gut-check: Is this decision coming from fear or freedom? Habit or truth?

Rewrite the Story of Who You Are

Your identity is not fixed. It was shaped by survival strategies, cultural conditioning, and early experiences. By the parts of you that were praised, and the parts that were shut down. You don't need to hate those layers. Just don't keep wearing them. Un-stitch what no longer serves. Reclaim what got buried. It's like swapping the nameplate on the door to your own mind. Every time you speak about yourself, you're either engraving the old title deeper or installing the new one. Start with curiosity:

- What do I believe about myself when I fail? When I rest? When I succeed?
- Who might I be without that belief?
- What part of me had to go silent to survive?

You can't rewrite your identity in CRASH, when your system is reactive and closed. Identity shift happens in COACH, when you're calm, connected, and open to new truth. Remember, it's not an affirmation, it's a declaration. Your identity is not a brand to manage. It's an ecosystem to tend. Let outdated names compost. Let new ones bloom in their place.

Story: *The Unshrinking of Holly*

Holly wore perfection like shapewear; tight, restrictive, and one deep breath away from a breakdown. She smiled like it was her full-time job, agreed with everyone (even when they were wrong), and made life easier for everyone but herself.

Raised in a family fluent in addiction and denial, Holly got the memo early: Don't be a problem. Be a placemat. So, she folded herself into the role of a peacekeeper. No needs. No noise. No mess. Just helpful, competent, and quietly simmering inside.

But emotional suppression isn't a long-term wellness strategy. She slow-cooked for decades on low heat. Until one day, she realized: "Wait, I'm not a fixer. I'm a person."

Coaching woke her up. She stopped treating her feelings like spam email and actually opened a few. Turns out, the shame, guilt, and buried fury she'd been avoiding weren't flaws. They were flags.

Her body waving the white one; begging her to come back home. And she did. Not all at once. Not with a dramatic life overhaul. But in tiny, radical ways: Saying no without an apology. Resting without guilt. Telling the truth without checking if it makes her likable.

Now? Holly doesn't contort herself to keep the peace. She doesn't smile through resentment. She's still kind; but not at her own expense. She no longer needs to be good to be worthy. She no longer needs to be easy to be loved.

Holly is whole. Spacious. Sovereign. And so are you, when you stop living as a paper doll version of yourself.

Pause & Reflect

- How are you speaking about yourself lately? What story are your words reinforcing?
- Are you offering the world the person you are, or the one you've outgrown?
- What would change if you stopped arguing for your old limitations?
- What would become possible if you let your new identity lead?

Live as the New You

The real test comes next: Will you show up as the person you've become?
- Serve from overflow, not obligation. Ask: Does this drain me or light me up?
- Express what's inside. Speak, write, build, dance. Not to perform, but to stay in alignment.
- Let your presence be the impact. Enter a room fully regulated and watch it shift.
- Lead from your values. Make every choice a reflection of: Does this align or betray?
- The people who need you won't find you if you're still hiding behind who you used to be.

Remember: Return is the Measure, Not Perfection

You will still CRASH. You will still forget. That's human. The difference now is you know how to come back and choose to do it. You recover with speed and self-compassion. You treat every wobble as a window. You stretch your capacity. You model repair instead of shame. And you keep walking.

Even in your hardest moments, remind yourself:
- I always find my way home.
- I know who I am, even when I forget.
- My nervous system is wise. I trust its rhythm.
- This moment belongs to the new me.
- I am no longer in the shape of my survival.
- This choice comes from freedom, not fear.

This is not about striving, it's about matching your life to your deeper truth. Matching your language to your liberation. Matching your presence to the path you've walked. You've done the work. Now let your identity reflect it.

This isn't self-improvement. It's self-remembrance. The truth of who you are was never broken, only buried. Let this be the moment your breath, your body, and your beliefs finally align.

Anchoring Insights

- Return, not perfection, is the real metric of maturity.
- Identity evolves with practice. If the label stays small, life shrinks to fit.
- True Self leads when choices come from freedom, not fear.
- Rewiring happens in COACH, not CRASH. Install new truths when you're regulated.
- Visibility, service, and expression are the proving grounds of your new story.

Exploration 23: Declare Your New Identity

This is a distilled version of Steve Hardison's identity document practice, and you've already done half the work. In Exploration 10, you named false beliefs and forgave yourself for carrying them.

Now it's time to name the truth, a reclamation, a homecoming to self, and a deliberate shaping of the ground you already stand on, claiming what your Higher Self has always known and shaping your identity in any way you choose.

Here's how to write your own living, breathing declaration.

Step 1: Revisit what you wrote in Exploration 10

Return to the old beliefs you forgave:
- I forgive myself for judging myself as lazy.
- I forgive myself for judging myself as someone who always messes up.
- I forgive myself for judging myself as not good enough.
- I forgive myself for judging myself as not belonging.
- I forgive myself for judging myself as someone who can't be trusted.

Step 2: Write the Truth

Turn each judgement into an identity statement: words to live by. Write them as who you are now. Let them be bold grounded, and so honest they move you to tears.

- Stillness is strength. My pause is powerful. Rest is holy; I owe no proof.
- I walk forward, my every breath an act of courage. Each step is mine, and that is perfection.
- I am worthy. No one gets to vote on my value. I exist; and that is proof.
- I belong, because I am. I carry home in my bones. I am never outside of it.
- I trust myself; even in the dark, even when I shake. My hands know the way. I am held.

Let your words be a mirror of your soul, not a marketing pitch. No "shoulds," no performance. Just truth.

Step 3: Make it your Document

Create your own identity document. Title it something that resonates: "Who I Am Now" or "My Self-Declaration." Include all the identity truths you've uncovered through this journey. Memorize it. Read it out loud. Daily if you can. Especially when the old voices creep back in.

This is your new baseline. This is your reminder. You've done the work. Now choose the language that matches. This isn't just change. This is the naming of your next self. Let it be said. Let it be lived. Let it be known.

Branch 24: Create from Truth

You've made it to the final branch, the place where all your inner work becomes something the world can touch. This is the moment to create, not from lack, proving, or performance, but from the wholeness you've fought to reclaim. You stayed with yourself. You said yes, again and again, not just to reading, but to remembering. To telling the truth, facing the mirror, unraveling old stories, and reclaiming your place in the world.

You didn't just consume information. You metabolized it. You walked with it. You traced it through your nervous system. You faced roots and shadows, and cracked yourself open to deeper self-trust. That's not light work. That's soul work.

At this threshold, the invitation is no longer to simply know yourself or tend your ground. It is to shape something true from it. This branch is where integration becomes expression. Where your healing takes form. Where your soul finds shape.

Let your growth give birth to something tangible: an art piece, a project, a movement, a business, a vow, an offering. You have journeyed far, from the hollow echoes of old wounds to the luminous architecture of your being. You remember your wildness. Your worth. Your wholeness. And now, you create from that.

The Final Act Is the Offering

In the mythic arc of transformation, this is the next step: the offering. The soul doesn't heal just for itself. It heals to serve. In Bill Plotkin's language, this is the shift from ego-centered living to soul-centric service. The adolescent matures not through age, but through integration; through purpose, presence, and contribution.

To become an adult in the deepest sense is not simply to age, but to awaken. To become a vessel for the unique gift only you can bring. When you do the deep work, your life blossoms, and you begin to live from the highest expression of your soul.

Think of a teacher with a difficult childhood incorporating trauma-informed care, a neighbor from a food desert planting a community garden, an artist releasing a deeply personal piece about her struggles and growth.

On your heroes journey you descended into the depths, transmuted shadow into gold, and are now returning with medicine for the village. Who you are is going to change everyone around you.

Creation as Mirror

In this process, some of you may become rich or well-known, but that is not the goal of this work. The deeper aim is to become real, to live and create in resonance with who you truly are. Whether you're an artist, healer, teacher, builder, poet, or guide, let your being shape something beautiful.

Everything you create from truth becomes a teacher. Your book teaches you. Your painting heals you. Your offering expands you. Creation is not a finish line, but a mirror. Let it reflect and refine you.

For me, writing this book has been a journey of self-witnessing. In revisiting stories long past, the ones that once defined me, I met them with the consciousness I have now. I saw them in a completely new light, as entry points back to myself. In telling them again, I rewrote myself: not only as powerful, but as limitless. The shift was not subtle. My identity upgraded in ways that felt undeniable and irreversible.

Let your hands make visible what your heart has learned. Let your voice carry the song that's been gestating in silence. Let your project, your art, your offering be a mirror, a testament to what becomes possible when someone chooses transformation. It's a precious gift for the world.

Soul Signal, Not Strategy

When you create from truth, you don't have to chase resonance; it finds you. Your words, your work, and your presence carry a frequency that only emerges from lived authenticity. That's what magnetism really is. Not strategy, but soul signal.

You are the observer, the architect, the alchemist. The life you shape now is not reaction. It is resonance. Let what has healed become what now creates. You no longer need validation or applause from outside, you know how to give it to yourself. You create because truth longs to take shape. And your lived, earned, sacred truth is needed in this world.

Your offering; however humble, becomes part of the living archive of remembrance. A prayer made visible. A seed planted in the collective field. Long after the applause fades, your truth will ripple forward as medicine in someone else's storm.

The branch doesn't stretch toward fruit without rooting deep first. And now; it's time. Time to give shape to the silence. Time to weave your resonance into the fabric of the world.

You don't owe your soul to the algorithm. Visibility isn't vulnerability without discernment. You choose what to share. When and with whom. Sharing in sovereignty.

May your hands become holy. May your voice ring clear. May your truth take form. And may that form ripple healing into the world.

Story: *The Poetry of Returning*

Kelly once wrote grants for nonprofits. She was meticulous, impactful, and invisible. She knew how to weave urgency into numbers and compassion into metrics. But over time, the very invisibility that made her good at her job became a kind of erosion.

Her voice faded behind the cause. Her days blurred with giving. She became spiritually homesick; longing not for meaning she could measure, but meaning she could feel.

One day she joined a poetry challenge: a poem a day for thirty days. She didn't think it would change her life. It was just a pause; a small rebellion of beauty in the margins. But something ancient stirred.

Each morning, before the world could ask her to be efficient, she sat down to write. Not to be read or liked. But to hear herself again. Some days, she had only ten spare minutes.

She stood in the kitchen, torn between breakfast, movement, and the blank page. And every time, she chose poetry. She chose what made her time feel sacred. In those few lines, she turned pain into pattern, and grief into grace. She shaped her story into something she could love.

It wasn't just catharsis or communion. Writing became a form of intimacy; with her own becoming. With the contradictions she used to fear. With the hard-won truths she now held with tenderness.

On paper, she told the truth she didn't yet understand. She let sorrow teach her softness. She let mistakes become metaphors. She let poetry become her mirror and her compass.

When Kelly writes, she remembers who she is, what she values, and how much love it takes to face the world with an open heart. Her poems don't rescue or solve.

They reveal. And in that revealing, they heal anyone who reads.

Pause & Reflect

- When was the last time you created something purely to feel yourself again?
- What truth in you is longing to take form?
- Where are you still trying to earn worth instead of expressing from it?
- If you trusted your voice was needed, what would you create next?

Anchoring Insights

- Creation is not performance; it's presence made visible.
- When truth is integrated, it longs to take form.
- Your offering is not about being seen, it's about being sourced.
- Art is what your soul remembers through your hands.
- Resonance, not strategy, is the real magnetism.

Exploration 24: Bring It to Life

Choose one tangible way for your truth to take form.
Not someday, now.
Let it be a letter, a dance, a retreat you design, a business you launch, a garden you plant, or a mural you paint in a forgotten alley. Big or small, it doesn't matter. What matters is that it's yours, and it's real.

Name it. Commit to it. Put it on the calendar. Break it into steps and start the first one today. Let the plan live on paper so it can breathe into the world.

Your truth has waited long enough. Give it shape. Give it roots. Let it be born.

Bonus Branch 25: Make it Mutual – The Art of Conscious Agreements

If Branch 24 reminded you that your truth wants form, Branch 25 will help you give it structure. Because when you're creating with others, structure isn't the opposite of freedom, it's what protects it. Without it, expression scatters and old patterns creep back in. The heart of it: expectations drain, agreements sustain.

Why Expectations Break Us

There are two ways to navigate relationships with others: through expectations or through agreements. The purpose of expectations is simple, to know who gets the blame when things don't turn out. The purpose of agreements is to get the job done. Expectations are mostly shaped by fear, habit, or upbringing. They sound like:

- You let me down again.
- I assumed you'd know.
- I thought we were on the same page.
- Why do I always have to say something?

We usually notice an expectation only when it's violated, and then our anger flares. Most of the time, we never actually state what we would like, so it's unrealistic to expect someone to honor it. Unspoken expectations are silent saboteurs; they breed resentment, confusion, and collapse.

What Makes an Agreement Work

A real agreement isn't a forced compromise. It's not giving in to keep the peace. It's two people saying: "Here's what I want. Here's what you want. Now let's find where those truths meet."

Agreements aren't about control; they're about clarity and care. A clean, powerful agreement includes:

- **Clarity**: What are we actually agreeing to? Spell it out.
- **Consent**: Do we both want this? Can we both be content with it, even if there's compromise?
- **Feasibility**: Can each person follow through with integrity?
- **Timeline**: By when? How often?

- **Check-in:** When will we revisit or revise?
- **Repair Plan:** What's our plan when we're out of agreement?

If even one of these is missing, you're back in murky water, swimming in assumptions, disappointments, and silent scorekeeping.

Agreements are not about good or bad; they're about functionality. No one person can be blamed. If an agreement isn't honored, all parties are simply out of agreement. The only step then is to acknowledge it and decide what to do next.

Story: *The Agreement That Changed Our Zoom Room*

My cousins (the ones from Huckleberry Woods) and I have a cherished Zoom ritual once a month. It is semi-chaotic, sometimes tearful, always soul-filling. For a while, one cousin was chronically late. If tardiness were an Olympic sport, she'd be draped in gold.

For her, it was evening: kids asleep, tea steeping, serenity. For me, it was Tuesday morning, prime coaching hours. I sat waiting, toggling between She's probably finishing something up and I should catapult this laptop into space. A telltale sign of having expectations.

At first, I let it slide. I'm "flexible," right? (Translation: I swallowed it. I abandoned my needs to keep the peace.) Eventually, I realized I wasn't mad at her, I was mad at me for never naming what I needed.

So, I finally said: "I treasure this call. I block work hours to be here on time. If you want to meet, arrive on time. Otherwise, I'm not interested."

She gave her usual mix of excuses: ADHD, laundry, and "time is a construct." Another cousin, our gentle peacekeeper, offered a solution: "What if I call you five minutes before?" We agreed. And you know what? It worked.

Nobody had to change who they were. We simply made a clear agreement. And that single act of clarity restored the joy to our calls.

Pause & Reflect

- Where are you expecting someone to do something they never actually agreed to?
- What agreement would bring clarity, relief, or repair?
- Where do you blame others for not doing what they were "supposed to" do?
- What have you been silently tolerating that a simple agreement could resolve?

Where This Shows Up

You can create agreements in any relationship:

- Romantic: "If we fight, let's check in within 24 hours."
- Business: "If either of us feels tension, we'll name it before it festers."
- Friendships: "Let's be honest about how often we actually want to connect."

Agreements are not about perfection. They are about sitting down and sketching out what this thing we're creating together will look like. Agreements are a powerful tool for building trust.

Agreements aren't just "good communication", they're liberation. They replace assumption with agency. They turn confusion into clarity. They transform relationships into mutual havens.

You want your life to work? Practice integrity. You want your relationships to work? Practice agreements. They're two sides of the same sacred coin. Let people know how to win with you. Don't leave them guessing. Don't leave yourself abandoned. Make it mutual. Make it clear. Make it an agreement.

Anchoring Insights

- Expectations live in silence. Agreements live in truth.
- Resentment is the receipt of an unspoken, unmet expectation.
- Real agreements are co-created, clear, and revisitable.
- Integrity becomes relational through agreements.

Exploration 25: Upgrade One Expectation to an Agreement

1. Identify a place where you feel frustrated or let down.
2. Ask yourself: What expectation am I holding?
3. Clarify: What do I actually want? What outcome would feel good and clear?
4. Approach the other person with curiosity and sovereignty:
    - "Can we make a clear agreement about this?"
    - "Here's what I realize I need. What's true for you?"
    - "I want us both to feel good about what we commit to."
5. Co-create the new agreement and document it, even if it's just a shared message, voice note, or calendar entry. Make sure it's mutual, specific, and time-bound.

Living Compass: Trunk 6 Summary: Expression

Integration, Celebration, Visibility

Core Distinctions

- **Integration vs. inertia:** Growth requires space to land, not constant motion.
- **Ritual vs. routine:** Marks the shift from change to identity.
- **Identity vs. role:** Must evolve with your truth or it defaults to the past.
- **Agreements vs. expectations:** Co-created clarity replaces silent resentment.

Core Practices

- **Honor nervous system rhythm:** Work, rest, and restore in cycles.
- **Mark thresholds:** Use Severance, Threshold, and Incorporation to seal transformation.
- **Update identity out loud:** Speak the truth of who you've become.
- **Create from soul signal:** Let truth; not performance, guide expression.
- **Make conscious agreements:** Protect your time, energy, and relationships with clarity.

Key Tools

- **Work-play_rest rhythm:** Design a weekly schedule that honors your capacity and prevents burnout.
- **Rites of passage:** Create personal ceremonies to mark growth, closure, or new beginnings.
- **Identity declaration:** Turn old self-judgments into bold, embodied truth statements.
- **Creative alignment:** Ensure your projects reflect your current values, energy, and purpose.
- **Create conscious agreement:** Co-create clear, mutual commitments in personal or professional relationships.

Guiding Truth

Expression is the final stage of integration. Transformation lives through how you speak, create, and show up.

Your Wake-up Call

Many do the work, face the past, learn to communicate, build resilience, shift habits, speak new truths. Yet even after all that, something still feels off. The outer life hasn't caught up to the inner growth. The transformation happens inside, but the calendar, the language, the boundaries, the art, the presence still echo an outdated self.

This is the final disconnection, subtle but costly. Even after the healing, doubt creeps in. You wonder if anything really changed. You forget to celebrate, hesitate to speak, downplay your power, and quietly shrink. Without conscious updates, you don't rise to your vision; you default to old nervous system conditioning.

This is your wake-up call, not to push harder, but to cross a threshold. That longing to be seen, to feel whole, to create from truth isn't vanity; it's your soul saying: The world needs you fully alive.

You don't have to start over. You simply have to let the life you've built reflect the self you've become. No permission required. No perfection necessary. No waiting for fear to vanish.

Integration doesn't happen in the mind, it happens in the mirror, in the ritual, in the creation, in the choice to be visible. This is the moment your whole life changes for good, because you decide it does.

You are no longer who you were. Now let your life speak it. Let your story shine. Create your masterpiece. Live in the harmony you've become.

Create from truth. The world is waiting. Don't go back to sleep.

Part 3:
Fruits & Flowers

Part 3: Fruits & Flowers

This is what we fantasize about: the turning point. The moment it all makes sense. Proof that the struggle wasn't wasted, the pain wasn't pointless, the path wasn't in vain.

But here's the truth not many dare to see: a flower blooms only because its roots dared to reach into the dark. Growth takes both sunlight and decay. And fruit? Fruit doesn't ripen on command. It ripens in the chaos. It ripens in the waiting. Yours ripens through the slow, faithful choices you make when no one is watching.

This last part is not the finish line. It isn't about perfection or arrival. It's an expression; the part where what's been growing inside you finally blossoms into the world.

The stories you're about to read aren't rewards for getting it right. They are proof of what becomes possible when you stop pretending, start listening, and choose to act in alignment with who you really are.

They reveal what blooms when you honor your roots, stand in your power, and take full responsibility for how you meet life. They show the kind of fruit that grows when you stop trying to be someone else and finally embody your wholeness, no filter, no apology.

This is where self-trust deepens. Where grit gives way to grace. Where intimacy with life; messy, tender, beautiful life, becomes the reward.

How to Read This Section

Read these stories not just as inspiration, but as evidence. As maps, mirrors, and reminders that if I can bloom from bankruptcy, heartbreak, shame, near-death, and decades of disappearing, so can you.

As you read, pay attention to your body. What stirs an ache in you? What makes you want to cry? Where do you flinch, itch, soften, or open? That's your cue. These are not just stories. They are frequencies. If you feel yourself resonating; if something inside you stirs, the field is working. We are co-tuning reality, one breath, one bold yes at a time.

Don't rush. Don't skim past the discomfort. The moment you think, I could never do that, might be the exact moment life will invite you to take a shot.

The fruit might look like a stack of cash, a long-awaited summit, or simply a day when you gave everything you had; especially when you thought you had nothing left. It's never easy, rarely loud or obvious. Sometimes the most radiant blooms grow from confusion and despair.

Let these stories remind you: you're not behind, not broken, and not too late. You are in the process. Maybe your bloom is slower than you wanted. Maybe you bloom in ways no one else sees yet. But if the roots are reaching, the fruit is forming.

And if you keep choosing yourself, especially when it's hard, especially when it's lonely, you won't just change your life. You'll change the field.

So read closely. Let it provoke you. Let it pull you. Let it dare you.

Because the bloom isn't out there. It's already in you.

Don't just read. Step in.

Fruit 1: The Universal Thumb
Lake Tahoe, California 2001

Sometimes "fruit" looks like freezing halfway up a mountain on the far edge of the world. Sometimes it looks like a hungover man in a black sports car, bloodshot eyes behind designer sunglasses.

Remember him from the start of the book? The man who pulled over one sunny Tahoe morning and gave me a ride to Squaw?

The wad of cash he handed me turned out to be four thousand dollars.

A miracle, a lucky break, maybe even God's intervention, money that cracked open the foundation of my life.

That solo South America trip I took later? Paid for largely by a stranger's belief in my dream.

At the time, I thought it was a wild stroke of luck. Now I know better. It wasn't luck. It was clarity. He gave it because I was clear.

When our words, choices, and energy align, when we stop apologizing for wanting something, the world listens. It throws us a Shaka.

That man didn't invest in me. He invested in the force of someone who had stopped asking for permission and was already in motion.

It wasn't the money that changed everything, though it helped a lot. The real lesson for me was the realization that the universe rewards courage and radical honesty. It meets you on the road. The path only appears once you start walking.

So dare to look foolish. Ask for rides with dust on your boots and conviction in your voice. Leap with your whole being and let the world catch you.

Clarity is power. Boldness is creation. And creation is magnetic.

This kind of clarity isn't constant, I don't live here all the time. But when I do, I win big. The flow fades, life complicates it, doubt creeps in. But every time I've found my way back, when I knew what I wanted and dared to ask for it, the magic returned.

Yes, the price is high. You might feel like a broke fool. You might thumb rides to a crappy gig for a while.

But it's worth it a hundred times over. Because the reward isn't just a check or a lift down the road, it's becoming the kind of person who keeps moving toward her vision in an uncertain world.

The one who risks showing herself. Who walks forward even when the map is missing and the destination is still a mystery.

And sometimes, when you follow the pull with nothing but trust in your heart, the reward isn't getting what you asked for. What you get instead is a pure and holy beauty of being fully, undeniably alive.

Fruit doesn't ripen by waiting. It ripens because you walked, across valleys and peaks, not knowing if you'd ever reach it, but moving anyway. Step by step, until the path revealed itself beneath your feet.

Uncertainty is the altar where magic gathers.
If you knew the ending, the journey would be just a stroll.

P.S.

Twenty-five years later, I told this story to inspire a client. At the time, I was helping fundraise for my little sister, who had just moved to Los Angeles from Warsaw to break into the film industry; a bold dream not unlike mine in Tahoe. A few days later, I opened my mailbox and found a check for four thousand dollars, along with a simple note: "I want to keep this tradition going."

I was overwhelmed by the beauty, the generosity, the echo of belief moving through time. The magic is both in the money and in the transmission of faith, passed from one bold dreamer to the next. My sister cried when I gave her the funds. Later, she wrote: "A stranger reminded me that kindness exists. It gave me the strength I needed to keep going, and confirmation that my dream is worth it."

What is Blooming in You Now?

You have a dream like this, too.
A vision so bold it feels too wild to voice
A whisper inside saying, "I'd do it… if only."
The road is listening. Speak your dream out loud.

Fruit 2: Aegialis Awakening
Kalymnos, Greece, 2017

Hanging from my fingertips high above the Aegean Sea, I moved; confident, committed, into the steepest part of the route. Every move felt marginal. If I fell here, I'd fall forever. My heart pounded. My limbs burned. And yet; I wasn't panicking, or even fighting. Just flowing. Total presence. Nothing else existed.

Trust and surrender, but never let go.

I had come to Kalymnos for a breakthrough. A small Greek island floating in the Aegean Sea, famous for its sweeping limestone caves, tufas and stalactites hanging like chandeliers from wildly overhung walls. The routes are long, exposed, powerful, and proud. Every angle is a postcard of bright azure sea and sculpted stone.

I arrived physically strong, mentally solid, and finally ready to step into something bolder as a climber.

No jackpot could hold a candle to what climbing gave me. Trade it for comfort? Fame? Certainty? Never.

Climbing gave me more than escape. It was a mirror that showed me who I was becoming, a medicine that kept me moving, and a map to find my way back to myself. It made me someone I could trust. Someone I could root for.

What began as a way to survive my monochrome teen prison became the very thing that brought my life full color. A homecoming to the self I had once buried and finally chose to reclaim.

Throughout my twenties, I was a volatile climber. Prone to explosive tantrums, self-loathing, and meltdowns whenever I hit a wall; literally, and figuratively. If I didn't send, I'd spiral. If I did, I'd downplay my performance through self-criticism, convinced I should have climbed it faster, better, with more ease. Then I would raise the stakes higher, trapping myself in a constant negative feedback loop. I'd rigged a losing game.

Eventually it became unbearable. So I coiled my ropes, moved to the tropical island of Hawaii, and adopted a new identity as a kitesurfer. A part of me still ached for stone, but I disregarded it, pushed it away, and tried to keep it silent.

After 10 years away from the vertical world, I decided to give climbing another shot. I told myself I was more mature now, that it was just a hobby. I'd stopped throwing tantrums, but I still wrestled with deep feelings of inadequacy.

I resumed handing over my leads, stuck to 5.11s, and became a solidly unremarkable climber, constantly in full nervous-system management mode. I wasn't chasing possibilities; I was managing risk. And I knew it.

After my divorce, I realized I didn't want to half-ass my life or my climbing anymore. I didn't want to keep outsourcing my courage to others. I wanted to try, for real, for myself. I wasn't here to conquer anything; I was here to reclaim my lead, on the wall, and in my life.

That's when I saw Aegialis.

Standing guard at the entrance to the Grande Grotta cave: It's the crown jewel of Kalymnos climbing. This colossal natural amphitheater adorned with massive tufas and king lines, is a three-dimensional playground for climbers; the epitome of what Kalymnos is all about.

And Aegialis… well it's one of the most iconic routes on the island; brilliantly steep, sculpted, and runout*. It's no surprise it graces the guidebook cover. It's the kind of line that makes climbers book a flight.

Standing at its base, staring upward, it scared the hell out of me. The first time I got on it, I didn't even pretend to try. I hangdogged* my way up it; resting at every bolt*, avoiding any real falls. The distance between the bolts felt massive; up to fifteen feet in places, meaning a possible fall of thirty to forty feet. I wasn't quite ready to fall that far. I came down, rattled and swore I wouldn't come back.

But I couldn't stop thinking about it.

I returned over and over. Each time, my body froze. My breath shortened. I hated how much it mattered to me. I hated how much I wanted to quit. But I kept showing up, its power and beauty holding me captive.

I rehearsed the moves, breathed through the fear, taught myself not to bail. I realized: this climb wasn't asking for more strength; it was asking for more trust.

Then, one crisp morning, I tied my figure-eight*, a knot I'd tied thousands of times before, but this one might have been my best yet. Calm and present, I started up the route, letting my body do what it had been practicing. My breath leading the way. Clipping the 5th bolt; the one with the biggest fall potential; I thought, *the universe loves me.* I moved with clarity, precision, and grace. The rock felt warm and waxy under my fingers. Gusts off the Aegean carried the scent of salt and wild rosemary.

When I clipped the anchors, there was no scream, no tears. Just stillness and a smile; ancient and whole; watching from within.

For years, I had chased climbs to feel worthy.
This time, I climbed because I already was.

Aegialis was the hardest climb I'd ever done, yet it felt easeful. It wasn't a physical breakthrough, it was a frequency upgrade. Surrender didn't teach me, it sang through me. The route I once avoided had became a portal into joy, flow, and self-trust. I'd broken the mold.

Aegialis was the doorway, and on that climb, I left the old story behind.

That's the fruit: Not just effort or grit, but the decision to come back when every defense says "quit" because an ancient part of you remembers: there's more.

For years, I'd climbed quietly, afraid to be too much. That day, above the Aegean, I didn't just take the sharp end; I bloomed. I wasn't climbing to belong, to escape, or to earn applause. I was climbing because I was finally willing to let the flower open.

A few days later, I watched a young climber named Timmy float up Aegialis onsight*. No falls. First try. I ran into him at the end of the season in a taverna in the village of Myrties, devouring souvlaki.

"Are you the guy who onsighted Aegialis?" I asked. "Aegialis? Where's that?" he said.

It hit me: what breaks you open might barely register for someone else. And that's okay. We're each playing a different game. It was never about the route. It was about who I became in the process of climbing it.

The prize wasn't the send; it was how I showed up: choosing presence over pressure, curiosity over control, joy over judgment.

What is Blooming in You Now?

You have a climb like this, too.
A challenge that mirrors your inner edge.
The shift is not in the final clip,
but in you choosing your joy.

Fruit 3: Knocking On 700 Doors
Warsaw, Poland, 2022

This is a story about you. About what becomes possible when we stop waiting to feel ready, perfect, or certain, and simply start knocking.

Hanna (my mom), grew up a sickly child frail, in and out of hospitals. Her body demanded caution before she ever had the chance to choose boldness. She was the younger sister, always trailing behind one who was wild, loud, and full of fire.

While her sister charged into the world, my mom disappeared; into books, into studying, into safety. Her intelligence became a safe harbor. If she didn't take up too much space, maybe she wouldn't get hurt. If she could just get everything right, maybe she'd finally feel safe.

Her disappearing act wasn't just personal, it was cultural. She came of age in 1950s communist Poland, where silence was survival. The system dictated what you could say, eat, and believe.

Her childhood was shaped by ration cards and the unblinking gaze of concrete proletariat heroes. Silent stone sentinels guarding a story Hanna never chose. The regime rewarded obedience and punished curiosity. In that environment, her quietness wasn't just a coping mechanism, it was the path of least danger.

She became invisible in the most respectable way possible: quiet, obedient, hardworking. Dissociation dressed up as discipline. Her strength wasn't loud; it was subtle, survival-born, wrapped in silence.

For most of her life, my mom lived inside a small, carefully constructed bubble. She raised two daughters, ran a one-woman graphic design studio, and stayed close to the safety of familiar routines. No big risks. No wild adventures. No public presence. A modest life, lived behind the scenes.

Her intellect was her gateway into the world; she read voraciously, was deeply educated, and quietly formidable. Her great spirit was never absent; it was imprisoned beneath a mask of modesty. Strength mistaken for smallness. Power camouflaged as politeness.

When my younger sister moved out and Hanna closed her physical office, her world shrank further. Some days she just stayed in bed. She read obsessively, binge-watched Netflix, tried new hobbies, but it all felt hollow.

She wanted to be of service, but when she reached out to volunteer at nonprofits, they told her, "thanks, but no thanks."

Then, the war in Ukraine began.

When you live in Poland, a war in Ukraine isn't a distant headline; it's at your doorstep. It's in your blood, your history, your DNA. For my mom and many others, it unearthed old wounds.

When Poland was invaded in 1939, marking the official start of WWII, the world looked away. In her bloodline lived the memory of that abandonment, and she knew, in an instant, she would never hand that fate to another.

She began by filling a bag with supplies and walking to the local school gym, which had become a donation drop-off point. Inside she found chaos: piles of bags, no system, no order.

The next day, she came to organize the bags. By the end of the week, she was running the entire operation. She created a system for accepting, sorting, and delivering supplies. She showed up every day; sometimes for fifteen hours; at sixty-seven years old.

As the needs grew, so did her leadership. She coordinated volunteers. Built supplier partnerships. Organized fundraisers. Met every challenge with creativity and grit. She didn't just wrangle chaos; she became the center of a movement that fed 500 Ukrainian refugees daily.

And in giving others relief, she started finding her own.

Hanna cried often; sometimes from despair, but more often the depth of human connection. She wept at the strength of the women she served, at the generosity of strangers, at how a fragmented community became a living, breathing circle of support.

Soon, she began thinking long-term. She launched a program to help Ukrainian women start small businesses: language classes, help navigating Polish bureaucracy, craft circles that sold handmade goods and raised funds for local causes.

She was no longer facilitating survival; she was fostering renewal, creativity, joy.

Her quiet efforts created ripples she never imagined. A family friend in Hawai'i, reluctant to give to faceless organizations, heard about what she was doing and donated enough money to fund the entire center for six more months.

All because she showed up; as herself.

She didn't stop there. When a seat opened on her local government council, she stepped up, and was unanimously voted in. One of the

optional responsibilities was collecting property taxes. Most council members outsourced it. Not Hanna. She saw it as a chance to connect; to meet her neighbors.

In just under two weeks, she personally visited seven hundred homes.

The one who once disappeared into books was now knocking on doors, asking questions, listening to stories, offering herself in service. She had once taught me to be careful, to not ask for too much. But here she was, knocking boldly. Not to be seen, but to see others.

Hanna had broken the cycle.

She told me that each door had its own scent: fresh varnish, cabbage soup; postcards from inside people's lives. When no one was home, she returned later.

When I asked her why she kept on doing it, she said: "I trust myself now. What will be will be. I can't force anything. I'm not perfect, and that's what makes everything easier. And I just feel better when I'm active."

Trusting herself and choosing to feel better is what allowed my 70-year-old mother to knock on 700 doors, sometimes twice, with heart and purpose. This was her fruit: fierce service, reclaimed agency, radiant visibility. No longer the quiet worker behind the scenes, she was a woman blooming in full light; a force for connection, dignity, and hope.

Her knock wasn't just a knock; it was also bloom. The unfurling of a woman who had once hidden, now showing up in motion. A walking flower. Not to be admired, but to witness others in their fullness. This wasn't the end of her story; it was her third act. The part where all the healing ripens into service. Where who you are becomes how you live.

The woman who said yes to something bigger than her doubt.
Who let service crack her open and give her back to herself.

This isn't just my mother's story, it's a cheatsheet. A reminder that reinvention doesn't require perfection. It requires showing up anyway, and letting life use you to love the world better.

What is Blooming in You Now?

You have a door like this, too.
A voice whispering, You're not needed.
But what if you were?
Knock. The truth will answer the door.

Fruit 4: Her Breakthrough Was My Shortcut
Rifle Mountain Park, Colorado, 2023

This is a story about a big climbing win, but it's not about climbing at all. It's about interconnectedness. Transmission. And the shortcuts we find through each other's courage.

Climbing has been everything to me. My way out of my gray country, my bridge to nature, my path to mastery, self-knowledge, and community. But even the thing I love most has its shadows.

Certain routes, like Beer Run, can spiral me into the old trap of tying my worth to my performance. Not only did you not climb well, but: You're a fraud. You don't belong here. You're fundamentally flawed. I know this pattern. I know how to tend to it. But it's still there, especially when I'm nearing my edge.

The harder I try, the more healing I require. Push too hard? I break. Don't push? I disappear.

This story is about one of those rare moments when someone else's courage carved me a shortcut. No mindset hacks. No journaling marathons. No striving. Just pure, radiant transmission.

I was facilitating a climbing outing for a small group. One young woman, Ady, a routesetter from a gym in New York, stood out; brilliant, skillful. She was also terrified. She told us up front she was fine just following, but leading? Too scary. Absolutely not.

There was a famous climber in the group; respected, well-known and Ady was drawn to her like sunlight. I paired them together. She didn't push Ady; she honored her sovereignty. But her presence held a kind of invitation. A mirror of what was possible. And Ady bloomed.

Inspired and challenged, she climbed like a different person: bold, free, alive.

And then she led a climb.

After years of telling herself she could never do it, she just… did. A quiet earthquake in her story. We all had tears in our eyes. This wasn't just a personal win; it was a deep identity transformation.

She left changed. And I knew she'd carry that transmission back to her gym, her people, her world. She cracked something massive open, and we all felt the ripple. Driving home, I was filled with joy; and something else: envy. The good kind. The kind that says, I want that feeling back. She reminded me of something I hadn't felt in years in my climbing: lightness, possibility.

After 25 years of climbing, my love was still deep, but the learning curve had flattened. Breakthroughs took more work, awe was harder won.

Her joy lit a fire in me.

The next day, I drove to Rifle Canyon and tied in for a climb I'd been working on for weeks. This time, I didn't bring grit or determination. I brought Ady's spirit: beginners mind, curious buoyancy. Chalk dust hung in the still canyon air, leaving a mineral tang on my tongue. I gave myself the same presence and encouragement I'd offered her.

Then something wild happened: I crushed my project.

The moves that had felt impossible just days before now felt effortless. My body moved with ease, joy and lightness, even on the moves I was normally maxed out on. Flow, not force. It wasn't me climbing; it was life, trying itself again through my limbs.

Most of my breakthroughs have come the hard way: Through storms, failure, grit. But this one? It arrived like a flower in bloom; unexpected, beautiful, shared.

Fruit is the reward of devotion.

But the flower? That's the beauty. The radiance. The part that touches others without trying.

Fruit can come from the long, slow climb through your own resistance. But sometimes, it arrives through someone else's liberation.

That's the power of this work. The healing doesn't just stay with us. It ripples. It travels faster than strategy because it's carried by presence. That's what it means to become fruit-bearing. That's what it means to be in bloom.

What is Blooming in You Now?

You have a spark like this, too.
A crack where the light gets in.
Your courage doesn't end with you.
It's contagious, it cannot be contained.

Fruit 5: High On The Ledge Of Love
El Chalten, Patagonia, Argentina, 2025

Sitting on a sloping ledge high on Cerro Chaltén (Fitz Roy), staring up at a sky drenched in stars, I finally understood something deeply true: Only Love Is Real.

But getting here? That was no small thing.

Months earlier, my client Molly and I had dreamed up an outrageous plan: a year-long mountain climbing and coaching journey to earn her Master's of Badassery. It was bold, audacious, thrilling. But as we mapped out the idea, one thing became clear: if I was asking Molly, who wasn't a mountaineer or even an athlete; to stretch beyond what she believed was possible, I had to do the same.

Fitz Roy came to mind straightaway. I'd seen it over two decades earlier during my solo trip to South America; a 6000 foot cathedral of vertical stone, windswept and dusted in snow. The native Tehuelche called it "Chaltén," the "smoking mountain," for the ever-present clouds that stream from its summit. Chaltén was what bold climbers dreamed of and dreaded.

That evening, my partner Steven pulled a guidebook off the bookshelf, "You know what I've always wanted to climb?" he asked, flipping through the pages. I already knew: Fitz Roy.

Synchronicities are shakas from the universe. Our plan was set.

We spent the rest of the year training as best we could; which was like jogging around the park to prep for the Leadville 100 ultramarathon. With training came fear. I'll never be able to do it. I'm too small. I'll die. I'll look stupid. I'll get wrinkles. Who do I think I am?

Fear doesn't just nag: it strikes.
And it always aims for the tenderest spots.

By fall, the epic tug-of-war between my goal and my fear felt like it might rip me in half. But this time time, I didn't shrink back. I leaned on the roots I'd grown: self-awareness, self-respect, courage. And I did something radical, for me: I asked for help; from mentors, friends, the people who see me clearly, who remind me of who I am when I forget.

I let myself lean. Asked without apologizing. And in doing so, discovered a different kind of wealth: not independence, but interdependence. The gift of being held when you can't hold yourself.

In the end I made it to Patagonia once again.

Now here I was: bundled up in eight layers, burrowed into my sleeping bag, precariously perched on the edge of a narrow snow-covered ledge, thousands of feet up Fitz Roy; reflecting on everything that had brought me here.

Everything I practiced; sitting with fear, asking for help, honoring my commitment; was being tested. This wasn't just a climb. It was the embodiment of my inner work. Up here, the I who wanted to prove disappeared. What remained was the pink purple sky, the most weathered granite in the world, and the silent joy of belonging to it all.

We'd arrived in El Chaltén four days earlier, right in the middle of a rare weather window. In Patagonia, clear skies don't last long. There wasn't a moment to lose. We exploded our gear across the floor of our tiny room. Meticulously going through each layer of clothing, every piece of equipment, every calorie of food. Forget a lighter, and you might lose the summit.

At dawn we loaded into a taxi and headed north to the Valle Del Río Eléctrico trailhead. Most climbers do the approach in a single brutal push. We opted to break it up into two days hoping to conserve energy.

Our objective: "Mate, Porro y Todo lo Demás," a 3000-foot route up the Pilar Goretta on Fitz Roy's north side, with another 1000 feet to the summit. It was a last minute decision, recommended by friends.

Two days of steep trails, unstable boulders, and rotten glaciers brought us to the northwest side of Fitz Roy The final stretch was 2,000 vertical feet of steep snow to the base of the pillar. The approach alone had taken a huge toll, and now we were staring up at our true ambition; an immense wall of cold, coarse granite, looming overhead, unyielding, and merciless.

But the sun was out, the wind was low, and for a fleeting moment, it all felt possible. We basked in that warmth, soaking in the stillness, letting our bodies settle before the challenge that lay ahead.

Early the next morning, in cold pre-dawn darkness, we slipped on stiff boots, strapped on icy crampons, and began kicking steps up the final few hundred feet of frozen snow to the start of the route. The air was sharp and perfectly still. Only the crunch of our boots and the rhythm of our breathing broke the silence.

As we reached the granite, sunlight spilled across the Cerro Torre range behind us, bathing it in a rich rose-gold alpenglow. I led the first pitches, weaving through a mix of rock, ice, and snow. The climbing funneled into a steep, continuous corner system that stretched impossibly skyward; a never-ending dihedral*.

The granite was solid and nearly vertical; physical, and sustained. It didn't take long to realize we'd made a serious mistake: climbing with our backpacks. The weight crushed our upward progress, the bulk snagging on every crystal, and every edge. Our progress was slow and inefficient.

We couldn't continue climbing like this. At the next belay, Steven dropped his pack and took the sharp end, leading pitch after pitch up the vertical ocean.

At each anchor, he resorted to the same grueling work-a-round, hauling his pack hand over hand with our tagline*, not ideal but it was all we had. His forearms cramped and screamed, but his determination was stronger than the alternative of going down.

High on the route we encountered a literal waterfall of snowmelt. We climbed through the icy torrent, dripping and shivering; still resolute but feeling the toll. A few pitches higher slumped at an anchor, Steven said, "I'm worked, it's your turn to take over." He was so cold, he could barely feel his hands.

I nodded, took the rack and kept leading. The sunlight faded, skewed behind the ice cap on the western horizon. Shadows lengthened. The wall loomed colder and darker. The final pitch to the bivy ledge was a cold, unforgiving chimney choked with snow, ice, and loose rock.

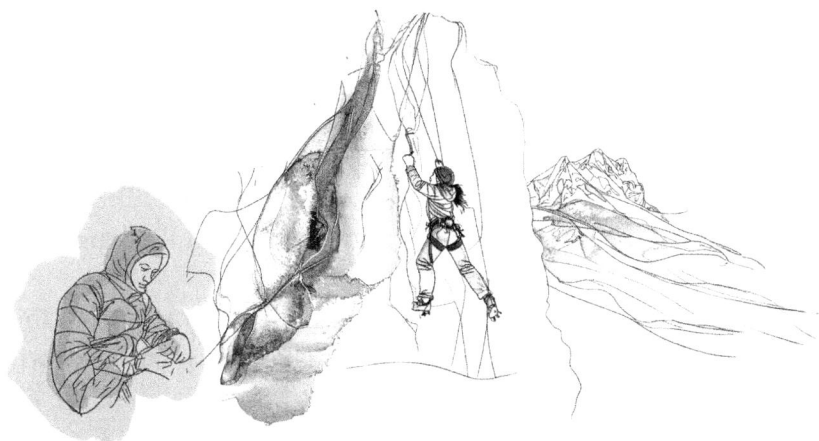

Fruit 5: High On The Ledge Of Love

In almost any other scenario, we would've bailed; too cold, too risky. But over halfway up Fitz Roy, turning back was an even more perilous option. I postholed through soft snow in rock shoes, tiptoed across unstable stones, and jammed my hands into icy cracks. My heart pounded, but underneath that urgency, something steadier stirred. A quiet witness. A knowing. After 150 feet of tension and grit, I pulled myself onto the only ledge big enough to bivy* on the entire route.

As night fell leisurely over the Patagonian wild, we sat in silence, legs dangling over the edge of our narrow perch. Below, a jagged sea of snow-draped granite stretched to the horizon, glowing softly in the last light. The sky layered itself in, burnt orange fading to indigo, crowned by a sliver of moon and a single bright star. Across the void, the Cerro Torre range pierced through the clouds like black shark fins, their flanks glowing in the reflected dusk. It was impossibly still. Stillness that makes you feel both infinite and small.

Fear would've kept me at home. Fear told me to cancel when my swollen toe wouldn't fit into my climbing shoe just days before our departure. Fear reminded me of everyone who doubted my place on this mountain. But the real mountain wasn't Fitz Roy; it was the one inside me: lined with old doubts, invisible critics, and all the times I'd turned back before.

Fear is powerful. But my commitment to love is stronger.

Love packed my bags, booked the flights, said goodbye to my dog, Aisha, navigated crevasse-riddled glaciers, and pulled my exhausted body up that relentlessly steep wall. Love whispered encouragement when Steven and I got off route on treacherous terrain. Love kept my eyes wide open all night, unwilling to miss even a second of the beauty.

With dawn came the infamous Patagonian rage: fierce winds, and bitter cold. No words were needed. The mountain had spoken: there would be no summit. We started our retreat, one rappel* at a time, eighteen careful drops down the Goretta Pillar, while the wind howled our names like a warning. Wrecked and humbled, we paused on a sheltered ledge to melt snow, our first sip of water since the night before. Then came more rappels, the return to the familiar snow slope, and the long, stumbling descent back to camp.

Our final night in camp, the wind nearly tore our tent from the earth. We jumped out in our undies frantically trying to anchor it down. Patagonia wasn't done with us yet. It whipped us real good on the hike out, with gusts so strong they nearly lifted us off our feet.

On that long slog home, I realized something essential: I'd once judged mountaineers as selfish. Maybe because my father left when I was young. Maybe because I carried guilt for prioritizing my own dreams. But the mountain showed me a flipside: every single moment offers a choice. We can slide down the icy slope of fear, or kick in our crampons and climb toward love.

Every step toward love is a gift; to ourselves and to the world. And whatever we give is repaid a hundredfold.

I thought I was doing this for Molly; to walk ahead, to show her what was possible. To earn some invisible credential as an elite mountain coach. But the mountain reminded me: we never climb just for ourselves. When we choose love over fear, that energy radiates outward. Molly felt it. I felt it. That's how transformation spreads.

This climb taught me that fruits grow from our commitment. From choosing love, courage, and resilience instead of fear. That bivy ledge; cold, terrifying, breathtaking; was the fruit. Not a summit. Not a pat on the back at the bar. Just a sliver of night that existed because we didn't turn back.

Whatever your soul is calling you to give; give it.
Don't wait. Don't let fear rob you of your abundance.

The fruit isn't waiting at the summit. The fruit ripens in the storm, in the missed turns, in the choice to keep going anyway. It tastes like grit and grace. Like snowmelt and sweat. Like silence after the wind. The fruit is the journey itself.

And the flower? The flower is what I became up there. Not harder, not more impressive. But at peace with everything that is. A soul who's learned to bloom right at the edge.

Love was the soil. And under alien stars, the cliff itself flowered, and we tasted its midnight fruit.

What is Blooming in You Now?

> You have a ledge like this, too.
> A fear whispering, Don't go.
> A love that says, You must.
> Take a leap. Your journey ripens the fruit.

Fruit 6: The Truth At 17,500 Feet

Pico de Orizaba, México, 2025

It's 11 PM on Thursday, and Molly is just waking up. No breakfast. No coffee. Just layers, boots, and the sharp bite of frigid night air at 14,000 feet.

We step outside the refugio into the piercing glow of a full moon. The wind claws at our Gore-Tex. Ahead, vast darkness stretches into the void, the summit nowhere in sight.

We are here to attempt an ascent of Pico de Orizaba, the highest volcano in Mexico, the third-highest peak in North America. This is the final mountain in a journey that has already tested everything: patience, plans, and personal limits.

This isn't just another adventure. For Molly, this is a threshold.

She'd been preparing for months; physical training, mental coaching. But life had other plans: altitude sickness, pneumonia, a death in the family. Still, Molly and I both knew she had to try.

By the time we arrived in Mexico, my carefully laid-out itinerary had already started to unravel.

On Sunday, we headed toward Nevado de Toluca, a 15,000-foot dormant volcano southwest of Mexico City; our first acclimatization peak. Nearing the trailhead, we passed through a chaotic stretch of vendors, cars, and crowds. A man flagged us down, demanding payment for an unclear entry fee. We questioned him, and when his attention shifted, we slipped past. "Just another toll scam in Mexico," we joked, winding our way up the dusty road.

The road ended at a gravel lot with a few scattered buildings. Most visitors were packing up. Only a few rangers and police remained. We'd heard there might be a hut available. I approached a ranger.

"The park is closed on Mondays," he said flatly. "What?" I asked, stunned. Strike one.

"You can stay tonight, but you have to be gone by 7 a.m. Technically, you're not supposed to be here."

I watched the disappointment hit Molly. Her first international mountain trip, and already the ground was shifting beneath her.

Change of plans. Early the next morning, we headed east toward Iztaccíhuatl. The drive took most of the day, cutting once again through the endless sprawl of Mexico City. But as we escaped the city's grip, the chaos faded into wide skies and winding roads, into the mythic saddle between Izta and her eternal lover, Popocatépetl.

We arrived at a deserted ranger station. A locked gate barred the road to the trailhead six miles beyond. By now we knew the park was closed on Mondays but hadn't expected to be physically shut out.

We jiggled the lock, scoured GPS for side routes, even drove down a random dirt road. Nothing. Sitting beside the gate, we spun plans we didn't want. Wait until 9 a.m.? Too late. Add twelve miles? Not an option. This was meant to be a warm-up, not a death march. Strike two.

Then a vehicle appeared; from the other side. *This is our chance,* I thought.

When a ranger emerged, I struck up a casual conversation. Friendly. Indirect. We both knew what it was really about. After a long exchange, we struck a deal. "2 a.m.? Yes," for a modest fee, of course.

Just as promised, the gate opened in the darkness. The plan had changed, but this was the path now. Life asked for openness, steadiness, and movement.

I realized this was the fruit of all the inner work: not a flawless plan, but the capacity to adapt without collapsing. To pivot without losing heart. To meet life as it comes and keep going.

Iztaccíhuatl is no casual warm-up. We moved slowly in the glow of our headlamps, gaining four thousand vertical feet into thinning air; every step a negotiation with gravity.

Reaching a ridge crest, we caught a glimpse of an alien world below: amber and fluorescent lights twinkling from the chaos of the valley city.

We continued upward, reaching a small col just as sunlight peaked over the eastern horizon.

Halfway to the summit. Two more hours of steady climbing brought us to a tin hut at 15,500 feet.

From there, the trail steepened into loose sand and unstable talus. Molly eyed the next section with unease." I'm not sure about this," she said.

We continued, slowly. The trail blurred into scrambling. Just like life, the ground can shift without warning. The gift is learning to meet it with presence, not resistance.

A hundred feet higher, we stopped. Six hours in. The summit was close; but so were exhaustion and altitude. Molly made the call, turn around. In that moment, I saw real courage. She didn't let fear drive her choice. She didn't push to prove. She listened; to her body, to the mountain, to the truth.

Watching her choose self-trust over ego reminded me: this work isn't about winning. It's about becoming the kind of person who knows when to keep going, and when to stop with love.

That day, Molly pushed beyond what she thought was possible. She climbed to 16,200 feet over an 11-hour day; 2,000 feet higher than she'd ever been. It was the hardest day of her life in the mountains.

But Orizaba was still ahead. And we had one more shot.

We spent Wednesday resting in Puebla, a city vibrant with history, color, and ice cream.

Thursday came; and with it, Strike three. Food poisoning.

We lingered as long as we could, giving Molly more time to rest. That afternoon we drove to Tlachichuca and organized our gear, hoping, praying, trusting that she'd recover in time.

The next morning she still wasn't feeling 100%, but she was good enough to try. We loaded into a 4x4 and headed up the mountain. By 7 PM, we were in our sleeping bags at Piedra Grande Hut.

At 11 PM, we started. We marched into the night. Like zombies; slow. methodical.

After a few hours we reached the Labyrinth: A maze of steep rocky spines, frozen snow chutes, and icy slabs. The technical crux of the route.

Molly had fallen in love with ice climbing the week before in Ouray, but this was different. This was technical alpine ice at 16,000 feet.

It was 4 AM, pitch black, bitterly cold; terrifying terrain lit only by headlamps.

By sunrise, we reached the base of the Jampa Glacier. Seven hours of grinding upward, one step at a time. The full moon set as the first light touched the peaks.

It was breathtaking. It was brutal.

At 17,500 feet, Molly could barely move. The air was razor-thin. Her body was spent. Her mind was lagging. The wind smelled of raw ice. The summit was 1,000 vertical feet away, but it might as well have been 10,000.

At 8 AM, she made the call: "We need to turn around." It was her decision. And it took as much strength as the climb itself.

The mountain wasn't an obstacle; it was a waveform. Each step: a crest and trough in the breath of becoming.

And we were far from done.

Seven more hours to get down, making it the new hardest physical day of her life. "Izta was hard." she said. "This was another level."

We didn't reach the summit that day. But we walked away with something rarer: the knowing that true power doesn't always mean going farther. Sometimes, it means honoring where you are. And that kind of self-trust? That's the fruit.

A few days after returning to the U.S., Molly sent me a letter. I still feel her words in my bones:

"Three months ago, I was sick with pneumonia. Now I've climbed to 17,500 feet. That takes my breath away. Effort got me further than I ever imagined, but eventually, willpower meets reality. That's where I found myself: breathless on the glacier.

This isn't the end. It's the beginning. I don't know yet what's next in my Badassery curriculum: more altitude? More skill? I know I'm not done."

One of the hardest parts wasn't the climb.
It was stepping away from my life of certainty and walking into the unknown. In my normal world, I am someone.
Out here, I was just a person in the elements.
Stripped down. Unsettled. And somehow, safer than I've ever felt.

"Now, three questions keep echoing through me:
What do I love?
What does it cost?
How much am I willing to pay?
Let this be my guide."

Molly's words carry the rhythm of a soul crossing a threshold. This was never about the summit; it was an initiation. A descent into unknowing, a shedding of borrowed identities, a raw encounter with the edge of her own becoming. When breath grew thin and willpower met its end, something deeper stepped forward.

That is the work. That is the fruit. Not a peak, but a pulse. Not a finish line, but a fire; ancient, luminous, uncontainable. The kind of fire that doesn't arrive… it awakens. I felt it too, radiating through every breathless step, calling us home to who we've always been.

At 17,500 feet, she met herself in complete uncertainty. No guarantees. No clear path. Just her breath, her limits, and a choice.

This is why I choose adventure as my training ground for leadership: because when I increase my exposure to uncertainty, complexity, and chaos. I expand my capacity to lead through it.

Not control. Not comfort. But courage; in the whiteout.

That day Molly went to 17,500 feet. A year before, she had never been above 9,000. Most people never will be. We approach these climbs thinking we'll conquer something. What we conquer, if we're lucky, is our illusion of control. What we come home with is a self that we finally recognize and admire. The flower wasn't forged in the summit push. It opened quietly, at 17,500 feet, in the space between effort and surrender.

What is Blooming in You Now?

You have an edge like this, too.
A place where certainty ends.
What do you love? What's the cost?
Name it, tune in when you're there.

Fruit 7: The Fall That Set Me Free
Baja California, Mexico 2015

Cataviña is like a prehistoric fever dream come to life. Giant granite boulders rise like ancient bones from the earth, surrounded by desert plants so strange they seem more alien than botanical. Towering cardón cacti, twisted ocotillos, and Dr. Seuss-like boojum trees give the whole place a surreal, dinosaur-era vibe; like you've stumbled into Jurassic Park.

It's remote: deep in the heart of Baja California, Mexico, tucked inside the Valle de los Cirios nature reserve. Hours from the nearest town. No gas stations. No cell reception. Just a barbed desert, and endless sky.

This was the backdrop to one of the most significant awakenings of my life.

My Polish friends and I weren't chasing anything grand. It was Christmas break, a brief escape from cold winds and looming responsibilities. That day, we were just scrambling across warm granite boulders, laughing in Polish, letting the Mojave sun soften our winter gloom. No plans. No pressure. Just movement for movement's sake, play laced with the desert's surreal magic. Until my foothold broke...

One moment I was moving across the face, the next I was airborne; spinning in the air just before impact. I landed hard on the side of my back with a sickening thud. My head cracked against the gravelly soil.

For a few long seconds I couldn't breathe. Just shock. Silence. My body flattened into the earth. And then the gasp came; air, pain, dizziness. My friends rushed toward me, panic in their eyes. But the first thing I said, without even thinking, was: "Let's not tell anyone."

That's what stuck with me the most; not the pain, but that instinct. To hide. To minimize. To pretend it didn't happen. I didn't want to ruin the trip. I didn't want to be the weak link. I didn't want to be seen as broken.

But I was.

I got up, somehow. I walked back to the car, every step a negotiation with pain. The December sun dipped below the horizon and the cold crept in like a shadow. My body began to shake uncontrollably; shock, hypothermia, or both. Wrapped in a sleeping bag, I slid into the car, my mind racing with visions of internal bleeding or shattered discs. We were ten hours deep into Baja, miles from help, driving north through dust and potholes, the road a narrow lifeline to an uncertain future.

I entered the strange, nonlinear terrain of grief. There was no orderly procession through the stages, just a storm of bargaining and sorrow, looping like a desperate prayer.

Please, Universe, just let me have climbing back. I promise I'll be better. I'll be grateful. I won't take a single move for granted. I'll earn it. My mind raced, trying to strike a cosmic deal. My only answer silence and pain. Then came the weight of despair; not just physical, but existential. Who am I if I can't do the thing that makes me feel alive?

Yet somewhere in that bleak, shivering uncertainty, a strange stillness arrived. Not peace. Not clarity. Just a soft surrender. I didn't know what was coming next, but I realized it was going to be a gift.

We drove through the night, stopping in village after village, searching for help. Each time: Closed clinics. No doctors. Nothing. The nearest real hospital was in Tijuana. But if I was seriously injured, I wanted to be treated in the U.S.; somewhere I had insurance. So we kept going. North. Past cacti, cliffs, checkpoints. Past every ounce of comfort.

At each one of the military checkpoints, we explained the situation. "I was injured. Trying to reach a hospital." And at every one, we were searched; car unloaded, backpacks open. No exceptions. Just protocol.

Fifteen hours of agony. Fifteen hours of stillness and space. Enough time to ask the real questions.

What if I was done climbing?

What if this was the end of the life I knew?

What if the fall wasn't a failure, but an invitation?

Something broke loose in me, and it wasn't just bone. I wasn't going to live afraid anymore. I wasn't going to keep disappearing to keep the peace.

I wasn't going to let the girl who got bad grades and felt like a nobody keep running the show. I was done waiting to be chosen. Done pretending that safety lived in mediocrity. Done tolerating what wasn't true.

Yes, I was hurt. But I was done being wounded.

Truth didn't arrive in words; it arrived as a trembling tone in my spine. It hummed: Now. I didn't choose this clarity. It chose me.

I had things to do. Divorce papers to file. A new life to walk into. No drama, just a clear decision. By the time we reached the hospital in Santa Barbara, the real healing had already begun.

The scans stunned the doctors. Yes, I'd broken my back, but only the spinous processes. No disc damage. No spinal cord trauma. Just a clean break. The kind that heals.

They called it a miracle. But the real miracle was in my choice: I didn't need the injury to be life-threatening for it to be life-changing. I chose to let it change me.

This fruit wasn't the waxed-to-perfection supermarket variety. I birthed it from the terror of realizing: This is my one life. No do-over. No second script.

I wasn't going to waste it pretending I was fine. This fruit ripened the moment I knew I couldn't keep betraying myself to belong; fertilized by truth, by fear, by the kind of clarity that scorches everything false.

It grew from the fire that ignites when you finally face it: You don't get to come back and do it differently. You either live like your life is yours, or you die a stranger to yourself.

That vow became my line in the sand. One week later, I ended my marriage.

That fall was the fruit of truth ripening. Messy. Painful. Unplanned.

From that vow came more than just a new chapter. It became the foundation of everything I would later build: my business, my freedom, my voice, and my service.

Just like the wildflowers that bloom in the Baja desert after rain; unexpected, resilient, radiant, and defiant, I bloomed too.

What is Blooming in You Now?

You have a fall like this too.
A moment that breaks the grip of your old ways.
You may still be mid-air, but know this:
The bloom begins the second you say: No more.

Interlude: Basket Of Roots

The screen flickers and geography dissolves. It's Mental Fitness time. Not a gym. Not therapy. Every Tuesday for the last three years, a circle of truth-tellers gathers to practice being real.

Jess clicks in first, Cascade wildflowers still clinging to her trail shoes. Brooke follows, somewhere sun-splashed, wolf-sighting, her grin as wide as the Alaskan frontier. Heather joins next, waving from a half-unpacked porch. Leif jumps on from Bellingham, Bas from a tent in Africa or a stone barn in the Pyrenees, Kelly from an office lit by civic devotion and soft defiance. I slide into my rain-hammered "car-office."

And then we begin the way we always do:

"Numbers, please."

Ten for dawn-wolve sightings, heli rides in the savannah, and Japanese powder. Six for the ache of a difficult goodbye. Two for soaking in a shit waterfall. Nobody flinches. Honesty is the cost of entry.

What follows is coaching only in the most expansive sense. The hot seat migrates by instinct. Brooke slips into guide-mode, threading parts-work questions through a unicorn laugh. Kelly scribbles a ten-line poem on the back of a grocery receipt and reads it aloud, punching skylight holes through someone else's panic.

We ask: "Are you moving from obligation or from joy?"

Then reggae playlists, five-minute regressions, or a bath scheduled like sacred liturgy. Tiny actions: clearing one cupboard for pleasure, sending a brave email, becoming physical proof of self-trust.

Part 3: Fruits & Flowers

Over the years, a private lexicon has flowered: Crash. Coach. Fuel. Tiny Step. Root Basket. With it comes a muscle memory of mutual holdfast. Name a spiral: "I'm useless with money, again" and five voices echo the reframe; "I am financially capable and clear," until your nervous system believes it.

When life detonates; accident, thesis meltdown, or financial cliff; the circle becomes a lattice of unseen hands: no advice vending, no getting into the pool of despair, no toxic positivity. Yes for witnessing, mirroring and the kind of rare silence that lets hard truths bloom without shame.

We don't fix each other. We don't cheerlead past the pain. Instead, we stay. We welcome what is and get curious.

One week, we're naming crash states and laughing about gnome-themed hotels. Next, we're touching the soft underbelly of being unseen, unparented, or quietly afraid that our best still won't be enough.

We trade roles fluidly: coach, mirror, witness, poet. Some days it's Brooke naming her need for celebration instead of endurance. Other times it's Kelly reckoning with spiritual bypassing and the grief of groundlessness.

Heather describes our weekly mass as: "Sometimes it feels like a blind experiment, where curiosity and vulnerability collide, and an old wound suddenly shifts into self-love. Other times, it's slow; a chipping away of layers that want to stay. This space helps me step out of my own way."

And Jess: "I see myself more clearly here, through the stories of others."

Brooke, describes three years of Mental Fitness like this: "I've stretched, practiced, risen, crumbled, and risen again. I've rooted. I felt supported. Been the supporter. Dissected old patterns. Aligned with soul purpose. Attuned to heart center and spirit need. My partner and sister both sit in this circle, now we speak a language of open-hearted communication."

This isn't a mere coaching group, it's a dojo for soul mastery.

Kelly writes in an email: "I came here thinking it was a place for strong women, for athletes, for the ones who already had their shit together. I didn't expect it to be the place where I could lay mine down. What I've found is a collective of humans who are brave enough to show their soft spots and wise enough to laugh through the mess."

"We don't perform here. We practice", Heather writes."I've spent most of my life managing emotions, trying to not be a burden. But here, when

I speak a truth I used to hide, someone echoes it with love. That's how I know it's real. That's how I know I'm real."

Bas: This group gave me more than tools: it gave me a way of being. A way to catch myself. A way to return to myself. And it's changed how I move through every other space in my life."

While our sages and saboteurs wrestle with life's paradoxical truths, fierceness shows up beside woundedness. Play doesn't erase the pain: it oxygenates it.

And somehow, amid poetry and playlists, community projects launch, boundaries get drawn, old fears get held instead of exiled.

It's not group therapy, or a self-improvement drill. It's a shared practice of being real, again and again, until truth stops being a threat and starts becoming home.

The miracle is cumulative and ordinary. Days get lived fueled by love. Cabinets for the new kitchen are built but no longer from martyr energy, instead from joy and happy participation from the kids. A thesis chapter crystallizes into publishable science.

Brooke meets a wolf at dawn and takes the omen straight to her clients.

And when I drop my own number: "ZERO: Crashed and crushed to my bones." They are all ready to catch me.

"Hand us the rope," Marta, Jess says. "You've been on the sharp end for all of us. Let us lead you now."

Bas goes straight into his heart, where he holds me. Leif sends his resilience playlist. Heather reminds me that every shitstorm looks different in hindsight. Kelly names our gallery view: "A basket of roots strong enough to cradle any fall." And just like that, the temperature in my chest starts to cool. The fire still burns, but the intensity has diminished.

Today I came convinced I was the fracture. I leave remembering: Wholeness includes the fracture. Not as damage, but as design. This too belongs.

This is what it means to be human. Not every fruit grows from a single tree. Some bloom from what we carry together.

What is Blooming in You Now?

You have a tribe like this too.
What's real cannot be threatened.
Reveal yourself, the basket appears.
Roots hold the rupture until you bloom.

Fruit 8: Not Just Free: 5.13 Committed
Europe, North America, Australia, 2017-18

It was a year for the record books.

December: I broke my back.

January: I signed divorce papers.

February: I moved into my Prius, rain drumming on the roof like a metronome, lulling me to sleep. Mouse in a trap, my only roommate.

With my marriage and my Yosemite job gone, I was suddenly passport-light: no house, no schedule, no plan.

I left Joshua Tree with nothing. I had been living out of my Prius for months. And now, money was getting tight. Just as panic started to creep in, a dear friend offered me a remote job: shaka. Two days a week. Just enough to cover expenses. Not enough to own me. It wasn't soul work, but it gave me an anchor; something I could show up for while staying wild and tethered only by choice.

It gave me freedom to roam, time to heal, and space to grieve. Inside the Prius, damp rope and stale peanut butter formed a musk that was as luxurious as it got. Uncomplicated. A kind of sacred scruff.

So I traveled. Across the American West. A month in Turkey. Another in Greece. Germany to see a friend. Poland to see family. Hawaii to shoot a wedding while on my way to Australia. Three months of climbing in

Tasmania and Queensland. A year of doing whatever the hell I wanted: mostly solo, always climbing, always in motion. My dream life. Or so I thought.

Sunset swims in the Aegean. On-sighting a 12d in Turkey. A thousand kangaroos leaping across the road at dawn. I should've felt invincible, but all I felt was tired.

Scrolling through the highlight reel, I felt… nothing. No victory song, no fist pump. Just a bone-deep exhaustion and a whisper: This can't be it.

Standing at departures in the Melbourne airport; backpack in one hand, duffel in the other, I could barely lift either. My stomach was still churning from the horse pill that murdered the parasite we'd nicknamed Tyndall Belly; an uninvited house guest that moved in during my visit down under.

My muscles were hollow, as if someone had vacuumed out the will to stand. Weeks of nausea, weight loss, and food aversion. Tyndall Belly had emptied me out, literally and metaphorically.

I wanted to go home, but I couldn't quite remember where home was. It used to be a place. A role. A routine. Now it was just a memory I could barely recall. So, for lack of a better plan, I booked a flight to Hawaii. Hoping for clarity, and maybe a lei.

My good friend Jiva picked me up in Honolulu. Five minutes in, she pulled the car over, gripped my shoulders, and says, "Dude, something's off. This isn't you. You need help."

The words split me open. Tears, snot, full dam break. Jiva didn't try to fix anything. She simply named the truth and handed me the compass: "Call Nancy Rubin. Just don't run if she pulls out her glass ball."

Nancy; part counselor, part oracle, listened to my rambling stories of divorce, loss, and grief for months. Then one day, she pierced me with a single sentence: "You're here to guide others. You feel it, don't you?"

I wanted to run. If I hadn't been such a people-pleaser, I would have slammed the door. *How dare you?* I thought. *How dare you hand me hope that I could matter. That I could lead. Be heard. Serve. That I could have a voice in the world. And damn it, yes, I could feel it; a calling I didn't ask for but could no longer ignore.*

And right there, in the gap between my resistance and my longing, I saw the truth. I didn't just want that. I needed it more than anything.

In December, I texted Tony Bonnici, a friend and master coach. He told me to schedule a Zoom call. It took me until August to gather the guts. The moment his face appeared on my screen, I knew: this was the next wall I had to climb.

I didn't know what coaching meant at the time. But I recognized the feeling; it was the same one I had the first time I heard of rock climbing, the same one I felt holding my first pair of Boreal Stingers. I didn't need the full picture. I just knew I was in.

When I started climbing, most people topped out at 5.8. Only the serious few ever reached 5.11. By the time I was stepping into coaching, little kids were already sending 5.13s in the gym. The mindset, training, and belief had all evolved so much in those twenty years. I didn't want to be mediocre.

So I decided: I would become a 5.13-level coach; In my first year.

Three weeks later, I was in San Diego at Rich Litvin's intensive, a conference for real coaches. Three hundred seasoned pros under one roof. Even my current coach Townsend was there. And me? The greenest bean in the pot. I didn't even have a paid client yet.

The first exercise was three-minute speed-coaching rounds. My heart was pounding. I improvised. I stumbled. I wondered if I was even making any sense.

By the end of the day, a man named HR found me. "Whatever you said in those three minutes: no one's ever said that to me. Will you be my coach?" Shaka. Lightning. Proof. Out of 300, he chose me. I don't remember exactly what I said; something about how he acted tough but was crumbling inside. He looked at me like I'd said something holy.

By February, I quit my two-day-a-week job and committed to coaching full-time.

This was the real dream. Not the one that looked good on instagram. Not the one that let me roam, hide, or escape. This dream didn't offer guarantees. It demanded everything. It came with no map, only a mirror.

The one that made me come alive. The one that scared me. The one that mattered. The one I didn't even know was there.

The first time a client cried on a call with me, something clicked. Not fear. Not imposter syndrome. Just presence. I was doing the thing I never thought I was worthy of: guiding someone through a fire I had walked through myself.

My voice no longer trembled. It rang.

The real dream wasn't the lifestyle. It was the life. That's the fruit: the moment I committed to something deeper than freedom; my soul purpose. The kind that demands my full weight on the sharp end.

When I laid purpose down in the soil of my life, freedom didn't vanish. It bloomed. It was no longer an escape but a force. Fruit: wild and uncontained.

I was no longer chasing freedom.

I became freedom.

What is Blooming in You Now?

> You have a dream like this too.
> One that's been tapping your ribs all along.
> Clarity lands when you commit.
> Notice what's yours. Fruit. Fire. Shaka.

Fruit 9: Sparkling Into Sovereignty
Twisp, Washington 2024

As I stepped through the door, it felt like falling into a glitter-soaked lucid dream: equal parts desert ritual and dance floor altar. Not stilettos and martinis, but magical shawls, fur tails, and freedom. One woman shimmered joyful and mythical wearing nothing but a unicorn cape. Another swished her tail like it had grown from her spine. Someone else resembled Jim Morrison reborn as a topless goddess in combat boots.

By day, we jammed our way up fractured crimson red sandstone walls and thrashed our way down sandy, rock-strewn mountain bike trails. Skin to stone, grit in our teeth, laughter ricocheting off canyon walls. By night, we danced beneath eternal starlit skies, swaying to the native drumbeat of our souls. This wasn't just a party. It was the return of the goddess.

It was my friends weeklong bachelorette party and her a crew that partied with purpose. By 9 p.m., we were back in our beds, bellies full of burritos, drinking water like sacred wine. Because tomorrow? Tomorrow was another chance to tear it up under the splendid Utah sun.

I'd finally gotten my long awaited girls-just-wanna-have-fun moment. And these girls wanted it all: to sweat, howl, bleed, chase each other naked through the sprinklers, and rise.

That's where I met Brooke.

She showed up with two suitcases full of costumes, ten gallons of glitter, and an energy that cracked the room wide open. A real-life unicorn. Not just sparkle. Not just shine. She had that unmistakable glint: the kind that says, I'm here to remember the sacred.

Brooke had spent over three decades guiding thousands of people through Alaska's backcountry. One of only two female heli-ski guides in Valdez. A woman who could belay you through a blizzard and, in the same storm, cook you dinner while telling stories so inspiring you'd forget the fear.

She was into personal growth and always first in line for anything I offered. Before I even had a business, she showed up. If I launched a group, she joined. If I led a workshop, she was there, front row, notebook open, heart wide. She wasn't just a participant; she was an anchor. The kind of woman who dives in headfirst, no matter how cold the water.

She brought her full self; grit, depth, and glitter; to every session. And every time she rose, she reminded the rest of us: this work works, if you do. Somewhere in our Mental Fitness group, she said it out loud for the first time: "I'm ready to quit guiding. I'm gonna be a coach."

The moment she claimed that desire, the universe responded. Within months, she sold her house in Alaska. Moved. Met the love of her life. And donated her kidney. Yes; her kidney.

She went on the donor list for Patrick, a lifetime friend, an artist, adventurer, and spiritual guide she's been deeply intertwined with for over thirty years. Not because she had to. Because she wanted to. Because something in her body said: This is mine to give.

Her actual kidney went to a stranger named Carl. But her decision gave Patrick a golden ticket, bumping him to the front of the recipient line. It was never about obligation. It was about alignment. A yes that came from the depths of her soul.

And something wild happened in that surrender: her life bloomed.

Her brand-new coaching practice took off. Clients signed up immediately. She started making a living faster than any newcomer I'd ever seen; including myself. Why? Because Brooke lives what she teaches. When a pattern appears, she doesn't just name it: she tracks it to its origin, guts it, studies it, and alchemizes it. That's what she brings to her clients: a devotion to truth that's been pressure-tested in the wild.

But it wasn't just sparkle and determination that launched her. There was fire in her journey. A final ignition that burned away any remaining doubt.

She'd been sent to work at the luxurious Sheldon Chalet, a remote lodge perched atop a rugged nunatak* in Denali National Park. Accessible only by helicopter, surrounded by towering spires and the vast expanse of the Ruth Glacier, the chalet was the dream gig; until it wasn't.

Brooke flew in to replace Edward. His satellite messages had been cryptic, but nothing prepared her for what she walked into. The moment she met him, his gaze sent a chill down her spine. Her instincts knew: something is terribly wrong with him. Edward was in the grip of a psychotic break; paranoia, violent ideation, and full-blown delusion. Brooke quickly realized that her life was in real danger.

Thankfully Edward left, but not before the damage was done. The encounter had left its mark: invisible shrapnel lodged deep, striking trauma wounds she hadn't known were still tender, surfacing old echoes of betrayal and abandonment she thought she had outgrown. She found herself completely alone in that remote alpine hut, left to process what had happened. She stayed calm, safeguarded herself, and handled the transition with quiet strength, but the impact lingered.

In the days that followed, she couldn't sleep. Her system was stuck in red alert. Hypervigilance. Flinching at shadows. Her body didn't know how to come back down.

Outdoor guides often override their nervous system, until one day the drop overflows. Until survival becomes collapse.

Brooke didn't just return from the red zone. She mapped the way back. Now she teaches others to listen sooner, soften faster, and stay sovereign. That experience became the foundation of her nervous system recovery and resiliency work.

Fruit 9: Sparkling Into Sovereignty

Today, she helps others regulate stress, reconnect with their bodies, and escape the trap of performance-based living. She calls it Wild World Wanderings, a reclamation of wildness, not just in nature, but within.

Brooke's fruit? Sovereignty. Not the spotlight. Not a summit. Power without pretending. She doesn't lead from a pedestal. She leads from the path; with sparkle and soil, guts and grace.

Sovereignty, for Brooke, isn't about control. It's about deep trust in her own ground, the kind that can't be taken by a storm, a summit, or a psychotic break on a glacier. She knows how to come back to herself, and that is the map she now offers others: a way home, no matter where they stand.

What is Blooming in You Now?

You've felt a pulse like this too
The humming of clarity beneath the noise
The moment you stopped asking and simply claimed
Let your unicorn light run wild. The world is waiting.

Fruit 10: When The Work Works You
Grand Junction, Colorado 2024

That winter held three initiations: one that broke the body, one that cracked the soul, and one that came disguised as work. Together, they taught me that real power doesn't come from teaching, it comes from being undone.

We'd been on the road for months. First climbing in Kentucky's Red River Gorge. Then to Poland for my cousin's wedding. Then four weeks in Ethiopia; the land of origin: ancient, diverse, breathtaking, and endlessly complex.

In the Omo Valley, we met tribes living beyond modern reach, mosaics of resilience and embodied tradition. In the Bale Mountains, underdressed and overwhelmed, we trekked high-altitude plateaus with only guides, Ethiopian wolves, and endemic birds for company. Each day stripped us bare, exposing the raw truth of a world far removed from Western comfort.

Then came Mexico: swindled, stranded, double car trouble. My bandwidth hit a wall. I just wanted it to be over.

By the time we returned home in February, we were fried. Starved for normalcy. Aching for routine and rest.

On my birthday, we went out for a short climb in Unaweep Canyon to catch some Colorado sun in late winter; warm enough to feel like a gift. We picked a brand-new four-pitch route our friend had recently put up. Pretty cruiser.

At the top of the third pitch, the wind picked up. I tucked myself into a little alcove to escape the chill and built an anchor. Steven came up, and we hesitated. The final pitch looked easy, but we were lightly dressed and getting cold. He decided to go for it.

I stayed huddled out of the wind, belaying as he climbed out of view. Forty feet up he placed a single piece of protection: a green Camalot*, three-quarters of an inch of lobes.

A while after that I heard it: a hellish scream and the thunder of a tumbling rockfall. Not the kind of sound that would just crack a helmet, but the kind that could crush a body flat. I curled inward, bracing. Then the rope snapped taut in my hand. Steven had fallen.

I looked up. Nothing. I scanned the rope line down: there he was dangling twenty feet below me. He was upside down. Silent. He'd fallen close to a hundred feet, a massive, tumbling fall that later made national news. His weight hanging from single piece of pro*, a green camalot.

For a timeless moment, the canyon held its breath with me: soundless, suspended - before the weight of what had just happened began to settle in.

I weighed my options. At sixteen I completed a mountain rescue course and I knew what mattered: I had to get to him, NOW. I unclipped from the anchor and lowered myself down. We were now both hanging on that single cam.

I reached him and flipped him upright. He began making low moaning sounds, murmurs from another world. But he was alive.

I lowered us to a tiny ledge. He sat, screaming in pain. "What happened? I don't understand what happened. Why are we here?" A minute later: the same words again. I connected to a satellite and dialed 911. Twenty minutes later, we heard a helicopter.

He kept saying: "What happened? I don't understand." And then: "This helicopter better be bringing some morphine." That's when I knew: he was going to be okay.

Rescuers arrived from the top and our friends climbed up from the base. Eventually, Steven was lowered to the ground and carried out by the Mesa County Search and Rescue.

I rappelled down, gathered the gear, and hiked back to the car. By the time I got home, Steven was already in the hospital. The trauma surgeon couldn't believe the damage wasn't worse: seven broken ribs, a couple broken transverse processes, fluid around his lung, a mild concussion, and plenty of scrapes and bruises.

I nodded along like everything was normal. Like I hadn't just watched someone I love nearly plummet to his death. Steven's birthday gift to me? Not dying.

In those first hours, I still hadn't felt anything. The part of me that builds a wall was running the show. I kept functioning: tying knots, calling for rescue, driving home; moving through it all like a pro. But the thing about carrying weight for too long is that it eventually starts to get too heavy.

Later, once he was safe and I was alone, I began dismantling that wall. Piece by piece. To feel the part of me that almost lost him. I thought I had processed it. I was doing my best. But I hadn't yet reached the core.

When the outer storm finally clears, the body takes its chance to speak. Mine didn't whisper; It screamed. Not in tears or trembling, but in fever. Fire. A total collapse I never saw coming.

What you bury in silence, the body remembers. Unfelt pain doesn't disappear; it just sinks deeper until it erupts as sickness, inflammation, burnout, or worse.

I had just started teaching a new course: a chakra class. At the time, I thought I was simply launching another program. I had no idea I was walking straight into my own fire. It began like many things do: with inspiration and a clear sense of mission. A client wanted to learn more about the chakra system, and I felt called to bring it to life in a grounded, practical way.

I mapped out a nine-week curriculum and opened the doors. It filled instantly.

The first two sessions went beautifully. Root. Sacral. Safety and creation. We explored energy leaks and protective blocks. The breakthroughs were profound: one couple said they hadn't felt this connected in nineteen years. Then came the Third Chakra: Personal power. The morning of that class, three days after Steven's fall, I had a fever. I dismissed it. I opened class with meditation. The energy was electric. People made deep, intimate discoveries in the breakout rooms. The lesson landed.

Hours later, my body exploded in sickness.

He had survived the fall. Now it was my turn. Not a bug; a rupture. Fever. Ice-pick headaches. ER visits. Hallucinations. Shadows clawing up from old places. Rage I hadn't spoken. Boundaries I'd broken. Ghosts I'd buried. My body was doing the work of un-doing.

In those vision-drenched nights, I prepared for death. Left instructions. Closed affairs. Said goodbye.

Then, in the ER, a doctor sat beside me; a man who felt like he belonged to another dimension. He told me a story about his Greek grandmother. He asked: "What if there's a place in you that already knows how to be still, even when everything else is on fire?"

It hit me like a lightning strike.

That was the place I had remembered in Tahoe; arriving with no plan and letting the unknown guide me. The place I dropped into on Aegialis, when fear gave way to flow and presence. The place D-Griff named high on El Capitan, when the summit stopped mattering and presence became the gift.

That place doesn't shout. It waits. Like a fire-lit cave in the heart of the storm. And when I remember it, I remember who I am beneath all the content of life. Unshaken. Whole. Already home.

**I am not just this body. Not just this pain.
I am the still presence behind it all.**

The next morning, I knew I would live. But I also knew I could no longer live the same way. I rose as a woman shaped by her own Chakra Class; one who no longer coddled comfort or enabled stories that stunted growth. I graduated one client with grace. Released another with love and truth.

Then I went deeper; into the bloodline. Named the family pattern we had danced around for forty years. Spoke the words I had been avoiding, not to wound, but to liberate. For myself, and for collective healing.

My re-entry to the world of living didn't feel triumphant. It felt like cleaning out the attic. The third chakra had done its work. The fire of personal power had burned through every false allegiance and invisible contract. What remained was mine to stand in; clean, clear, and uncompromised.

That was the fruit. Not a new method. Not better boundaries. But a deeper devotion to myself; unapologetic, unwavering, and true.

This is what it means when the work works you. I thought I was teaching others, but I was actually the offering on the altar. And here's the kicker: remember how people used to say I was too sensitive?

That sensitivity became my superpower in this breakdown. I felt everything: what others couldn't or wouldn't. The sacred fever burned the rest of the barriers. It turned my belonging fears to dust.

I tracked my parts through the madness and came out with a clarity that now shapes my life and work. People pay me for this attunement. For this depth. What bloomed wasn't a new job title. It was the flowering of perception itself; sensitivity, not as fragility, but as sight.

This is what power really is. It is allowing life to break you open; and then choosing, again and again, to stand up differently.

What is Blooming in You Now?

You have a fever like this too
It waits for its rightful moment
Let the unraveling be sacred
In the cave of your fear the jewels await.

Fruit 11: The Film That Didn't Make Me A Filmmaker

Honolulu, Hawaii 2010

There was a time when I thought I'd become a documentary filmmaker.

I had the training: an art degree from Spain, a film school in Brazil. I'd edited TV shows and cut sports documentaries with clean structure and sharp rhythm. I had the eye, knew the tempo of a cut, the build of a scene, and I loved it.

Then I Just Love to Paddle landed in my lap.

My always-inspired friend Cliff had a vision: to paddle all nine channels between the Hawaiian Islands in six consecutive days; something that had never been done before. He planned to go with five companions. One of them - Uncle Nappy Napoleon, a legendary waterman, sun-worn and timeless, whose presence on the ocean felt ancient and true. Uncle Nappy paddled like it was prayer, like the ocean remembered him.

I joined the journey, fighting nausea between swells, filming from a wobbling deck, wrapping camera gear in garbage bags under salt-crusted tarps. We caught a marlin. We dropped a wallet. Nine days blurred into strokes, swells, and the big bright Hawaiian sky.

The film became more than a project. It was a soul offering; a portrait of a man who never stopped showing up. A meditation on ancestral presence, rhythm, and the sovereignty born of simplicity.

Shot across vast stretches of open water, I Just Love to Paddle captured Nappy's unwavering spirit: a steady current of humility and service. In his thick Hawaiian Pidgin*, he dropped truths that stirred the ocean's song:

"Jus' cuz I neva ask fo' be born, no mean I gotta be all pissed wit da world. Do yo' bes'. Nothin' come free, brah."

Translation: (Just because I never asked to be born, doesn't mean I'm gonna be pissed off with the world. Do your best. Nothing comes free.)

In one line, he distilled a lifetime of resilience and grace. Freedom wasn't found in arrival; it was found in rhythm. In the daily choice to show up, paddle forward, and live your life as an offering.

His devoted wife, Auntie Anona, came with us on the trip, adding a deep, soulful tone to the journey. She wasn't there to watch from the sidelines; she was woven into the heart of it, holding frequency. There was something about her that made the whole crossing feel more anchored, as if her presence stitched us into the lineage we were paddling through. Her words have led me more than I can recount: "Life is as great as you want it, as grand as you want it. Don't stop. Whenever there's an adventure, say yes. And if you can't say yes, ask for a second chance. It will come."

She said it like she'd lived it; not from a book, but from a thousand choices to keep saying yes when comfort would've been easier. It wasn't advice in the transactional sense. It was blessing, invitation, and challenge all in one.

During the interview Nappy told me "I never had much education." He laughed softly, eyes drifting toward some old memory. "In fac, I wen to a school where you make chairs, and you make all these kine coffee tables, because I was pretty good with my hands. But for's remembering fengs? I wasn't much good. I can study all night, den nex day I fo'get what I study."

When Auntie Anona got a scholarship to Stanford for her PhD, Nappy stayed back in Kaimuki to raise their four boys. No drama. No wounded pride. Just a shrug, "Dey was pretty growed up already" - he recalled.

Fruit 11: The Film That Didn't Make Me A Filmmaker

For a Hawaiian man of his generation, that kind of humility, and role reversal wasn't just rare. It was revolutionary. In a world still unlearning the noise of toxic masculinity, Nappy didn't need to give speeches about equality. He just lived it. Quiet and unshakably free.

At sea during the nights, I'd crawl into my bunk, hands still trembling from the day's swells, and review the footage. Editing became communion. I let the water speak. Cut by feel, not formula. Let silence breathe.

Every frame became a love letter: to him, to legacy, to endurance, to presence. It took a whole year of labor; and it was love, through and through.

The film did well. It won awards. It made people cry. The Honolulu Star even called me "a Polish-haole-local." I thought I'd begun my life as a documentary filmmaker.

My next project was already set: a sadhu on pilgrimage to the Kumbh Mela. A ten-year journey of the sacred. I was ready. But the project unraveled. The trip disappeared like mist.

The agents I'd trusted with the Nappy film turned out to be frauds. The money vanished. The dream collapsed.

What was meant to launch me became a quiet grief. No second film. No Sundance. No career in lights.

Just a story lodged in my body; and a question I stopped asking: What would've happened if…

I lingered near the film world for a while afterwards. Applied for film jobs. Shot photos for Patagonia and Climbing Magazines. But the arc had already turned.

Years later, someone stumbled upon the film. They watched it and wept. "It stirred in me something ancient and real," they said.

A tiny cultural center in Minnesota screened it. Afterward, strangers stood up and hugged. And me? I still carry the edits in my spine. I still see the world through Uncle's eyes, even when the camera's gone.

Cliff smiled once, his eyes distant with memory. "I learned so much from Uncle Nappy," he said. "He just assumes everything's going to be hard. So if it isn't, he's pleasantly surprised. And if it is, well, he already expected it. Either way, he keeps moving."

Auntie Anona blessed me with a farewell mantra:

"On top yo' canoe, you can bring all yo' kupuna (ancestors). Dass yo' dream, yo know, do what you like in yo' dream."

The fruit is what we made: A film that outlived its plans and landed in people's hearts. It stirred tears, it sparked hugs. It reminded someone of their grandfather. It remembered a sacred ocean hum.

The flower is what bloomed in me: stillness, reverence, the rhythm that never left. I don't need a title to know I'm a maker of beauty. I don't need an audience to know I'm a witness.

This is how I live now: less proving, more offering. This is what remains.

And beauty, when it's real, doesn't need applause. It just needs to be seen and shared.

The film didn't make me a filmmaker. But it made me true.

What Is Blooming in You Now?

> You have a reel like this too
> That never went viral but rewired your soul.
> Not meant for fame, but for rooting.
> Expression as devotion, the outcome is beside the point.

Fruit 12: After The Diagnosis, The Mission
Warsaw, Poland 2020

Before the diagnosis, Zofia worked in media. She held a respected role at one of Poland's major TV stations. Life was messy, full, and fast, with two careers, two young kids, and a house outside of Warsaw. There were dinners made in a rush, toys underfoot, emails at night, and soft bedtime moments tucked into the chaos. Her daughter Joanna was thriving in kindergarten. Her toddler son, Jerzyk, was curious, bright-eyed, and full of delight, "the sweetest boy on earth."

Life was busy, and it worked, mostly.

Jerzyk had just started running, playing, and discovering the world on his feet.

Then the falling began. The stiffness. The curling wrists. His body stopped cooperating with his joy.

The doctors said he was fine.

Then at a barbecue, a family friend, a pediatrician, shook her head while watching Jerzyk fall. "This isn't good." Not long after, the diagnosis landed like a detonation: Metachromatic Leukodystrophy. A life sentence.

The air changed. Time slowed.

MLD is very rare, and unforgiving. It unravels the nervous system, slowly and relentlessly, eating away at the protective coating of nerves. It takes children who once ran, laughed, and played: and strips them of

movement, language, independence; often while they are still aware of what's being taken.

There's no cure. Only treatments that might slow the progression if caught early enough... Zofia, and all of us, began combing the internet in a panic. Searching for miracles. For something that could be reversed or cured. But the internet was a pit. One story all ending the same way. No survivors.

Receiving the diagnosis was like watching the floor drop out from under them. One moment, Zofia and her husband were managing diapers, daycare, and busy work schedules. Typical young family chaos. The next, they were told their son had an incurable, degenerative disease that would slowly rob him of every ability he had just begun to master.

There was no roadmap. No promise of survival. Just a name, Metachromatic Leukodystrophy, and the shattering realization that they would have to watch their child regress, suffer, and eventually die.

The only possible cure for MLD is gene replacement therapy, but it has to be performed before any symptoms show up, which points to the importance of doing prenatal screening. And bone marrow transplant therapies are incredibly expensive, upwards of 3 million dollars.

The grief was immediate and ongoing, but so was the urgency. Within days, they were researching clinical trials, gathering medical records, and applying for emergency passports. The heartbreak never left, but it sharpened into motion.

They had no choice but to act, even with the weight of devastation sitting on their chests. They didn't have time to collapse. Their son needed them to be alert, advocating, and clear. So, they moved forward, grieving, terrified, nothing would ever be the same for this family.

Over time, Jerzyk lost the ability to sit up, then to crawl, then to move with intention at all. He never got the chance to speak in full sentences, MLD stole that before the words could form.

Eventually, he lost the ability to swallow safely too. To express pain. To smile with his whole face. His mind still flickered behind his eyes, but his body froze into stillness. This is what MLD does. It takes away everything, piece by piece, one nerve strand at a time.

Zofia's life changed overnight. She left her job: not by choice, but because Jerzyk needed full-time care. She stopped being a producer of stories and became the steward of a single, fragile story: her son's.

She took Jerzyk to the United States so he could participate in a clinical trial at the Lurie Children's hospital in Chicago. He was the second child in the world admitted. Weekly spinal injections. Hours spent in fluorescent-lit hospital rooms. Medical terms she didn't yet understand.

In Chicago, they stayed at a house run by a Polish foundation for families with critically ill children receiving treatment abroad. The rooms were filled with parents carrying impossible stories, kids in wheelchairs, post-surgery, mid-chemo, post-diagnosis. There were tears in the kitchen, prayers in the hallways, and small, fierce moments of connection between people who didn't need to explain a thing.

For Zofia, it was a revelation. A sense of community. A mirror. A reminder she wasn't alone. And it planted a seed. The knowing of how vital it is to have people around who understand exactly what you're going through. Later it inspired her to support other parents who received heartbreaking diagnoses, and to offer the kind of presence she once so desperately needed.

Fear translated through every appointment. Six months in, they returned to Poland but now traveled weekly from the suburbs of Warsaw to a hospital in Antwerp, Belgium. Every week: bags packed, flights taken, spine tapped. A growing, disabled child in tow. Hope stitched to survival: the treatment doesn't reverse the nerve damage. It slows it.

No one tells you what that does to a family. A scenario one shouldn't complain about: the pharmaceutical company was providing life support for Jerzyk. Zofia didn't crack, but life was extraordinarily difficult.

Three years in, havoc had become her rhythm. The spinal injections, the flight schedules, the feeding tubes, the appointments. What once felt impossible had become routine. But that didn't mean it got easier, it just became familiar.

The exhaustion was deep and cellular. Not the kind that sleep fixes, but the kind that builds in the bones from years of vigilance, of grieving on a loop, of holding steady when nothing in life is. Her son was still declining. The disease was still incurable. The caregiving was still relentless. And yet, her capacity had grown wider than she ever imagined it could.

The woman who had once been crushed by the diagnosis was now fluent in medical jargon, bureaucracy, and emotional resilience. She was still tired, but she was also powerful. She knew how to advocate. How to read a single change in breath or mood. How to fight for both her children, in different ways. She knew how to catch moments of joy like fireflies in the dark, silly dances in the kitchen with Joanna, Jerzyk's eye contact when he liked a song, the softness of their family curled up together on the couch.

On January 7th, 2025, Zofia stood before members of the Polish Parliament and told the truth. It was during a national conference on MLD, newborn screening, and gene therapy. She didn't speak in statistics or policy language. She told the story of her son. Of the missed signs. Of the doctors who looked but didn't see. Of the vague symptoms that slowly became a nightmare.

She spoke of fear, helplessness, and the breathless urgency that every MLD family knows all too well. She called it what it is: a diagnostic odyssey, one that costs lives. She made it clear that only testing children at birth can save them from the brutal fate this disease brings.

In a room full of lawmakers hardened by politics, tears fell. That's the power of truth, spoken from the heart: an impact of one mother refusing to stay silent.

Some truths arrive like moonlight. Not to illuminate, but to soften the dark. She no longer lived in denial or panic. She lived inside a reality most people can't even imagine, and she had made it a home.

There was still heartbreak. There always would be. But there was also laughter. Love. Beauty. And a kind of strength that came not from having it all figured out, but from continuing to show up, day after day, with an open heart.

Joanna, still just a child herself, struggled to understand why her parents were never fully present anymore. She felt invisible. Her needs came second, third, never. At school, she started withdrawing. At home, she was alone, even with everyone there. The emotional cost of survival has its own diagnosis: and it doesn't come with a treatment plan.

Day in and day out, Zofia became the nurse, the interpreter, the advocate. She lived in rooms most people don't even know exist. What she quickly became aware of was this: there was no map. No language for what she was going through. No space that spoke to the agony of watching your child slowly disappear.

So, she made one.

Zofia created @po_diagnozie, a space for parents navigating the unthinkable. She wrote about the grief of regression, the trauma of diagnosis, the heartbreak of hope. Her posts gave shape to what so many felt but couldn't say. And in doing so, she created a community. Belonging. A torch in the dark. She had crossed the invisible line from surviving her own crisis to becoming the voice others depended on.

But she didn't stop there.

She became an advocate: not just for Jerzyk, but for every child yet to be diagnosed. She began pushing for the inclusion of MLD in Poland's newborn screening program. She spoke out about the need for access to gene therapy. She teamed up with other parents, turning private anguish into public pressure. She provided space and listened to other parents with difficult diagnoses. The very person she wished she could have talked to when this was happening in her life.

Zofia's experience caring for her son with MLD reveals the profound challenges families face with this rare disease and many others. Her journey, marked by relentless caregiving, heartbreak, and unshakable devotion, embodies a fierce tenderness. It is a love that doesn't flinch, one that fuels her advocacy not just for her son's well-being, but for greater awareness, support, and hope for every family touched by terminal illness.

She gave her pain a purpose.

This is the fruit. Not resolution. Not recovery. But devotion, repurposed as action. The quiet, fierce commitment to fight for lives that will never even know her name.

That is fierce tenderness. The kind that doesn't collapse. The kind that transforms everything it touches.

What is Blooming in You Now?

> You have a heartbreak too.
> The kind that split you open.
> Let it become more than survival.
> Let it become your reason to rise.

Fruit 13: The Marriage is His Wildest Adventure

When I first met Bas at a friend's wedding, I was dumbfounded that anyone could have a life like his. He was the guy who scouted locations for epic adventure shows and races like Eco-Challenge, venturing into the wildest, and most remote places on the planet to map out the courses that pushed human limits.

Bas lived the kind of life most people only see in movie trailers. He hacked through the Amazon with a machete looking for routes fierce enough to break elite athletes. He drank frog venom with shamans in Peru, negotiated with Siberian villagers on snow-covered borders, and leapt from helicopters onto Alaskan glaciers to map terrain no human had ever even touched.

While most of the world sipped cappuccinos in coworking spaces, Bas was waist-deep in swamp water chasing anacondas, dangling from vines in Borneo, or arguing with tribal chiefs in Fiji over the logistics of a zipline so high, no insurance company would sign off on it. His passport was bloodstained, duct-taped, and bursting with stamps from places most people couldn't find on a map.

A living blueprint of an adventure man.

One day, Bas reached out. Something in his life was going terribly wrong… he was terrified.

As we started working together, we uncovered a thread of pain that stretched far back into his childhood: the trauma of his parents' divorce, and a deep, cellular knowing that if he didn't change course, he'd lose his marriage in the same way. He feared most that his children would inherit the same ache he'd been trying to outrun his entire life.

The universe had already delivered his wake-up call.

Two years before our work began, Bas fell asleep at the wheel driving home on New Year's Day. The crash was catastrophic; three rescue helicopters were called to airlift his family, all in critical condition; to the hospital. Bas's body was declared dead.

Bas describes his near-death experience as "melting into the singularity; an experience outside of time and space." It turns out it was not his time, and "the consciousness of my kids put a halt to that melting"… A heli came back for him.

On January 2nd the prognosis was not good. With multiple breaks in both legs, Mary faced the possibility of having at least one, if not both legs amputated. Callum and Jeanne had massive internal organ damage with kidneys, livers and spleens all heavily compromised…doctors gave them a "40% chance of survival".

With a broken neck and back comprised of 14 fractured, compounded or displaced vertebrae, Bas entered surgery with a "50% chance of survival and guaranteed paralysis"… if he made it through.

This is not the place to try to describe the incredible, some would say miraculous, events of the next three weeks; suffice it to say, beyond anyone's wildest imaginations Mary, Bas, Callum and Jeanne defied all the predictions, all the odds. Twenty days after that fateful prognosis they were reunited in a single hospital room.

In that moment, he didn't just survive, he reclaimed the rest of his life.

That moment: raw, unimaginable, crushing, became his core memory of love.

Our coaching work began from that fire. Bas got commited, he met his grief, his patterns, the CRASH state in his intimate relationships he'd mistaken for normalcy. He committed to daily practices. He started coming home to himself, and slowly, his relationship with himself… and hence with his wife and children began to heal.

I remember a session when he pressed his hand to his chest, Locator Button, named his feeling "Terror," breathed, and said, "Welcome, terror. I'm here." That practice became his north star. Every time the old adrenaline itch hit, he'd tap his chest, breathe, and choose presence instead of escape.

At some point, Mary (who did walk again) took a job abroad. Bas stepped into a new role, as a solo parent, mirroring the years Mary had carried the domestic weight while he disappeared into jungles, satellite phone his only tether. In our weekly Mental Fitness group he admitted, "I'm terrified to parent alone for a month, but I'm up for the challenge. I now see how much Mary had been doing."

Nobody starved, and the kids even somewhat enjoyed the role reversal, joking about their new Mr. Mom. Bas and Mary also began seeing each other differently. Respect replaced resentment, frustration shifted to compassion. Weekly Sunday State Check-ins, dog walks together, and a shared calendar took root.

When we first began coaching, Bas proposed something unexpected: he would pay my high coaching fee by bringing me onto one of his TV productions.

So, we spent a month in Vietnam filming a "water-based survival series." Translation: a floating circus of city slickers who treated the ocean like a personal insult. They cursed the tides for ruining shot lists, moaned when waves rocked the camera pontoon, and threw tantrums at the clouds for daring to exist. The executive producer sneered, "I hate nature," while standing at the edge of a turquoise bay that poets would die to portray.

Reality-show producers don't hunt for real adventure: they manufacture drama in a sterile lab of storyboards and soundbites. They'll fake a fight over cold coffee, script a meltdown because the sunset isn't "on brand," and call it authenticity while the world's raw beauty sits ignored just outside the frame.

I was hired for one purpose: to create a rock climb, a line that contestants would climb in the finale. I spent days rigging the selected rock wall, hauling gear by boat, marking holds in the tropical heat. On the morning of the final shoot, I asked the producer for the climbing timeline. He barely looked up from his phone. "The climbing? Oh, we killed that segment," he said, waving me off like last week's prop.

Manufactured drama had elbowed out real adventure again. A tragic misuse of human fire.

We wrapped up the gig, but Bas walked away different. Right there, knee-deep in wasted beauty, he drew his line: No more soul-sucking projects. No more selling wonder to people who despise it. From that day forward, his work had to mean something, or he wasn't interested.

And slowly, meaningful opportunities started to arrive. Until one project showed up that checked all of the boxes.

An unconventional philanthropist had recently started a project where she would spend the rest of her life, and not inconsiderable wealth, travelling the world supporting amazing people and their worthy humanitarian projects. At the same time, she would make a documentary shining a light on them and their incredible work. She needed help overseeing and guiding the adventure and ended up offering Bas the opportunity to create his own dream job… doing just that.

The project had heart, soul, and service. He said "Hell yes."

One day, he joined our coaching call from a helicopter. He had just taken a group of Kenyan kids up for their first flight. He smiled. Mid-air. Mid-transformation.

Close the arc: among other important things, the documentary raises awareness about the plight of so many souls in the world that don't have access to clean water. His new boss's donations fund the installation and upkeep of clean-water systems; Bas sees kids drinking from a new tap and whispers, "This is the real summit."

That's what happens when we stop bullshitting ourselves. When we sit in the pain on purpose, meeting our deepest fears head on. When we stop making excuses and start creating meaning from our truth.

The fruit is the marriage: not the wedding-day demonstration. It's the hard-earned, rebuilt union forged in grief, humility, and renewed devotion.

The flower is presence: Bas, no longer chasing adrenaline, instead savoring tiny moments, like dancing with his daughter in the kitchen, or holding space for his wife in silence. He traded unleashed and numb for present and rooted. And found something even rarer: peace.

"I used to chase danger to feel alive. Now I breathe with my kids and feel more adventure in their laughter than in any Fijian jungle." He reflects.

This isn't a Hollywood ending. It's better. It's a man who chose to return. To stay. To love. To live the wildest life his heart could dream of.

What is Blooming in You Now?

You have a crash like this too.
A moment that asked whether you'd stay or slip away.
If you stay, who will you be?
The pressure that bends you, is all in your mind.

Epilogue:
The Soul, The Sky, And The Silence

I had a dream.

We gathered in a clearing beneath the stars, silence wrapped in pine and firelight. The sky had fallen into that sacred indigo dusk. A fire crackled with spirit. Around the blaze, faces glowed; familiar, weathered, beloved. People I'd once met at thresholds: trembling, shedding, aching with questions.

Now? They emanated. Not perfect. Not finished. Just true, rooted, risen, fruit-bearing.

D-Griff spoke, his voice as slow as snowmelt over granite. His words, few, landed like a well-placed cam in a runout stretch of becoming.

"I've lived long enough to know: the stone remembers.

It remembers who we were when we touched it,

chasing glory, fleeing ghosts, or finally listening.

I came for the topout. But I stayed for the stillness.

The kind that doesn't shout or rise.

It just waits. Until we remember we were never separate."

Molly's cheeks were wind-chapped from Orizaba. "My fruit? Breathing self-trust at 17,500 feet, and bringing that altitude home."

Little Marta swung her legs over a mossy log, heart-shaped patches on her knees. "Mine is a promise: I don't have to vanish to be loved."

Bas stirred something fragrant, laughter echoing. "Mine is a marriage once buried. Now it's the ground I bloom from."

Forest Marta, hands stained in huckleberry, smiled into the dark. "The forest taught me abundance."

Zofia held Jerzyk close. "I once whispered our story through tears. Now, I speak it to Parliament."

Kelly stood with ink-stained fingers. "My fruit? Choosing beauty when urgency demanded speed. Every poem, a homecoming. Every line, a thread back to myself."

Performer Marta sat quietly. No applause. Just breath. Just being.

Maria; my grandmother; raking leaves in invisible rhythms. "By sweeping the yard, I was keeping the storm at bay."

Brooke twirled a sequin scarf. "My fruit? A kidney, a wilder heart, and a constellation of client light."

The Girl in the Tight Boreals, fifteen and sovereign. "I saw a film I loved, and stepped into it."

Hanna, stitched in thread and thunder. "I knocked on 700 doors. But the one that opened everything… was mine."

Thumb-Out Marta, roadside in Tahoe. "I'm so glad I dared to follow my dream and asked for a ride."

Ady, chalked and steady. "That lead wasn't a climb. It was a vow."

Bufo Marta, soft as breath. "I screamed my way into being. Now I chose to stay."

Steven, ribs healed, hands steady. "My fruit? This. I never quit so that I can be here in this moment. Still here to live the unfolding."

And me? I just tended the flame. I was never the journey, the map, or the traveler. I am the space in which it all arises.

Then, in the hush that follows when a log is offered to the fire, they turned, not toward a guide, but toward a center we shared.

Because this was the fruit. Not a summit. Not even a story. But the soil we remembered together. The root we became.

And I said the only thing that felt real: "I'm so grateful."

No one answered. We didn't need to. The flames kept dancing. And we sat in the glow.

Nothing left to climb, no more peaks to reach. Just sky, and a soul that had become the world.

Next Steps / Getting Help

Resources and Contact

My work is rooted in one truth: every human carries far more capacity than they believe. Coaching is not about adding something new, but dissolving the veils that keep us from our wholeness. The path is remembrance: returning, step by step, to the pulse of our own power and belonging.

Below are pathways into this work: rites of passage, bold circles of women, accessible daily guidance, and bespoke one-to-one arrangements.

Wild Threshold Year

A one-year rite of passage, rooted in the seasons, mythic ritual, and deep resonance with land.

This journey is for those called into authenticity, grief and joy, eldership, true adulthood, and service to Earth and soul.

Across twelve moons, participants move through the six trunks and twenty-five branches of Masters of Badassery – a harmonic upgrade for the whole being. Ceremony, somatic practice, nature immersion, movement, grief tending, storytelling, and council weave a living curriculum of transformation.

At its heart is a ten-day resonance quest in the wilderness: a ceremonial fast and solo time on the land, where the soul listens again to the harmonics of cosmos and self. This is not a retreat or a training, but a passage – an ancient weaving of descent and renewal that carries each being across the edge of who they have been, toward who they are becoming.

For those ready to walk themselves home, and never forget again. www.mastersofbadassery.com

Bold & Free

Step into a circle of visionary women who reach beyond ordinary success. Together, we explore untamed landscapes and deep inner journeys, creating lives where goals align with the deepest authenticity.

This is your invitation to thrive: boldly, unapologetically, and on purpose. Reclaim vitality: feel alive and energized again.

Build confidence: grow strong, capable, and resilient.

Adventure with purpose: create challenges that spark growth.

For women at life's threshold who feel the quiet ache of "What's next?" and are ready to answer with courage. If you've ever felt isolated, stagnant, or unsure whether it's too late to begin again, this is your reminder: you're not alone, and it's not too late.

www://mastersofbadassery.com/bold-free

Innerverse App

For those seeking daily touchstones of guidance, the Innerverse App offers a living stream of individualized coaching, an accessible way to bring rhythm, reflection, and accountability into everyday life.

Powered by AI yet rooted in human wisdom, Innerverse is designed to help you deepen self-awareness, strengthen your inner compass, and access practical and affordable tools for transformation. Whether you are navigating transition, longing for meaning, or simply ready to step into a higher octave of your life, Innerverse becomes coaching in your pocket, a resonance you can carry anywhere.

www.innerverseapp.com

Private & Adventure Coaching

For those ready to go deeper, I offer bespoke coaching for individuals, couples, and groups who are done settling and ready to live from truth and desire. Each arrangement is crafted around your story, your thresholds, and your deepest commitment.

Often this means leaving the familiar. Adventure Coaching takes you into the mountains and wild places, where nature strips away distraction and reveals your raw edge. Out there, you discover resilience, clarity, and the freedom that comes when you step beyond what you thought was possible.

Wherever you begin: whether with a step, a practice, or a plunge across the threshold, know that the path is already alive within you, waiting to be remembered.

Connect with us on Social:

https://mastersofbadassery.substack.com/

https://www.instagram.com/mastersof_badassery/

https://www.facebook.com/Mastersofbadassery

Acknowledgements

Twenty years ago, my mother Hanna planted the seed: *"Why don't you write a book."* This is the tree that grew from that whisper, rooted in memory and watered by time. She put in endless hours formatting this text. To her, I offer both the genesis and the closure of this twenty-year arc, a circle now complete.

Her words became a blessing for this book: *"I've designed and formatted thousands of books in my life, both beautiful and wise, but this one is the most important to me. Not only because it was written by my wonderful daughter, whom I constantly admire and am proud of, but because Marta's experiences brought back memories and revealed how difficult and twisting her path, our path has been. From those tangled roots have grown magnificent flowers and fruits. This is an incredibly wise and inspiring book that everyone should read."*

To Maciek, thank you for always cheering me onto my wildest, most untamed expression.

To my grandparents, for the sacred gift of the forest cabin: a sanctuary where I learned of the infinite abundance.

To Steven, who stood with me on every page, never accepting the surface when depth could be summoned. This book would not have happened without him. Thank you for being relentless with me.

To Kellan, for never doubting my limitlessness, you anchored this expansion in me. And to Leah, whose eyes missed nothing, your diligence wove clarity into the weave.

To: Amber, Kate, Sumit and Tom for the investment of your time, holding my hand while asking the right questions in the early stages.

To all of you: this is not just my work. It is a mirror. You were the field that shaped its reflection.

Glossary

Aid Climbing – A climbing style where progress is made by pulling on gear placed in the rock, ice, or wall rather than using natural holds. Climbers often use ladders called "aiders" or hooks to move upward. This style is common on very steep or featureless terrain, such as big walls, where free climbing (using only hands and feet on the rock) would be extremely difficult or impossible.

Alpine – Climbing in high mountain environments, often above the tree line. Alpine climbs may involve rock, snow, ice, or a mix of all three, along with hazards like sudden weather changes, avalanches, and altitude sickness.

Anchor – A secure connection point to the rock, ice, or wall, built to hold a climber's weight and catch a fall. Anchors can be made from bolts, cams, nuts, slings, or natural features like trees. They are the foundation of safety in climbing systems.

Belay Device – A small mechanical device used to manage rope friction when belaying. It allows the belayer to stop the rope if the climber falls, lower them safely, or feed rope smoothly as they climb. Common types include tube-style devices (like the ATC) and assisted-braking devices (like the GriGri).

Beta – Information about how to do a climb or specific move. Beta can range from a short tip ("Use the left crack") to a detailed sequence of body positions. Receiving beta can make a climb feel easier, but many climbers prefer to figure things out themselves.

Big Wall – A very large vertical or near-vertical cliff that typically takes climbers more than one day to ascend. Big wall routes can be hundreds to thousands of feet tall and often require hauling gear, sleeping on the wall (in a portaledge or bivy), and using aid climbing techniques for the steepest sections. Famous examples include El Capitan in Yosemite and Trango Tower in Pakistan.

Bivy – Short for "bivouac." A lightweight or improvised overnight shelter, often used during multi-day climbs or mountaineering trips. A bivy can be as simple as a sleeping bag on a ledge or a small waterproof bivy sack to block wind and rain.

Bouldering – Climbing short but often very challenging routes ("problems") without ropes. Climbers use crash pads (portable foam mats) to cushion falls and usually work on powerful, technical moves close to the ground.

Bolt – A permanent anchor drilled into the rock, typically made of stainless steel. Climbers clip quickdraws and ropes into bolts for safety in sport climbing. Bolts are usually placed where natural protection is scarce.

Cam – A spring-loaded piece of climbing gear that expands to fit into cracks in the rock, creating a secure point for protection. When weighted in a fall, the cam's lobes press outward against the rock to hold it in place.

Camalot – A well-known brand of camming device made by Black Diamond. "Camalot" is often used generically to refer to any cam, though it's technically a trademarked name.

Climbing Grades – A system for rating the difficulty of a climb. In the United States, roped climbs are most often graded using the Yosemite Decimal System (YDS), which starts at Class 5 for technical rock climbing and goes from 5.0 (easiest) to 5.15 (hardest). Each grade above 5.9 is split into letter subgrades a, b, c, and d, with "a" being the easiest and "d" being the hardest in that number range (for example: 5.10a < 5.10b < 5.10c < 5.10d). A "+" sign can be used in some guidebooks to show a climb is on the harder side of a grade. While these ratings give a general idea of difficulty, they are subjective and can vary depending on the area and style of climbing.

Couloir – A steep, narrow gully on a mountain, often filled with snow or ice. Climbers and skiers use couloirs to access routes or descend steep slopes, but they can be dangerous due to rockfall or avalanches.

Crux – The most difficult section of a climb. It could be one hard move or a sustained sequence. Many climbers focus their energy on figuring out and practicing the crux because it determines whether they'll complete the route.

Dirtbag – A climber who chooses a minimalist, low-cost lifestyle to spend as much time as possible climbing. Dirtbags often live in vans, campgrounds, or out of their cars, traveling to different climbing areas.

Dihedral – An inside corner in the rock formed by two intersecting planes. Climbers can use stemming (pressing feet against one wall and hands against the other) to move upward in a dihedral.

Dyno – Short for "dynamic move." A jump or lunge made to reach a distant hold, often requiring explosive strength and precise timing. Unlike static moves, dynos commit the climber fully to motion before making contact with the target hold.

Figure-eight – A strong, easy-to-check knot used to tie in - attach a rope to a climber's harness and many other applications.

Follower – The climber who goes second on a rope. They clean (remove) the gear placed by the leader and are belayed from above. Also called a "second."

Free Solo (Soloing) – Climbing without ropes, harnesses, or protection gear. A fall is almost always fatal. Famous free soloists include Alex Honnold.

Gear – All equipment used in climbing, such as ropes, helmets, harnesses, cams, nuts, quickdraws, belay devices, and carabiners. "Rack" is another term for a climber's gear set.

Hangdogging – Working on a climb by resting on the rope rather than climbing it in one continuous push. This is common when learning the moves of a difficult route.

Haul Bag – A large, durable, waterproof bag used to carry food, water, clothing, and gear up a wall. On big wall climbs, haul bags (also called "pigs") are pulled up behind the climbers using a separate rope.

KT-22 – A steep, expert ski run at Palisades Tahoe in California. The name is sometimes used in climbing and skiing culture as a reference point for something challenging or iconic.

Kneebar – A climbing technique where the climber wedges a bent knee between two holds or features to create a hands-free rest or increase stability.

Leader – The climber who goes first on a pitch, clipping the rope into protection along the way. The leader faces more risk because they could fall farther than a second.

Lead Climb – A style of climbing where the climber starts from the bottom with the rope trailing, clipping it into bolts or gear as they go up.

Lockoff – Holding yourself in a bent-arm position, often with one arm, so you can reach for the next hold with the other. Strong lockoffs help on steep or overhanging routes.

Mecca – In climbing slang, a "mecca" is a world-class destination that attracts climbers from around the globe for its exceptional rock, variety of routes, and climbing culture. The term can refer to an entire region, a single crag, or even a particular style hotspot. Examples include Yosemite Valley for big wall climbing, Kalymnos for sport climbing, and Hueco Tanks for bouldering. It implies not just high-quality climbing, but also a vibrant community and history tied to the area.

Nunatak – A rocky mountain peak or ridge surrounded by glacier ice. Nunataks often serve as navigation points in polar or alpine environments.

Offwidth – A crack too wide for hands or fists but too narrow for the whole body. Offwidth climbing requires unique moves such as arm bars, knee jams, and hip squeezes.

Onsight – Completing a climb on the first try without falls, rests, or prior detailed knowledge about it.

Pitch – A section of a climb between two belay points, usually the length of one rope (about 50–70 meters). Multi-pitch climbs have several pitches stacked on top of each other.

Pidgin – A local creole language spoken in Hawaii, mixing Hawaiian, English, and other languages. It's often heard in Hawaiian climbing communities.

Portaledge – A hanging tent-like platform used by climbers for sleeping on the side of a cliff during multi-day climbs.

Projecting – Working on a climb over several tries until you can complete it without falling or resting on the rope.

Pro or Protection – Climbing gear such as nuts, cams, bolts, and pitons placed into the rock to catch a fall and reduce a risk of injury. The more protection placed on a pitch, the safer the climb.

Rappel – Descending a rope in a controlled way using a belay device, usually to get down from a climb or reach the start of a route.

Rigging – Setting up ropes, anchors, pulleys, and other equipment for climbing, hauling, or rescue.

Rigger – A person skilled at setting up and managing rope systems for climbing, rescue, or industrial work.

Rope Gun – A strong climber who leads the hardest pitches for a partner, making the climb possible for the team.

Runout – A long stretch of climbing between protection points. Runouts increase the distance one could fall, making the climb riskier.

Second – See Follower.

Send (Sent) – To complete a climb from bottom to top without falling or resting on the rope. "Sent" is the past tense ("I sent the route").

Sharp End – The lead climber's position on the rope, where the risk and responsibility are highest.

Slackline – A length of flat webbing stretched between two points for balance practice. Popular among climbers for building core strength and focus.

Spraying – Talking excessively about your climbing accomplishments, often to impress or one-up others.

Spraying Beta – The act of overexplaining how to climb a route, by giving step-by-step instructions for every move, which floods the climber with overwhelming details, removing the joy of discovery and sometimes even making the climb harder.

Tagline – A thin rope used to haul gear or retrieve a main rope after rappelling.

About the Author

Marta Czajkowska is a Polish poet, cliffside philosopher, and part-time feral goat whisperer. Born in communist Poland, she grew up believing dreams were for other people, until she started hitchhiking toward them in a front-loader.

She has climbed El Capitan, stared down the shadow of her childhood wounds on six continents, spooned through alpine nights without water, and once moved across the world after watching an outdoor adventure film, all in service of remembering who she really is.

A climber, coach, and storyteller, Marta writes about the messy, mythic path from shrinking to sovereignty, blending memoir, myth, and soul-medicine for the wild-hearted. A professional tangler of roots, climber of towers, and drinker of rivers, she hopes this book inspires you to do at least two of those things. She believes the best maps are drawn in metaphor and dirt.

When not coaching clients or chasing granite or meaning, she's picking mushrooms and berries in wild places, plotting her next improbable soul adventure, and reminding humans that their joy is not optional. It's planetary.

Marta is available for soulful nature walks, myth-soaked retreats, and group or personal coaching.

Invite Marta to speak in front of your group, and she won't just give a talk. She'll deliver a paradigm-shifting, soul-remembering, mythic field activation disguised as a keynote. Whether you're gathering leaders, seekers, artists, or entrepreneurs, expect poetic grit, laughter, truth bombs, and just enough wildness to stir something ancient awake.

Bring a notebook, a compass, and maybe a machete.

Printed in Dunstable, United Kingdom